ANIMOSITY AT BAY

PALLAVI RAGHAVAN

Animosity at Bay

An Alternative History of the India–Pakistan Relationship, 1947–1952

HURST & COMPANY, LONDON

First published in the United Kingdom in 2020 by

C. Hurst & Co. (Publishers) Ltd.,
41 Great Russell Street, London, WC1B 3PL

Printed in India

A Cataloguing-in-Publication data record for this book is available from the British Library.

ISBN: 9781787382145

www.hurstpublishers.com

My parents,
TCA Raghavan and Ranjana Sengupta,
and sister, Antara Raghavan,
are the truest owners of this book.

CONTENTS

List of Acronyms and Abbreviations ix
Acknowledgements xi

Introduction 1
1. Bilateral Solutions 23
2. The Nehru–Liaquat Pact 47
3. Evacuee Property 73
4. No War Pact: 'All Men of Good Will'? 99
5. Indus Waters 117
6. Shaping International Personalities 139
7. Trade and Financial Relations between India and Pakistan 161
Conclusion 183

Appendix I 187
Appendix II 193
Notes 195
Bibliography 221
Index 235

LIST OF ACRONYMS AND ABBREVIATIONS

BL	British Library
MEA	Ministry of External Affairs (Government of India)
NAI	National Archives of India, New Delhi
PRO	Public Records Office, UK

ACKNOWLEDGMENTS

Those who are familiar with this project, will know that it went through several stages–both in its writing as well as *non-writing*. It evolved as a manuscript-in-waiting at the Centre for Policy Research in New Delhi, as well as an almost-there manuscript at Jindal University and Ashoka University. Each of these institutions was important in the shaping of this work, because they enabled interactions with individuals who pushed me into writing a stronger, and more rigorously argued, book.

My supervisor at Cambridge, Prof. Joya Chatterji, indelibly shaped my understanding of the discipline of history, and equipped me for life to navigate the world with an invaluable set of intellectual tools. Joya's insistence on attention to a closely crafted historical analysis, based on empirical research, as well as carefully rounded and historicised interrogation of the archival material, have immeasurably added to the strengths of this book—though all its shortfalls are, obviously, mine alone. In addition, I would also like to thank Dr. David Washbrook, and Prof. Sumantra Bose for their close reading of the thesis, as well as their subsequent encouragement. I am also grateful to the Cambridge Trusts and the Nehru Cambridge Scholarship for funding my PhD research.

The evolution of the project from a PhD dissertation to a study of India's early bilateral relations with Pakistan could not have found a better mentor than Srinath Raghavan, whose generosity with intellectual support, when coupled with a phenomenal patience over what now seems like a remarkably prolonged gestation, have greatly enriched the substance and depth of the arguments in the book. These have also benefitted hugely from my interactions with fellow scholars of Nehru's world and modern India's international history—an exciting, and newly resurgent field of study.

In particular, I would also like to thank Mahesh Rangarajan and Pratap Bhanu Mehta, for their inputs at various stages of the manuscript, as well as for acting as entry points into scholarly communities where the ideas and arguments of the manuscript could be further tested and strengthened. The circles they introduced me into, moreover, of researchers from different fields engaged in questions about India's Cold War, the process of the shaping of international relations, as well as state-making in India and Pakistan during the 1950s, have also contributed enormously to my understanding of this field.

Delhi's historian circle consists, I think, of some of the loveliest people in the whole world—I have loved interacting with them, and benefitted enormously from their bracing concern with the adherence to the requirements of the discipline, alongside an equally important engagement with the question of how our toils can also enable a more large-hearted, humane and compassionate world around us. In particular, I would also like to thank the 'JGU Historians Group'—its accredited, 'card carrying' members, as well as those for whom, on occasion, we deigned to make honourable exceptions. They provided the support system that a close-knit community of scholars can bring for dragging a book across the finishing line, along with consistently useful insights about how the chapters in the manuscript could be further developed.

This book has also been written while in the companionship of fellow travellers, who will know who they are, and whose friendship I have treasured. I want to express my deepest gratitude to them for this, along with the hope that they will enjoy reading the subsequent pages.

I am also hugely indebted to Michael Dwyer and the team at Hurst, who have shepherded this book through production while displaying amazing fortitude and professionalism. The book has been hugely improved as a consequence of their efforts, and I have greatly enjoyed working with them during the finalisation of the manuscript. I will always be grateful for their diligence, as well as kindness to a first-time author.

INTRODUCTION

An over-wrought despatch from the Indian mission in Lahore in 1948 had concluded: 'There are no parallels anywhere to the nature of the diplomatic relations subsisting between India and Pakistan, or to the type of system evolved for conducting these relations.'[1] The writer, M. K. Kripalani, the deputy high commissioner of India in 1948, was referring to the bewilderingly manifold nature of the tasks that the Indian High Commission in Pakistan confronted. These related not only to defence, or security or intelligence gathering, but covered rather just about all aspects of life: who lived where, who could marry whom, where they could travel, what they could own, and how they could meet their parents. Nowhere else in the world, Kripalani continued, would the staff of a High Commission be called upon to perform as many different sets of tasks, as those in the offices of the Indian High Commission in Karachi and Lahore.

But this statement also strikes one as curious, given the subsequent characterisation of the India–Pakistan relationship as one of high stakes brinkmanship and a volatile and all-consuming strategic rivalry for territory. Given this kind of characterisation—of a high stakes security game, based on a zero-sum rivalry—the writer seemed to be painting a slightly different picture: pointing to a far more wide-ranging and deeply ingrained set of problems than could be mastered by pinning down the mechanics of winning a geopolitical game. It seems incongruous that the writer, in 1948, rather than speculating, say, on the preparedness of the armies for a war in Kashmir between India and Pakistan, should have been lamenting the burden of the weight of the diversity of administrative responsibilities his office had to bear.

The bilateral relationship between India and Pakistan occupies a strange place at the heart of the process of state-making in the subcontinent in the years that followed the partition. Along with shaping the direction of bilateral relations between the two states, they were also participating in the conversation about just what these states were for, and having to arrive at definitions of their jurisdiction and sovereignty. This process, Kirpalani seemed to realise, was far more complex, more difficult to grasp, than simply following a set of rules about conflicting claims to land. What it also acknowledged was that the relationship between India and Pakistan was not as simple a matter as only achieving the goal of obtaining paramountcy in Kashmir: while this was obviously true, something even more difficult and intractable lay at the heart of the knotty relationship. In fact, the writer seemed to be saying, a broader set of approaches would have to be adopted, those that went beyond territorial conflict, in dealing with the India–Pakistan relationship.

In many ways Kirpalani, in performing the acts of the state, was also creating it. Issues around marriage licenses or educational degrees Kirpalani seemed to lament, should not have been part of his responsibility, and ought to have been settled by someone else, preferably very far away from his desk. Yet, he found himself, a year after the partition, having to plod through interminable requests for verifying bank details, property deeds and the minutiae of questions relating to the wellbeing of religious minorities in Pakistan. What the writer was actually alluding to was the process of both India and Pakistan embarking on a process of state-making, that had to be mutually constituted. The disagreements between the states were obviously present: but what also had to be done first was for both to define what the purpose of their states actually was.

At its heart, the India–Pakistan relationship contains a collaborative element. It assumes a mutual acknowledgement of the validity of both states. In the aftermath of the partition, the central leadership in both countries were aware of the intense fragility of the nation-state project in South Asia. The legitimacy of their existence could be called into question in any number of ways—citizenship in both India and Pakistan could not be defined on the basis of religion, or race, or ethnicity, or language. Ties that primordially held people together—kinship networks, language and dialects, familial relations, and religion—cut across boundary lines, even after the partition. Exactly why people ought to have an innate appreciation for giving their exclusive allegiance to the states of India or Pakistan was not in fact clear to many people at the time: logic, if anything, dictated otherwise. The reasons for why state structures ought to be invested with the greatest amount of faith as being the ultimate arbiter of power or decision making had to be asserted, rather than being self-evidently true. Collaborative exercises in bilateral relations were thus carried out as part of the exercise of willing the post-colonial states of India and Pakistan into existence.

This mutual aim led to cooperation between the two governments on a variety of levels. Partly, this was also based on the elite convergences of Indian and Pakistani society—exclusivist, self-serving and occasionally brutal though they could certainly be—that gave the most impetus to a collaborative framework in the bilateral relationship. What this also enabled, however, was a realisation that the process of disentangling the uncertainties of the partition was vital for upholding two mutually exclusive, sovereign, and self-contained states. In order to do this, both governments sought resolutions to lingering uncertainties brought about by the separation. They quickly recognised that the process of separation needed to be as complete as possible. Anchored quite deeply within the logic of the bilateral relationship, therefore, is a kind of partnership that enables giving a firmer shape to the definitions of the Indian and Pakistani states.

The object of this book is to highlight how an alternative history of the India–Pakistan relationship, which is based on acts of bilateral engagement and cooperation in the years that followed the partition, is also possible. This book examines how a joint—and immediate—recognition of the necessity of finalizing the partition was transcribed into the shaping of bilateral relations, while dealing with difficult questions such as the rehabilitation of abducted women, negotiating a settlement on minorities, getting to grips with the question of evacuee property, negotiating on the division of the Indus rivers, and engaging with one another at international forums. These processes required the shaping of a parallel process of engagement and cooperation in India–Pakistan relations, which simultaneously took place alongside acts of hostility and violence.

The task of emerging out of the partition required not just the mechanics of waging warfare in Kashmir, but also an intensive effort to flesh out the state structures for India and Pakistan, often in a more collaboratively determined fashion than appearances would suggest. This particular dynamic has been insufficiently addressed in a great deal of the literature on India–Pakistan relationship, and should be incorporated further into the analysis of the set of ingredients that contribute to the shaping of the relationship. Therefore, this book charts out the avenues of cooperation between India and Pakistan were laid out as part of the process of demonstrating the viability of their state structures as separated entities, and examine what the reasoning for undertaking these tells us about the broader India–Pakistan dynamic.

The Overlooked Dynamics of the India–Pakistan Relationship

An alternative history of the India–Pakistan relationship is long overdue. Its terms of reference are frayed and well-worn; and its trends are monotonously predictable. India and Pakistan have entered into three full-scale wars, border skirmishes take place almost daily, and both pursue their diplomatic spats thoroughly and with zeal. They point out each other's shortcomings at the United Nations, and spend vast sums of money on maintaining armies on the border in preparedness of an attack. A slice of land, approximately 90,000 square miles in size, has been contested between the two for more than six decades. The dialogue process moves along in fits and starts, and is seen as being held hostage by a variety of interests that benefit from a further deterioration of the relationship. A state of 'thaw' between the two countries is the exception, rather than the rule, and, in general, the two countries are considered to be in a situation of a powder keg close to an accidental match.

These conclusions are not unjustified—but are also incomplete. What they do not address are a mutually held basis of reasoning that undergirds the existence of the Indian and Pakistani states. Much of the literature on this issue is often couched in the metaphors of a bitter family feud, and described through the terms of two 'blood brothers',[2] caught in a 'deadly embrace',[3] in pursuit of a suicidal 'sibling rivalry', which dates from when both were born in difficult circumstances, under the aegis of a misguided 'midwife'.[4] This relationship, so the argument goes, was doomed to violent showdowns and hostile acrimony from the very beginning, because of the bitterness left on both sides by the traumas of partition, and the continuing conflict in Kashmir.[5] The analysis is sometimes based on the assumptions that the very nature of the personalities of the two countries—democratic as opposed to authoritarian; Muslim as opposed to Hindu; secular as opposed to theocratic—suggested that the relationship was always doomed to failure. The most simplistic of these explanations roots the reasons for the tensions between India and Pakistan to what is essentially an extension of a thousand-year rivalry between Hindus and Muslims in the subcontinent, or, in slightly more nuanced versions, of the old rivalry between the Congress and the Muslim League.

In the 1970's, for instance, S. M. Burke had argued 'It is difficult to think of any two religions more antithetical to each other than Hinduism and Islam', and this, Burke argued, has prevented any lasting solution to the Indo-Pakistani hostility. Burke suggested that these tendencies came to the fore in the making of bilateral relations between India and Pakistan, when 'this deep seated reluctance on the part of Hindu leaders to accept the separate existence of Pakistan has been a principal factor in hindering reconciliation between India and Pakistan'.[6] These factors are believed to have exercised a vice like grip in subsequent dealings between India and Pakistan, and ensured that bilateral relations could not be freed from a mutual suspicion and jealousy. In such circumstances, an innate and bitter rivalry was deemed inescapable; and the choices made with regard to bilateral relations seemed too entangled with these emotions, which led to both sides compulsively taking action that would be to the detriment of the other.

But, even to the most hardened sceptics of the capacities of this relationship, the explanation of a primarily religiously driven animosity for the India–Pakistan dynamic is a stretch. For one thing, a surfeit of personal religious piety did not, by and large, characterise the domineering personality traits of the actors involved in this story. For another, they do not offer a consistently workable explanation for all the dealings between India and Pakistan. But more importantly, for our purposes, they also do not account for the necessity of the states of India and Pakistan consistently working to protect, and, where necessary, mutually acknowledge, the basis of their establishment. The process that led them to demarcate the extent of their responsibilities towards refugees and migrants in the 1940s, are the same that also require them to act in ways that emphasise the importance of the state, rather than the religious community. The same set of processes, moreover, also led them to work out the extent to which bilateral trade ought to be continued, and to carry out negotiations about the division of water, as well as explore the contours of a potential 'No War' Pact, between India and Pakistan.

Another set of explanations about the differences between India and Pakistan—those based on the institutional inheritances of India and Pakistan—also do not wholly account for these considerations. The different kinds of institutions that underpinned the states of India and Pakistan, it is argued, are also responsible for shaping the quality of their mutual interactions. The preponderance of the military in Pakistan, the argument goes, is also responsible for a perpetual state of warfare being advanced against India.[7] The weakness of Pakistan's institutions are unable to balance out the emphasis that Pakistan's army places on the threat perception from India. This, in turn, is responsible for the perpetual state of warfare between India and Pakistan.

But this book suggests that the relative strengths of different institutions in India and Pakistan are not always the causal link for the way in which the relationship between the two were shaped, and do not always offer consistently applicable explanations for all the twists and turns in the trajectory of the relationship. Choices about war and peace between India and Pakistan often seem to straddle the ideological and institutional leanings across governments. One glaring example of this is how Parvez Musharraf—the head of Pakistan's army, and president of the country—engaged in, what seemed at the time, serious attempts at constructive dialogue with Atal Bihari Vajpayee—the head of a government that represented beliefs about giving greater voice to political expressions of Hindu ideology.

A little closer to our period of study, General Ayub Khan presided over the signing of the Indus Water Treaty, even while acknowledging some of its shortcomings. Similarly, the size of the electoral majority in the Indian legislature is not always an accurate guide to the hostility of its government towards Pakistan. Indira Gandhi for example had embarked on the Bangladesh war, while Vajpeyi made sustained efforts towards dialogue with Pakistan. Explanations about the different institutional underpinnings of the states of India and Pakistan therefore—while in themselves not incorrect—cannot always offer a correlative account about the state of bilateral relations. While the fact of a religious divide, or the differences of institutional and ideological orientation of both states do occupy a space in the conduct of the relationship, this is also tempered, I would argue, by the necessity of both states having to acknowledge the basis of their separation.

The nature of this imperative, to acknowledge the validity of the state structures of both India and Pakistan, is not given adequate weight by such explanations in much of the literature on this subject. In analysing the relationship as merely a complicated set of exercises that ultimately only advance brinksmanship, shaped by ideologically or institutionally pre-determined factors, important qualifiers are missed out that also contain within them the equally viable possibility of breaking down a narrative about unremitting and relentless hostility, with no other possible option in sight. For example, although calls for resorting to outright war were repeatedly made in the subcontinent, there is also a reason that this rhetoric is not consistently followed through which greater force. Indeed, in the instances of bilateral negotiation I examine, the approach that both governments took in forming their bilateral positions, were very consistent. The calculus on which conversations with regard to the negotiations in the inter-dominion conferences were shaped, were based on how much, and whether, they could help in ending the uncertainties arising out of the partition. If the dialogues could help in giving a cleaner, more defined shape to the state structures of India and Pakistan, then there was every reason for them to be carried out further.

The disputes between India and Pakistan in the early 1950s—as well as, needless to say, in the current context—certainly were diverse and numerous. They included the control and occupation of

Kashmir, settling the question of control over the Indus Waters Canals, evacuee property, division of assets, and the financial settlement to be competed between two countries. Indeed, by January 1950, relations between the two were mired in deadlock. Outright war had seemed dangerously close to the horizon for many months, and continued to remain a distinct possibility even as the correspondence progressed. The two new armies had already been in conflict in Kashmir by December 1947. The question of the accession of Hyderabad had come to a head by September 1948. In 1949 and 1950, many questions relating to bilateral cooperation seemed to have stultified into non resolution. The evacuee property conferences had largely failed in terms of securing concrete compensation for either government. Inter-Dominion trade had come to a halt entirely following the currency devaluation crisis of 1949. A fortnightly report from the British High Commission in Karachi in January 1950 stated: 'If there is any comfort in the situation, it must be sought in the fact that relations between India and Pakistan have now reached a stage where it would seem impossible for them to deteriorate further, short of open war.'[8]

But alongside these events, the chronology of the 1950s—much like the decades that followed—is littered with events which suggest that the relationship was not necessarily inevitably predisposed towards conflict, and that the leadership of both sides repeatedly, and carefully considered avenues that could enable a stable coexistence. During the same time as relations seemed to deteriorate particularly dramatically in 1950, for instance, Nehru and Liaquat Ali Khan were also, simultaneously, exchanging letters that explored the possibility of a 'No War' deal, according to which neither could be legally able to declare war on the other first. Instances of bilateral engagement and dialogue occurred particularly regularly during the 1950's. This decade also saw a slew of highly constructive inter-governmental exchanges, including a number of major ministerial summits and conferences, frequent—indeed, sometimes almost daily—communication between the two prime ministers, numerous meetings between provincial delegations from either side of the border, and dense engagements between cabinet ministers, bureaucrats and diplomats, on the questions of minorities, Inter-Dominion migration, and evacuee property.

Several of these questions had been extremely fraught at the time, and could conceivably be compared to Kashmir in terms of their ability to destabilize the India–Pakistan relationship. This book will detail the circumstances in which each of these agreements was arrived at, and therefore show how, when the situation demands it, acts of engagement and cooperation are as integral to the interests of both countries, as those that perpetuate hostility. The shared goal of finalising the partition—and thereby creating a stable coexistence of two permanently established entities—shaped the contours of their relationship to a significant, but also under-acknowledged, extent.

Nehru and His Foreign Office

A recent surge in the studies of India's diplomatic history, Nehruvian foreign policy, as well as the junctions between the subcontinent's history and international relations, have also contributed to the arguments of this book. Srinath Raghavan, in his definitive account of the strategic history of the Nehru years, shows how India's relations with both Pakistan and China might be successfully categorised as exercises in coercive diplomacy, whereby, in order to achieve the optimal amount of stability in the subcontinent, it was also necessary to use military levers to achieve their ends. Raghavan shows that in the decade that followed the partition, Nehru used militaristic postures, not necessarily with the intention of subjugating the neighbours once and for all in a zero-sum conflict, but rather in order to defend a fixed set of criteria, along with also exploring options of greater political conciliation to achieve these criteria.[9] These approaches were most clearly evidenced, Srinath Raghavan shows, during the process of the integration of the Indian Union—the processes of the accession of Hyderabad, Junagadh and Kashmir were deeply shaped by Nehru's abilities to handle a crisis so that a more peaceful outcome could be pulled out from the face of a calculated strategy of escalating risks of violence.

Nehru's foreign policy—his balancing acts with idealism, and manipulation of his various domestic and international constituencies to his government's objectives—have received a growing, and more sophisticated degree of attention in recent years, from a range of historians of Indian foreign policy. Nehru was the inheritor of various legacies: of a continuity of British patterns of strategic thinking in India's immediate neighbourhood; of anti-colonialism; an affinity with decolonised nations who professed an equidistant relationship between communism and capitalism; the negotiator of a ultimately failed, but nonetheless arguably sensible set of principles with China for a peaceful coexistence.

What these works also underline is the importance of several other actors—bureaucrats, politicians, and ordinary citizens in the shaping of India's international relations. Indeed, it is important to move away from Nehru's own personality—which, partly due to his prolific writings, has undoubtedly left a larger than life impression—and to appreciate the extent to which, in day to day matters in the implementation of policy minutiae, Nehru was certainly not an omnipotent figure. Indeed, what also comes across is how Nehru was as often as the receiving end, as at the initiating end, of the decision-making agenda on foreign policy. In fact, several gaps between Nehru's own soaring rhetoric, and the realities through which they were implemented on the ground also allows us to appreciate the enormous leeway that a variety of actors had in shaping foreign policy. Moreover, if a closer examination of the archival material shows us anything, it is how India's diplomatic history had always been the subject of intense dissension, debate and the source for criticism, both from within and outside the government.[10]

While using many of the insights of the recent writings on India's diplomatic history extensively, the arguments of this book are also at a slight remove from their under-girding concerns. For one thing, this book does not offer a strategic history—the attempt here is not to evaluate the diplomatic posturing of India and Pakistan in terms of their ability for furthering their long term pursuits. And for another, this account will also place a greater degree of emphasis on the personnel of the early foreign policy establishments, as opposed to the individual inclinations of Nehru himself with regard to the shaping of the relationship with Pakistan. But, more significantly perhaps, according to this reading, bureaucrats in India and Pakistan were not merely instruments for carrying out Nehru's, or the government of India's already-mapped out pursuit of the state's interests, or world-views: instead, they were the shapers of how these interests were constituted. Their actions, therefore, should also be read as the pursuit of a path of statehood that they would feel had the most potential, and entail an examination of which kinds of assumptions went into shaping these appraisals.

But even more important to the concerns of this book is an attempt to examine the extent to which the states of India and Pakistan are mutually constituted entities. They were not already-formed, or even particularly internally consistent entities—their contours are held in place by one another. The assumption of the state, and its ability to pursue an international agenda, were thus upheld because of the mutual recognition of the finality of partition, rather than only being a product of the ideological orientation of their leadership. Exercises in determining the pursuit of war or peace—or, in the case of the pages that follow, protracted negotiation—were also, this book would argue, the product of a joint agenda of recognising the finality of partition. This, more than any other consideration, the book argues, is the causal driver that determined the courses of actions taken by India and Pakistan in the early years of their international existence.

The Durability of a Partition

All this brings to us a consideration of whether the fact of partition can be viewed through a different lens than it has been. Variously described as short-sighted, self-serving, opportunistic, valorous, or simply the tired surrender of a departing empire, the idea of partition has usually been given a negative reading in many historical accounts of the twentieth century. But, point out Dubnov and Robson:

> Scholars and policy makers alike, have failed to understand [partition] as the product of a particular global moment, when decolonisation, ethnic nationalism, and new forms of international organisation came together to create a kind of toxic miasma around the idea of physically separating ethnically or communally defined populations.[11]

A less explored set of questions that historians should also ask include: to what extent did it actually work in offering a new basis for setting up different, and more lasting, traditions of governance?

To an important extent, the kinds of explanations about the nature of threats from Pakistan to India seem to hinge on the partition. For example, arguments about irredentism, or the attempt by Pakistan to change the 'status quo' by being revisionist, are also partially based inside the logic that partition was not able to adequately provide for two stable states. In Sumit Ganguly's explanation of the basis of hostility between India and Pakistan, for instance:

> Pakistan is a revisionist state [since] it is intent on reordering the territorial arrangements that were reached at the time of British colonial withdrawal from the subcontinent. To Pakistani policy makers the status of Kashmir remains the 'unfinished business of partition'. The roots of this revisionism can be traced to the very ideological basis of the Pakistani state. It was created as a putative homeland for the Muslims of South Asia to escape Hindu domination.[12]

While, however, an analysis of how partition did not enable two self-contained states to arise have frequently been made—and not without reason—it is also important to look at the extent that it did.

Similarly, Stephen Cohen had identified the process of partition as being a foremost reason for the continuing hostility between India and Pakistan: that the state of Pakistan came to be defined almost exclusively in terms of the aftermath of partition, and through its relations with India. He argues, 'Pakistanis considered India's failure to adhere to the terms of partition—such as the defaulting on the division of assets, manipulation of the international boundary, and over the accession of princely states—as the supreme betrayal'.[13] Moreover, he continues, over the decades that followed partition, the continuing India Pakistan tension led to 'the vision of Pakistan as a homeland had been supplanted by that of Pakistan as a fortress—an armed redoubt guarded by the Pakistan army, safe from predatory India.'[14] Pakistan's foreign policy, therefore, stems from it being an 'insecurity state… that perceived itself not only as small and disadvantaged, but as on the defensive against a real and present threat, with its survival at stake'[15]

It is thus also important, in the light of such analysis, to interrogate the assumptions about partition as an administrative solution. The argument I will develop in the coming pages is about how the experience of partition, rather being analysed in a purely negative light, can also be viewed as a way of building a set of commonalities of interest between the successor states. In the years that followed the partition, bitterness over the violence in Punjab and political divisions between the Congress and the Muslim League did not necessarily predispose the leadership of either country towards only a unceasingly violent relationship between both states. Instead, the book dwells on how their acts of recognizing the finality of the partition, and deliberating how it could be given a long-term shape also contributed to the making of the India–Pakistan dynamic. Finally, it attempts to evaluate the success of the bilateral relationship in this light: in terms of its ability to fully implement the provisions of partition by providing for the establishment of two viable successor states.

One of the objects of this book, however, is to study the ways in which the legacy of a partition can provide for productive spaces of innovation for a state. In fact, this book will argue, the experience of partition was also seen as an opportunity for both governments to strengthen their hold over state-building, and to fashion a platform of legitimacy in the eyes of some sections of their public—particularly those within majority communities, or those who had newly arrived into India and Pakistan and made strong claims for the state's active help. It was on the basis of consolidating their grip on these constituencies, that the states of India and Pakistan also further entrenched and strengthened themselves. What the present work also seeks to show, however, is that this was also, and foremost, a bilateral and collaborative exercise: many of the questions of state making in India and Pakistan had to be done in consultation with one another—they could not be unilaterally achieved. In was in the necessities of strengthening the state that the bilateral dialogue between India and Pakistan proved to have its greatest value.

I thus try to examine the process of how issues arising out of the aftermath of the partition was used to bolster the basis of both states, as well as provide spaces for commonalties between them. In fact what also needs to be integrated further into the discussion about partition is the set of interests that come about in then upholding the state, and the extent to which they attempt to finalise the process of partition, partly as a means of consolidating their own position further. In carrying out these activities, can it also allow for the development of areas of commonality and synchrony in inter-state relations, that can lead to a furtherance of the basis of a stable coexistence? It is to the extent that these were fashioned that the success of the relationship between India and Pakistan can be gauged, but the answers, I would argue, are more nuanced than a more straightforward delineation between yes and no; or even the exclusive adherence to the rules of a zero-sum game.

Setting this process in motion did not necessarily, as this book will show, preclude the possibility of a more accommodative arrangement with regard to the subcontinent's minorities, the possibilities of a water sharing agreement, or even the prospect of occasional collaboration at the United Nations. For example, in the process of deciding who their citizens were going to be, or in deciding which sets of people would be compensated for having left their property behind, it was frequently the bilateral dialogue between India and Pakistan that most critically impacted onto these issues. Indeed, it was critical that the numbers of those allowed refuge in both states be calibrated carefully: any unilateral decision in favour of this or that community would have been disastrous for both governments, since this would only lead to the excluded community coming in their scores to the other dominion. It was on the basis of this kind of consultation, which was being conducted on the premise of two states having been viably partitioned, that the state-making processes India and Pakistan were cemented further.

As might be expected, the question of whether or not partition as an administrative device should be accepted as a viable solution to ethnic conflict, is fiercely contested.[16] But for our purposes here, it is important to point out that during the 1940s, this was widely regarded as a pragmatic approach to resolving conflict. The Irish historian T.G. Frasier remarked, for instance, 'It is important to remember that in the period when the question of the division of India on religious lines arose, partition seemed to have provided a relatively painless way out of the Irish problem'.[17] Indeed, the process of partition, and the questions that it raised were not unique to the subcontinent, they had already been rehearsed several times over the twentieth century, including for example, in the debates around Brexit. They revive the question, in other words, of what to do when someone raises the claim of feeling allegiance for a different kind of community than the one they are currently in, gains enough political traction, and succeeds in being in a strong enough position in shaping the process of the re-drawing of boundary lines. Subsequent to this chain of events, the question of what kind of relationship the two new entities ought to have between them—and with minorities communities within them—become particularly important.

Indeed, one way of looking at the partition is to examine it in terms of a case study within a broader conversation being had around the world during the 1940s, about how to reconcile the position of minority rights within a larger majoritarian framework. The dominant argument about the role of partition in the 1940s was frequently one of resignation and realism. The tendency to administratively regulate divisions on the basis of ethnicity only grew in the aftermath of the Second World War, and included, for example, the expulsion of some 9 million ethnic Germans from Poland, Hungary and Czechoslovakia in 1945, many of whom had lived in those places for several generations. 'During the 1940s', notes Yasmin Khan, 'refugees were being created by and left in the wake of the Second World War *everywhere*'.[18] Partition, in several instances, had been seized on as a means of resolving this dilemma. Both India and Pakistan were a part of what the historian of partition Robert Schaeffer calls the 'first generation' of partition—a process that was initiated and abetted by receding colonial powers, and which resulted in the division of multi-ethnic communities who constituted large minorities and majorities along religious lines, and which resulted in the partitions of Ireland, Palestine and South Asia.[19]

South Asian policy makers had to repeatedly engage with the soundness of the reasons for the viability of partition in their international dealings. To many, partition seemed the best administrative solution to a familiar problem of representation and minority protection, rather than being seen as the consequence of the inherently impossible relations between Hindus and Muslims. By 1946, Zafarullah Khan, for instance, says in his interviews with the historians Ainsley Embree and Wayne Wilcox, after the failure of the Cabinet Mission Plan, 'there was no doubt in my mind that the only way out was partition.'[20] The instincts of many of those present was to solidify the event further, rather than to erode it, and served as the basis of the decisions which prevailed. The account I relate is of individuals who were determined to make the partition last, to follow its logic through, even, and especially when this also required a measure of cooperation.

What also sometimes comes across in some of the early negotiations between India and Pakistan is the attempt at emulating models of statehood and sovereignty that had been designed during the inter-war period in Europe, in the context of newly drawn boundary-lines along ethnic majoritarian considerations. Some of the dilemmas that arose as part of this exercise were not dissimilar to the questions that Indian and Pakistani bureaucrats faced in the aftermath of partition; and, to some extent, the solutions they attempted to put in place were influenced by the types of administrative devices that were used in prior decades in other parts of the world. For example, the shaping of the Nehru–Liaquat Pact in 1950 also bore striking similarities with the provisions for minority protection by the League of Nations. The League of Nations had designed an inter-state approach to the question of the security of minority populations in the context of a substantial redrawing of territorial boundaries in the aftermath of the first world war.[21]

The Pact, as we shall see in the pages that follow, envisioned a system of protection of minority populations in Bengal, by making the governments of India and Pakistan accountable to one another about the treatment of minorities within their eastern provinces. What this also demonstrated, paradoxically enough, was that it was only after the fact of a partition that more collaborative solutions on the issue of minorities could be taken by both states. Such jointly constituted attempts at working through the aftermath of a partition were engaged with in a fair amount of detail by both India and Pakistan, and, I would argue, significantly impacted the mould within which subsequent engagements between the two countries would be carried out.

Islands of Agreement

In the case of ethnic conflict between two rival communities, the political scientist Barry Posen argued that the features of a security dilemma itself—a mechanism for gauging the propensity of the outbreak of violence, based on calculations of perceived threat towards oneself, and potentially to be defused by the perceptions of decline of such a threat—manifests itself particularly clearly. The shifts that take place during the break-up of an erstwhile regime most often present themselves along the lines of rival communities that are seeking to ensure their security from the other.[22] In such conditions, the different perceptions of what it would require to achieve the access to security for different groups—for example, the differences about adequate representation voiced for the Hindu and Muslim communities by the Congress and Muslim League in the midst of the departure of the British from the subcontinent—lead to the demands of differentiated sovereignties, and the uncertainties of this process exacerbates the security dilemma. Eventually, the best way that the dilemma can be resolved is when both groups act in ways that best consolidate their ways of acquiring security.

In such cases, the well-being of minority communities left behind as a consequence of the redrawing of boundary lines become a particularly important determinant of the intensity of the security dilemma. The creation of Pakistan itself had also been envisioned as a means of providing a bulwark that had the institutional heft to represent the interests of minority communities across South Asia. The dense set of bilateral negotiations between India and Pakistan during the 1950s, therefore, also served to bring the issue of minorities and their continued security into the agenda of both governments. An inability to protect the rights of such communities, surrounded by the majority population, Posen had argued, hurtles the state sharing the identities of the minority further along the security spiral, and thus towards a war.

But the consequences of a 'partitionist' line of thinking, Posen also points out, need not always point to a predisposition towards violence and hostility. The consequences range from outright violence and ethnic cleansing, to more collaborative and negotiated administrative arrangements, as were put into place in the case of conflicts between the states of Ukraine and Russia in the years that followed the break-up of the Soviet Union. Placing the early deliberations between India and Pakistan within this spectrum would also enable us to have a broader study of the politics of all post-partition states, beyond only those of the individual machinations of the Congress and the Muslim League.

But it is on this set of yardsticks—the ability of both states to be able to answer their security dilemma, while at the same time being able to uphold themselves as viable entities—that the progression of India–

Pakistan relations should also be measured. This book attempts to chart out a process in which the pursuit of security and self-sufficiency by India and Pakistan was collaborative—it was only on the basis of a bilateral dialogue, conducted on the basis of a finalised separation, that the foundations of both states became stronger. Paradoxically, a deeper set of connections and dialogues between India and Pakistan, on the basis of them being established as mutually exclusive states, would, therefore, seem to further enhance the stability of both states.

But what also comes across from an analysis of some of the discussions between the two governments is the requirement of a different set of measures for gauging what actually constitutes conflict. In India–Pakistan relations, instances of actual warfare have—given the nature of the toxic rhetoric that is voiced so frequently on the subject—been remarkably restrained. While the threat of warfare and violence forms a daily part in the rhetoric of both states, the actual violence between the two seems to be on a smaller scale in comparison to what the rhetoric would suggest. A recent episode of militarised conflict, for instance constituted heated debates about the whereabouts of a single aircraft, and the launch of the strikingly coined 'Non Military Pre-Emptive Action'. The single-minded and consistent pursuit of a policy designed to entirely eliminate the threat of the other seems, to this author at least, to not provide an entirely satisfactory descriptor of nature of the India–Pakistan dynamic, and the array of options that it contains for engagement.

For example, the legal scholar Gabriella Blum points out that in the most difficult conflict zones of the twentieth century—all relating to the aftermath of a partition, including India and Pakistan, Israel and Lebanon, as well as Greece and Turkey—the exclusive description of sustained warfare is not in fact entirely correct. Instead, Blum shows, these relationships also contain 'Islands of Agreement'[23] between two states that are also perpetuating a mutual hostility. The causes for hostility between each of these states might well continue to stay unresolved; but mechanisms for managing the conflicts are also devised in this process, and continue to operate simultaneous to the conflict. Such mechanisms constitute 'Islands' of cooperation, and it is in the expansion of such islands, that the best set of solutions for intractable disputes are to be found.

Once they do come into being, a set of calculations that uphold a state's interests also kick into the calculations of all actors. They take actions that will ensure their long-term survival. The better set of explanations about the nature of the India–Pakistan dynamic, therefore, lie in assessments of the extent to which 'finalised' state structures of India and Pakistan are being brought about, even in the midst of their conflict. The questions are not about the scale of the violence in itself—obviously, that is a given—but rather whether or not they can be read as acts that further the objective of 'state-completion'. In the pages that follow, I relate the accounts of a set of negotiations which were based on the assumption that the process of 'state completion' was not a mutually antagonistic process—it also had to be collaboratively defined and achieved.

The assumption, therefore, that the differences out of implementing the partition oppositionally placed India and Pakistan onto slippery slopes for furthering their conflict was not always borne out. There were also ways in which the exercises of reconciling the different requirements for resolving the security dilemma—could be mutually beneficial in further acquiring the object of state completion. Such exercises, moreover, were a product of the finalisation of partition—they took place because the partition had happened, and aimed to put in place measures that further bolstered its effectiveness. Analyses of India and Pakistan relations that assume rules of an oppositional, zero-sum game, therefore, cannot account for processes of consolidation of states interests, which also require a measure of collaboration.

What is also interesting is the extent to which both governments of India and Pakistan were willing to accept a similar set of rules about what defined norms for international behaviour. Their objectives for what a viable state ought to be able to achieve are the same, and, in the 1950s, both governments were in a sense engaged in the pursuit of a similar set of goals. Both states, therefore, were also willing to accept the definitions of what constituted viable entities in the international arena, and were engaged in putting in place a series of measures that would enable them to arrive at these. But the ways in which this could be done, however, also call for wider set of tactics than a stark set of facts about the battlefield, which should also be further integrated into the theorisation of the relationship.

Sources and Structure

Kashmir, and the disputed succession of other princely states, are important omissions in this book. Partly, this was because of an element of choice: there are several excellent studies on each of these topics already. The sheer volume of material on additional aspects of the India–Pakistan relationship also merited, I felt, a book on its own term. But my concern was also to identify topics in which the bureaucratic machinery of the state—as opposed to its army, or police—had a prominent role in determining the course of events. My attempt was to understand under the imperative of state building the processes that swing into action during the creation of a state, even those that are incompletely aligned with the idea of the nation.

The sources I have used are weighted in India's favour. Although I have relied extensively on memoir and some amount of primary literature in the form of government publications from Pakistan, the Constituent Assembly Debates of Pakistan, Legislative Assembly debates of East Pakistan, newspaper records, and some archival material from Dhaka, London, as well as in the United States for piecing together Pakistan's considerations in the shaping of the bilateral policy, my account of India's discussions on bilateral policy necessarily has a more granular and more multi-dimensional aspect. Partly, this is to do with this work being the product of thus far un-accessed archival material on Nehruvian foreign policy from the archive of the ministry of external affairs; and partly it is also to do with the existence of a more sophisticated historiography around Nehruvian foreign policy in comparison to that of Pakistan's early years. But what was most evident from reading files in the Indian Ministry of External Affairs about evacuee property, trade, water, and minorities is the extent to which they could probably have been a clean mirror image of the exercises carried out in Pakistan on the same questions.

In the next chapter, I will briefly offer the outline of instances of how the domestic imperatives of both new governments compelled a cooperative bilateral agenda. In particular, I will examine the discussions around the establishment of two separated foreign offices, and consider what these reveal to us about the nature of the bilateral relationship. Secondly, I will consider the trajectories of jointly constructed institutions designed to grapple with the immediate consequences of the partition, such as the Abducted Women's Cell and the Punjab Boundary Force. My argument is that the workings of such institutions were premised on a mutual recognition of collective dangers posed by the uncertainties around partition, although the day-to-day proceedings of these establishments were undoubtedly rocky. Through these discussions, this chapter addresses a broader concern: how sorting through the messy 'domestic' vicissitudes of the consequences of partition, necessarily impacted on the shaping of the external relationships of both these countries. Furthermore, breaking down the elements of this story is also important to see where the often highly subtle—but strong—threads of cooperation and conjunction between the two nation states are. Arguments premised on the viable coexistence of two separated nation states are the ones that last the longest in bilateral relations.

1

BILATERAL SOLUTIONS

Amongst the earliest actions that the Partition Council took was to establish an office of the High Commissions for India and Pakistan. In this chapter, I highlight how the administrative response to the immediate fallout of the partition, was determined foremost by how it could be bilaterally handled, rather than being governed by any other consideration—including, for instance, the necessity of bringing immediate relief to the law and order question. I examine how the Partition Council approached the question of setting up the foreign ministries for India and Pakistan in August, 1947, and the importance that was given to having a diplomatic architecture in place that could handle the inter-face between India and Pakistan on issues relating to abducted women, and the Punjab Boundary Force. In many ways, notwithstanding the glaring inadequacies of the state apparatus in being able to contain the violence around partition, what was given importance was the ability to produce a bilateral mechanism to deal with partition's fallout.

Therefore, I look at how the process of implementing the early consequences of partition were handled through the shaping of an administrative architecture that was aimed at establishing a mutual recognition between the governments of India and Pakistan. I argue that the actions of bureaucrats and politicians engaged in preparing this architecture were determined by a variety of considerations: how best to promote their own interests within the two states, as well as a determination that the response to the partition had to be driven by two separated entities. Indeed, one of the critical priorities for both governments in the midst of the chaos and violence of the partition rioting in Punjab, was not tackling the question of law and order on its own terms, but rather that India and Pakistan do this separately. What mattered more was not the inadequacy of the state apparatus in either country in being able to contain the fallout of violence across north India and Punjab for their own sake, but rather that this should also be seen to exist within a bilateral framework of action.

'The first step,' Mountbatten decided, on 6 June 1947, 'should be to set up a Committee on the highest possible level which would be charged with the duty of enquiring into all matters connected with the partition.'[1] The immediate decisions of the Partition Council were about the final demarcation of boundaries, the division of the armed forces, division of the staff of the various branches of government, the division of assets, the jurisdiction of courts, the economic relations between the two dominions, as well as methods of deciding how domicile should be determined.[2]

H. M. Patel and Chaudhury Muhammad Ali—both of whom went on to have very successful careers over the 1960s and 70s—were representatives on the 'Steering Committee' of the Partition Council, who would sort through the minutiae of dividing up assets. Chaudhry Muhammad Ali's memoirs describe the relatively cordial functioning of the Council—he suggests that left to themselves, bureaucrats were better placed to be able to quickly work through the conflicting requests by either government. H. M. Patel, his Indian counterpart largely agreed with his assessment: indeed, he went a step further and remarked 'We worked against the backdrop of savage rioting and bitter political animosity. My colleague Muhammad Ali and I, nonetheless managed to clear the substantial portion of the work allocated to us. God knows how much more tension these would have been otherwise'.[3] Ali went on to become Prime Minister of Pakistan in 1955, and before that, was Finance Minister in 1951. Patel, for his part, became Defence Secretary in the years that followed partition, and went on to become Finance Minister under the Janata government. Neither of these officials advocated a particularly intractable approach to dealing with the other country over the issue of splitting governmental assets. But both were very clear that the partition itself, and the ensuing process of creating two new states had to be administered as fast as possible.

Indeed, as we noted above, the moment of independence and partition served many uses for the elites manning the states of India and Pakistan.[4] When the partition plan was announced, many experienced bureaucrats decisively threw in their lot with one or the other dominion, rather than attempting to resist the changes. For some in the bureaucracy, a more tenuous set of decisions were shaped in the aftermath of partition about which state they would 'choose': some staying on for a period; others wanting to return after a few years.[5] Yet for others, and particularly those who went on to have distinguished records in either government, the writing on the wall was clear. Many, in fact, chose to use the creation of the new state as a vehicle for further professional advancement.

In many ways, Ali's and Patel's assumptions during the partition council meetings are of central importance to historians of India–Pakistan relations. They were based on acknowledging the finality and validity of partition as an administrative solution, and creating frameworks for the viable co-existence of successor states, as opposed to attempting to critique this logic in the first place. The most pressing concern for this group of actors was not with the unanticipated nature of the chaos of the partition riots, or even a sense of unreality about the movement of events, but rather with putting in place methods of administration which were consonant with nature of the nation states of India and Pakistan. At the same time, however, they also reveal a curious kind of partnership between the two states: having separated, the best chance for any hope of stable coexistence or amicability lay in first accepting the principle of separation, and then collaborating between institutions that recognised this fact.

The infrastructure for the foreign policy establishments of both countries was planned during the discussions of the Partition Council, which contained within it a separate sub-committee relating to the Department of External Affairs and Commonwealth Relations. The Sub-Committee—named Expert Committee IX—was instructed to make recommendations on relations between the two Dominions, and with other countries; what the diplomatic representation of the two Dominions would be abroad; on membership of international organisations; and on existing international treaties and engagements. Its members included Mr. A. V. Pai, P. Achuta Menon, Lt. Col. Iskander Mirza, and Major Shah.[6] They met daily from 22 June 1947, and submitted their report to the Partition Council on 19 July.[7] The Expert Committee considered the division of assets which belonged to the External Affairs and Commonwealth Relations department of the Government of India, and their holdings abroad, as well as assets which had been jointly owned by other governments in India.

The exchange of High Commissioners between the two new Dominions, moreover, was a task of the highest urgency. While discussing the question of relations between India and Pakistan, the Partition Council's Expert Committee on the External Affairs department declared:

> in order to facilitate mutual cooperation in the solution of the numerous complicated problems that are bound to arise, at any rate in the initial period, in the course of adjustment between their relations, the committee recommend that as soon as possible after the 15th August 1947, there should be an exchange of High Commissioners between the two Dominions. The Steering Committee have considered this matter further and come to the conclusion that it is desirable that the two Dominions have their respective High Commissioners in place by 15th August 1947.[8]

This need not necessarily be seen as an obvious step—against the backdrop of the communal rioting in the Punjab, for instance, it would also have been conceivable to postpone the question of setting up a bilateral machinery for the time being, and decide how the law and order situation ought to be handled. Yet, it did bring home the importance of a separated machinery dealing with the fallout of partition. The Partition Council, moreover decided on 6 August that the two governments would give 'reasonable assistance to the High Commissioners of India and Pakistan in finding the office and residential accommodation they required.'[9] The Council decided that the current High Commissioner for Pakistan, Mr Mirza Ismael, would represent his government at the Partition Council meetings after 15 August. Amongst the earliest diplomatic acts of the government of Pakistan, therefore was related to the completion of the division of assets.

The discussions of the Partition Council reveal little desire to break with the structures of administration and governance of the previous decades, and represent, rather, concerted efforts to secure them within new nations. Moreover, their tone is suggestive not of individuals overwhelmed by the violent turn of events, but those of cool headed bureaucrats making pragmatic calculations about how to secure more assets for their side. The operations of the Partition Council therefore are indicative of the nature of bilateral engagement: while fraught with minute disagreements, it was nonetheless necessary to both to ensure the completion of its tasks, so that two viable centres of government could be established.

The Council oversaw the work of a Steering Committee, which would organise the minutiae of division of the various branches of the government into the new governments of India and Pakistan. The immediate decisions of the Partition Council were about the final demarcation of boundaries, the division of the armed forces, division of the staff of the various branches of government, the division of assets, the jurisdiction of courts, the economic relations between the two dominions, as well as methods of deciding how domicile should be determined.[10]

Agreement on a decision by the Steering Committee was rarely unanimous. For example, representatives for India and Pakistan respectively at the Steering Committee of the Partition Council differed strongly with regard to the framing of the terms of reference for deciding how to divide the material assets of the government of India. H. M. Patel had argued that the existing assets of the government, such as irrigation canals, railway lines and telegraph lines, should simply remain in place. Muhammad Ali, however, pointed out that merely the accident of geography should not have priority over an equitable distribution of assets, since 'it was only fair that both the successor governments should in the matter of efficiency of services start on an equal a footing as possible.'[11] Although the Partition Council worked amicably enough, and did succeed with much of the work of the division of the government, it was also a forum for the articulation of the differences between the two governments. There were many—and some lasting—disagreements over the ways in which the partition was being implemented. Yet, even so, the need to carry this through formed the basis of a kind of cooperation between the two governments.

An Expert Committee within the Partition Council also examined methods of recruiting officers into the Foreign Service of Pakistan, as well as the question of transfer of those who had 'opted' to serve in Pakistan. A functional foreign ministry establishment, and the personnel required for this were rapidly recruited. Officers who had been in the government, and served abroad in various capacities, were highly valued. A recruitment board, which interviewed officers in the government of India, who had opted for Pakistan, and wished to join the Foreign Service, interviewed a number of candidates who had previously worked in the Princely States, as well those who represented India's economic and trade interests in the Commonwealth. It became increasingly important to both countries that a specialised, and professionalised service handle the question of India–Pakistan relations, rather than allowing looser arrangements to remain in place. In India, as in Pakistan, most of these men were those who had been active in the Indian Civil Service before independence, and had worked outside India in the diplomatic establishments of the government of India including South Africa, Washington, and China. By the end of August, a new foreign ministry was established in Karachi, and its foreign secretary, another senior bureaucrat in the partition council negotiations, Ikramullah Khan. The expert committee had envisaged this to be a comparatively small establishment to begin with: it noted that by September, 'one secretary, two joint secretaries, four deputy secretaries and eight junior officer', would have to be in place. Between them, they would manage the various sections under which external policies would need to be made; such as the Middle East, the United States, USSR, Commonwealth countries, India, emigration and Hajj travel, international conferences and UNO documentation, protocol, and passports.

One of the candidates who was interviewed for recruitment into the Foreign Service of Pakistan was Aga Hilaly. In many ways, his trajectories are similar to those described in this book. A member of the Indian Civil Service, Hilaly had worked in the province of Mysore, as well as in the Commerce Department of the government of India. He had travelled in Europe and Egypt as part of the Indian delegations for various conferences, and, the report concluded, 'had a fair acquaintance with current problems, political as well as economic, national as well as international'.[12] Hilaly had a law degree from Cambridge, went on to have a long and successful career in the Foreign Ministry, and, in 1969, went on as Ambassador to the United States. What this also shows is that far from questioning the soundness of the reasons for partition, many officers eagerly embraced the opportunities for success in Pakistan; and were eager to participate in the making of the state. For them, the best options for advancement lay not in preserving links with the un-partitioned subcontinent, but in contributing to carving out a separate, and sovereign state identity, with a clear foreign policy agenda of their own. While this agenda would come to include differences with India—differences, moreover, which were serious and lasting—it was also important to both to establish machineries which could clearly differentiate the governments of both countries.

For India, the report noted, few changes would need to be made to the existing Commonwealth Relations department, apart from one major exception:

> There will be substantial addition of work to the Commonwealth Relations Wing of the department arising from India's relations with the dominion of Pakistan Commonwealth Relations Wing will require one joint secretary, one deputy secretary and one under secretary and one additional Pakistan Section to deal with a large volume of complicated work connected with the dominions of Pakistan.[13]

The erstwhile External Affairs and Commonwealth Relations department, set up in 1937, had been a large and sprawling affair, and dealt with a diverse set of issues. The Government of India had acquired increased prominence in international affairs during the inter-war years. Its representatives were frequently attached as additional members to already existing British missions abroad. A large part of its work concerned the issues relating to Indians settlements elsewhere in the Commonwealth, most prominently, as far as their representation in the administrative apparatus of the Government of India was concerned, in South Africa, Australia, Ceylon, Malaya and Burma.

The infrastructure for conducting a foreign policy was quite well established for the government of India before to the transfer of power. The new Foreign Secretary for India would be Sir Girija Shankar Bajpai—a veteran of the colonial foreign policy department. In 1942, for example, he had signed the Atlantic Charter on behalf of the Indian government. Astute and exacting, he had worked in the Indian Civil Service for some decades before independence, and had been Agent General for India in Washington during the Second World War. Nehru asked Bajpai to oversee the structuring of the Ministry of External Affairs in July 1947, and he retained the position of Secretary General in the Ministry until 1952, when he became the Governor of Bombay.[14] Alongside him worked Subimal Dutt, a senior official in the Ministry in Delhi, and, during the late 1940s, an influential voice in the making, and execution of policy on Pakistan.[15]

By all accounts, the government of Pakistan was badly under-staffed and under-funded in the immediate period after independence. The ministry of foreign affairs was based in Karachi, itself a city which was undergoing a seismic shift under the onslaught of partition migration. On 6 June 1947, Liaquat had circulated a memo cautioning that the needs of the future central government of Pakistan in Karachi were urgent, and that 'A survey carried out by the Sind government has shown that even if the Sind government move out of Karachi, the available accommodation will be far short of the requirements of the Pakistan government.'[16] Therefore, Liaquat continued, the partition council should 'issue a directive to all departments of the government of India that they should give full assistance and provide the necessary facilities and the required priority for the establishment of the headquarters of the Pakistan government at Karachi.'[17] The early high commissioners, moreover, had often been involved in the Pakistan movement, and were, by and large close to Jinnah's own faction of the Muslim League.

Zafarullah Khan was appointed Foreign Minister of Pakistan in 1947, and worked closely with Liaquat Ali Khan in shaping Pakistan's initial foreign policy. Within a few weeks of taking over as Foreign Minister, the dispute over the line of control in Kashmir broke out, and he was despatched to the United Nations to represent Pakistan's case.[18] Pakistan's membership at the United Nations had been approved—unanimously—in September 1947, and Zafarullah's time in New York in January 1948 was busy. While putting forward Pakistan's case for the Kashmir dispute, he also remarked—unoriginally, as any listener of Indian and Pakistani conversation will know—'As a matter of fact, the stage members around the table were rather surprised at how much agreement there was between the two governments despite the differences which had arisen'.[19] It was thus important to both sides to show that the fact of the partition was being upheld by both government, and that India and Pakistan operated as separate entities from the beginning.

Much of this process—of the necessity of creating state infrastructure to deal with the consequences of the partition—was based on the acceptance of the principle of separation, and the necessity of recognizing the other in terms of its functioning as a state. In doing this, greater possibilities for collaborative dialogue were also created, based, in turn, on the necessity of completing the state- making process in India and Pakistan. Indeed, what also comes across from the early discussions about the nature of bilateral interactions is that, to a large extent, the 'blue-print' for the way in which the relationship would be conducted was set in place within a very few weeks of the partition—and may well, in fact, have already been in place during the time of the interim government.[20]

The Punjab Boundary Force

The existing capabilities of the state machinery, however—these parallel attempts at consolidation by both governments notwithstanding—were clearly inadequate. Indeed, the Chief of Army Staff in India, Arthur Smith, warned a colleague, 'The situation in Alwar State is appalling. Muslims are being murdered left and right, and we are pretty certain that State Troops might be responsible for this, as well as for burning crops. There are bound to be reprisals'.[21] The crux of the problem, though, Smith felt, was a total lack of jurisdictional demarcation of the institutions concerned—the efforts of the army to control the situation were hampered by the fact that 'while most of the disturbed areas lie in Punjab, a portion of it extends into the United Provinces. Troops in the Punjab have the backing of an Ordinance which gives them wider powers—those in the UP have not'.[22]

That the Punjab province, stretching from New Delhi, Gurgaon, across the plains into Lahore via the princely states of Bhatinda, suffered an irretrievable break down of law and order in the summer months of 1947 is well catalogued. The sense of helplessness and powerlessness against the savagery of the rioting—which led to widespread ethnic cleansing of minority communities—is documented in memoir after memoir of civil servants and observers of the time.[23] But the reasons for its failures were also not surprising.[24] The Boundary Force was working in a climate when neither state actually had a monopoly on the exercise of violence. The princely states of the province also acted within legal spaces where they were not answerable to either central government, and whose activities were not aligned with the objectives of the Boundary Force. Indeed, the Governor of the Punjab province, Ivan Jenkins, rightly foresaw that the administrative machinery of the Punjab would not be able to handle delivering a more orderly partition. He warned for instance that there existed at least three private armies' in the province—the RSS, the Muslim League National Guard, and the Akal Sena.[25]

Notwithstanding such assessments, however, the early governments of India and Pakistan chose firmly not to pool their resources jointly when dealing with the question of the horrific communal violence across the Punjab boundary line, or even with the question of abducted women. At a meeting on 29 August in Lahore of the Joint Defence Council, Nehru and Liaquat Ali Khan agreed that:

> it was of paramount importance that the psychological welfare of refugees travelling from one dominion to the other be considered. It was necessary, therefore, for both countries to lend soldiers to each other, who would conduct the bands of refugees safely across the border, and with whom the refugees themselves would feel secure with.[26]

A joint statement was issued subsequently, signed by both prime ministers, which assured refugees coming into both countries, of protection by soldiers of their own religion.

Moreover, the statement continued, 'from 1 September, the governments of India and Pakistan have taken over in West and East Punjab respectively the full military responsibility of law and order which previously was vested in the Punjab Boundary Force'.[27] After 15 August, the dominion governments of India and Pakistan would have to approve the decisions of the state governments of East and

West Punjab to reverse this order. It was also accepted at this meeting, however, that the Joint Defence Council could not have the authority to intervene in the 'disturbed areas' of either state, or be vested with the authority to declare a district to be a 'disturbed area'.[28]

But the cause for or of the failure of the boundary force, due to an insufficiently delineated structure of authority and jurisdiction is interesting for our purposes here. The instincts of both governments from the very first were to work separately, rather than jointly, even on issues where the objective was similar. Subsequent scholarship on this issue has shown how the failure of the Boundary Force was unsurprising, given the ambiguity in the structures of command at the time.[29] The Punjab Boundary Force was also serviced by personnel many of whom were concerned with which country they would serve in, and whose sympathies often extended further for one community than the other in this situation.

Major General Shahid Hamid, who was Private Secretary to the Commander in Chief of the undivided Indian army, Auchinleck—who, in 1947, was Supreme Commander of all British forces in India and Pakistan—noted in his diaries that the Punjab Boundary Force had virtually crumbled under the onslaught of the Punjab violence. The entry in his diary for the 19 August noted: 'The situation is explosive... There is even communal tension within the Punjab Boundary Force, and there is a likelihood that the troops may be shooting at each other....'[30] Similarly, Auchinleck himself, in a meeting of the Joint Defence Council on 28 August, declared that the Punjab Boundary Force should now be closed down, and that the units of the Boundary Force now be distributed between India and Pakistan.[31] It was no longer clear which institution prioritised the control of communal violence. And an organisation that could contain both Indian and Pakistani personnel engaged in the preservation for law and order in Punjab was no longer feasible.

Similarly, the Pakistani diplomat and politician, Jahanara Shahnawaz for instance, also pointed to the politicisation of the Punjab Boundary Force from both sides, writing 'some unwise Punjab officials whom the public had approached, had been saying that its policies were being framed by the British General in command of the Boundary Force and Hindu Generals'. Ayub Khan—who was at the time

Pakistan's representative on the Punjab Boundary Force. Ayub Khan, unsurprisingly, given Jenkins assessment of the situation, realised that the use of the PBF was increasingly unreliable. In a telephone call to Jinnah, he grimly got to the root of the problem: 'The Force is not doing what it was meant to—it is better simply to shut it down, and then to look after our own side.'[32]

The story of the Punjab Boundary Force does not provide a particularly edifying example of the possibilities of peacefully implementing a mandate for partition. But its failure is revealing: this was because, once a partition is announced, then the loyalties of the personnel of the state has to decisively swing in one direction or the other. This way of thinking was obviously not going to go away, and was already evident in the weeks and months that followed the partition, that destabilising the administrative certainty of the fact of the partition by suggesting that there could be methods through which this should be diluted when meeting common challenges—such as aiding in the flow of huge numbers of migrants—was seen as presenting a challenge to the new states' individual sovereignties. The focus was on establishing two separate structures of governance, rather than carrying on with one which could work for both sides. Nonetheless, it is also important to note that this process did not always preclude the possibility of also furthering a certain amount of cooperation between the two states.

Destructive though these processes obviously were, they also opened up other spaces for collaboration and engagement, as well as a sense of possibility, that the duties of the two state could also lie in implementing a better set of cooperative actions with the other, as in perpetuating a violent relationship. But this is also an illustration of the ways in which the two nascent states chose to cooperate: a single 'joint' mechanism run dually by members of both governments was out of the question, but one in which two separated entities of two states could work in parallel, in consultation with one another, in ways that strengthened the claims to legitimacy of both nations, was not.

Dialogues on Abducted Women

'Partition', note the historians Arie Dubnov and Laura Robson, 'is having a moment.'[33] In the present context, a re-emergence of interest of what newly divided states do in the aftermath of their separation, and the actions they take in order to solidify the lines of division, offers new perspectives on the actions that the newly established states of India and Pakistan took in the aftermath of their separation. The trajectories of the Punjab Boundary Force and the Abducted Women's cell also provide us with case studies of how post-partition states get to grips with the question of implementing a partition. The ability to effectively govern over a situation of partition, furthermore, is also related to the amount of planning and resources provided to governments to be able to handle its aftermath. For India and Pakistan, noted the political scientist Radha Kumar during the 1990s—another moment when the processes of partition had acquired renewed interest—the situation was also particularly difficult because the pressing need to 'quit' India meant that the plan to partition the subcontinent was drawn up and executed within five years of each other. In other instances, partition plans were 'incubated' for far longer stretches of time, in between dilatory arrangements for home rule and mandate arrangements.[34] Unlike the case of the Cyprus partition, for instance, or Ireland, the making of South Asian partition policy, its implementation, and its finalisation were all achieved within a relatively short period of time—a mere six years—to Cyprus' twenty and Ireland's seventy.

A particularly clear manifestation of such concerns were evidenced in the activities of both governments to 'recover' women who had been abducted during the partition riots. Questions about what was required from the state with regard to abducted women during genocide violence were not new. In a different context, the historian Keith Watenpaugh argues that the responses to mass murder and ethnic cleansing in the twentieth century were themselves constructed—these responses were also about establishing collective solidarities amongst a certain profile of European middle-class women who wished to be associated with humanitarianism in the aftermath of the Armenian genocide, and who identified with an early wave of reformist, missionary feminism. The exercise in the recovery of women also acted as a basis of shaping the constituency of those who belonged within a political community.[35]

The activities of the 'Women's Wing' of the Ministry of Rehabilitation in Delhi, or the 'Women's Relief Section' established by Fatima Jinnah, ought also to be contextualised alongside these attempts. Indeed, the parallel with the League of Nations' 'rescue' operation is worth recalling: not because of an exact correlation of developments in the two very different political contexts, but because of the precedents which had already been established in the creating of political and social solidarities around the rescue of women during fluid political circumstances. The rhetoric around the recovery of abducted women in India also served to consolidate a political platform around the necessity of rallying around notions of national honour, and with it, the legitimacy of the state.[36] It is no coincidence that the two governments—not otherwise known for the alacrity with which they respond to challenges to law and order—acted fairly promptly on the issue of abducted women: their existence posed a powerful reminder of the existence of the uncertainties of the division, as well as a compelling argument for the impossibility of adhering to a single loyalty.

Such responses, moreover, were jointly constructed—and mutually reinforcing. In the shaping of the question of the repatriation of abducted women in India and Pakistan, both governments were also simultaneously, and in a similar fashion, using the issue to establish a specific set of solidarities: defining a sense of who belonged to the nation state, and why these bonds had to be respected. In turn, these solidarities were about demonstrating what their states were for, and how they were viable as administrative and political entities, which necessitated a measure of cooperation. In this, the two governments worked collaboratively—and highlighted this cooperation, vocally, and visibly, as if needing to prove that they could surmount this challenge.

Such discussions also reveal the beginnings of a debate about 'civil society' in India and Pakistan, and ideals of how actors outside the bureaucracy ought to behave. In fact, in many ways the recovery process was central to the sense of self of both nations, and the politics around it shaped coalitions of groups that could have a stronger voice after the partition. The activities they undertook were indeed mammoth: Pippa Virdee notes, for instance that Liaison Agencies established by the government of West Punjab, which worked with the Ministry of Rehabilitation, the Military Evacuation Organisation, as well as social workers, 'recovered' some 20,695 Muslim women and brought them back to Pakistan, over the period of a decade.[37] When in 1957 the government of India allowed the Abducted Persons Act of 1949 to lapse, the government of Pakistan quietly followed suit.

At heart, regardless of the incessant disagreement about intentions and methods, these early activities of the governments of India and Pakistan with respect to one another, were collaborative: they were a joint attempt at achieving a clearer definition of the responsibilities for both governments. The decisions to engage at all with the mutually constituted mechanisms of the separation, were motivated by finding stability in the aftermath of the partition, rather than seeking grounds for the further deterioration of relations, or seeking revenge for the chaos it wreaked.

This was not a smooth process. For instance, Mrs Premvati Thapar, wrote to Gopalaswami Ayyangar, stating that a number of Hindu and Sikh women recovered from Pakistan were being housed in the women's jail in Lahore, rather than at the Provincial Transit Camp, which had been agreed upon in the Inter-dominion Agreements of September 1948. But, she said, 'no list [of the women recovered] is sent to our workers at Lahore or to any of our recovery officers in India.'[38] Recovery operations ran into hindrances with the classification of 'closed districts'. Pakistan restricted the access of Indian recovery workers to the districts of Jhelum, Sialkot, Gujarat, Rawalpindi and Campbellpore, as a security measure in connection with the Kashmir war. India, meanwhile, had closed off Gurdaspur and Kangra. By December 1948, Ayyangar was receiving letters of complaint from workers charged with this job. Actions by the West Punjab government to restrict access to some women who were in Pakistan—actions that may well have reflected the desire of some to simply stay where they were—were also sometimes highlighted as yet another instance of the obduracy of the government of Pakistan.

Legislation around the issue of abducted women was passed on both sides fairly quickly, and was designed to set up machinery for the process of recovery of 'abducted women', as well as to define what such a category constituted. The question was thrashed out in detail in an inter-dominion conference on the aftermath of partition in December 1947—the same month when, it is worth recalling, India and Pakistan were engaged in a small war in Kashmir. The conference delegates decided, nonetheless, that a sizeable infrastructure be built around the rehabilitation of abducted women. A separate 'Women's Wing' of the Ministry of Relief and Rehabilitation was set up, which drew from the talents and experiences of an array of formidable social workers, including Rameshwari Nehru, Mridula Sarabhai and Sarojini Naidu.[39] By March 1948, the Partition Council ruled that the governments would provide abducted women with rehabilitation regardless of whether they were accepted back into their families. In 1949, the Indian government finalised legislation through which they were entitled to recover Muslim abducted women—a piece of legislation that stayed intact until 1957. A corresponding ordinance was passed in Pakistan, and a coordinating officer was appointed by the governor general, whose task would correspond to the officer overseeing the recovery of abducted persons in India.[40]

Mridula Sarabhai, in addition to being a prominent voice in Congress politics in the early 1950s, was a formidable and well connected social worker who had been actively engaged in framing policy regarding abducted women. In the early 1950s she worked closely with Y.D. Gundevia, an official in the Indian Ministry of External Affairs then working on the Pakistan desk. In his memoirs, Gundevia records how Sarabhai was also very well connected with the machinery of the government of Pakistan, and in regular contact with Liaquat Ali Khan. She could, he pointed out, work far faster through her network of contacts than what the Indian mission would achieve.[41] He describes how an inter-dominion agreement came into being regarding the joint machinery for the recovery of abducted women on either side of the Punjab.[42] This was a fraught process, and they recognised that the 'recovery' of women was not a simple task: many were unwilling to return, fearing condemnation and stigma from their original communities; others simply wished to stay where they were, because of the new links that they forged, in private, and away from demanding questions about loyalty and allegiance from their governments.

Nonetheless Gundevia, mirroring the efforts of the government of West Punjab, directed the deputy high commissioner in Lahore to include the clerical establishment of the recovery office into the staff. A small office for social workers aiding in the recovery of abducted women in Pakistan was set up as a wing in the office of the Deputy High Commission in Lahore. It was financed by a variety of sources within the government, and also received separate funding from the office of the High Commission.[43] In May 1949, Gundevia received a letter from M.R. Sachdev, Chief Secretary in the East Punjab Province. The letter complained of a disparity in the numbers of cases of recovery between East and West Punjab. The government of West Punjab, Sachdev argued 'are indifferent, if not actually hostile to recovery work, and despite verbal promises made by West Punjab leaders that recovery work will be pushed on with rigour in that province, their declarations have so far remained mere pious hopes'.[44] Moreover, he continued:

> The East Punjab government consider that the attention of the Pakistan Government should be specially invited to this disparity in figures and that it may be brought home to them, that the higher recovery figures in East Punjab do not show, as is likely to be stated by them, that there were more abducted women and children in East Punjab.[45]

The matter was taken up with officials in the Pakistan government and corrective action was subsequently taken. In March 1949, Ms Sarabhai had a meeting with the Pakistani ministers for rehabilitation, Khwaja Shahbuddin, and with the minister without portfolio, M.A. Gurmani. These questions were dealt with in detail by the offices of the deputy high commissioners, in both India and Pakistan. In March 1949, the deputy high commissioner in Lahore, Mr Y.K. Puri, held a press conference, in which he entreated the All Pakistan Muslim League to utilise its resources for the recovery of abducted women and children. He added 'both governments were far from lukewarm in their endeavours to complete this work and that they would certainly not relax their efforts,' since this 'was a humanitarian task which everybody was anxious to see completed with the least possible delay'.[46] Although the question of abducted women was important to both governments, what was recognised from the outset that these efforts could not emerge from a joint system of governance, but rather, needed to be tackled by both separately. The deputy high commissioners' remarks thus also reflect a system of working whereby both governments, although working towards a similar objective, had also recognised that this did need to be carried out on a separated basis.

Capitalising from the Partition

In this section, I will present a spectrum of opinion across the foreign policy establishments of India and Pakistan on the question of the welfare of minorities, and consider how they represented different approaches to the question of finalising the partition. In doing so, I will also consider the limitation of certain forms of arguments, that appeared to represent a desire to 'undo' the choice of the partition, while highlighting how, those who advocated a transition to both states being present in the task of regulating the impact of partition in fact also enjoyed a certain amount of success.

In order to do this, I will also consider the trajectories of two individuals who started out as being central to the discussions about partition in India and Pakistan, and ended up being at a relative distance from the most critical centres of power. Sri Prakasa, the first Indian high commissioner for Pakistan, and Chaudhry Khaliquzzaman, the first Pakistani minister for minority welfare, had many commonalities. Both were from the United Provinces, and had cut their teeth in the agitations of the 1920s and 30s in the Congress and Muslim League. Both also had to navigate the treacherous waters of internal struggles within their own parties and, in 1947, could assert a reasonable degree of proximity to Nehru and Jinnah respectively. But they were also overruled when they tried to advocate a slower transition from the systems of joint governance operating from both India and Pakistan.

In his memoirs, Sri Prakasa, the first Indian high commissioner to Karachi, dwells on these dilemmas at great length. Within a year of his arrival at Karachi, Sri Prakasa had had to contend with the differing, and often more rigid views of his deputy high commissioner in Lahore, who, Prakasa felt—on the whole, probably correctly—had closer ties with the ministry in Delhi. Sri Prakasa himself had been active in the Congress, and in the politics of UP during the 1920s and 30s, and had, over the years, developed many close relationships with various members of the Muslim League who had eventually migrated to Pakistan. For these reasons, he wrote in his memoirs, he was a good candidate for being India's envoy to Pakistan—within days of his arrival, he 'felt immediately at home, meeting old friends and acquaintances everywhere I went'. His tenure was short-lived, and mostly successfully hampered by his colleagues in Delhi, as well as the deputy high commissioner in Lahore. His first few days in this position were uncomfortable—in his memoirs, he describes how, immediately after his arrival, he stayed in the house that had once belonged to Lala Lajpat Rai: 'His hospitable house was also full of refugees, and there was scarcely room enough to move about'.[47] Indeed, the substantial portion of the work of his high commission related to dealing with refugees, to and from India. His office was flooded with requests for help by departing Hindus and Sikhs in the Punjab, and later, from Sind.

During his time in Pakistan, Sri Prakasa was vocal in his criticism of the Two Nation Theory and, in his memoirs, records the many private conversations he had with prominent personalities in Karachi about the futility of the partition. For peoples who had similar language, lifestyles, cultures, and—from his point of view of being an active member of the Congress Party in India which still had a reasonably strong presence in Karachi—politics, he argued, partition seemed to have achieved no useful result. But, for the most part, these reflections suited neither government. His endeavours to be more lenient with Muslim migrants who wished to return to India were also generally thwarted. He repeatedly complained to Delhi about not being included in the making of policy with Pakistan, but was generally met with polite unhelpfulness.

In 1948, Sri Prakasa became concerned at the impact that Patel's and other Indian leaders' statements on the option of exchanging land for refugees had had in the Pakistani press, as well as the frankly ugly tenor of the statements about the rights of minorities in either country. His dispatches to Delhi argued that it 'is necessary for responsible Indian authorities in public statements to credit [the Pakistan] Government with good intentions, [since] if we attack the Government, Hindus will be encouraged to leave.'[48] Sri Prakasa delivered the same message in the Pakistani press himself, and made a statement to the effect that the government of Pakistan 'were trying to do justice to Hindus and had issued instructions to their officials to treat the minorities well'. This, however, evinced a strong reaction in India. Sri Prakasa received an angry telegram from the Premier of West Bengal, B.C. Roy, the very next day, demanding 'further explanation' of such a statement.[49] Sri Prakasa's argument was that the best strategy would be to withhold statements hostile to the government of Pakistan, until the Indian government had 'finally decided to take strong action'. In the interim, an openly hostile stance would only stoke further unease. This approach, however, failed to cut ice with any of the Indian leadership. An additional terse telegram arrived from Nehru, stating that 'Unfortunately what Pakistan Government says is not reflected in local policy in East Bengal.'[50] As the year drew to a close, the number of migrants entering India from East Pakistan increased, and with this grew the tide of angry complaints from state governments.

To some extent the positions taken by Chaudhry Khaliquzzaman are comparable. Khaliquzzaman too came from the heart of the Muslim League's political circles—from a wealthy landowning family in Awadh, to whom the decision of going to Pakistan represented many difficult choices. If he himself was divided about the prospect of working in Pakistan, he also included in his memoirs the fact that several members of his family were eager to do so. His brother in law was also told by Jinnah to report immediately to Karachi to become Pakistan's first advocate general. Khaliquzzaman counselled his brother in law not to rashly accept this offer, but to consider, after all, 'his considerable properties besides his average income of Rs. 10,000 a month and he could never expect to keep his large family on the salary which he would be able to draw as Advocate General in Pakistan'.[51] But the brother in law, Khaliquzzaman also made sure to mention in the book, was not convinced, and staunchly disagreed: 'he kicked at the walls and said "I am not going to sacrifice my conscience for mortar and brick..."'.

As the numbers of refugees flowing across the boundaries swelled, Zafarullah Khan raised the issue at the United Nations, condemning the government of India's persecution of its minority citizens, and declared: 'Unless the government of India took steps to end the slaughter of Muslims a formal complaint would be filed with the United Nations. If satisfaction is not obtained, the Government of Pakistan may have to resort to direct methods'[52] For Khaliquzzaman, however, these speeches did not represent the correct solution to the problem, as, he pointed out in his memoirs, the danger was, this would only hurt the minorities left in India further. At a press conference in India, Khaliquzzaman attempted to play down such attacks, and said that the Zafarullah statement did not have the backing of the government of Pakistan, and had not, moreover, 'correctly appreciated the situation...'. Khaliquzzaman even went as far as to say that 'it is not correct to say that the Government of India is responsible for what has happened'. If a satisfactory arrangement to the situation of minorities and their migration had to be reached, then a better relationship with India was crucial.[53]

In the short term, this stance did not seem to play well in Khaliquzzaman's favour. To his dismay, at a meeting with Jinnah in October, he found himself struggling to contain the damage. Jinnah, he says, curtly informed him that this statement had 'hurt us very much',[54] and his subsequent attempts at coordinating a more accommodating policy with India were met largely with non-committal silence from the new government:

> What pained me most in the Quaid-e-Azam's reception of me was that he had been mainly responsible for putting the burden of the leadership of Indian Muslims on my shoulders, but at the time of my interview with him, which was the last in my life, he did not realize my responsibilities towards the Indian Muslims who were facing a situation never before experienced in the history of a thousand years.

In a sense, this also captured the nature of the dilemma that the shapers of the bilateral relationship had faced: the partition had taken place so that Pakistan could provide security to the subcontinent's Muslims, and provide an state apparatus that could have parity with one for Hindus. Yet, at the same time, in the midst of the transition between the political rhetoric of the partition, to the process of creating viable states of India and Pakistan, any attempt at undermining the basis of the existence for the states of India or Pakistan, through the rhetoric of trying to highlight commonalities, was not, under the circumstances, as Jinnah was trying to point out to Khaliquzzaman in this instance, helpful.

Indeed, Zafarullah Khan's own trajectory also offers a contrast in terms of the different kinds of positions that could be adopted about the validity of partition as a solution. The historian Victor Kattan argues that Zafarullah Khan's career also involved an encompassing of the major questions that the Empire had faced in the 1940s: the questions of decolonisation, the process of transferring power to minorities and majorities; and the legal standing of the entities created in their wake. Above all, in fact, Zafaruallah had grappled, over some thirty years, the question of the rights and wrongs of redrawing boundary lines and the implementation of partition. Furthermore, the tenor of the decisions that he took at the International Court of Justice, whether on the matter of South and South West Africa, Palestine, or, for that matter in front of the Radcliffe Boundary Commission, in fact involved quite a consistent principle: the transfer of power had to be completed with the support of the majority communities in the countries concerned.[55]

What Khaliquzzaman and Sri Prakasa were up against, however, were not necessarily those who opposed a measure of cooperation between India and Pakistan in principle—or even to the equality of rights of minorities: it was against a set of officials determined to give meaning to the finality of partition by enforcing a cleaner division. The rhetoric of the need to finalise the partition, which included—but was not necessarily limited to—a majoritarian interpretation of South Asian politics, became the predominant feature of dealing with bilateral relations, within the first few months of the existence of both states. Cooperation between India and Pakistan, moreover, had to be conducted on this basis. Neither Sri Prakasa or Khaliquzzaman had in fact made public statements which went against the nation states of India and Pakistan. The points in their arguments, however, were about saying that relations between the two ought to be better because of their pre-partition ties. This, however, was out of step with the requirements of either government: pre-partition ties were neither here nor there; what was more relevant was how the question could be framed in ways that allowed for both states claims to existence clearly recognised.

In 1950, however, the dangerousness of the refugee crisis in Bengal seemed to provide a context where Khaliquzzaman's suggestions were adopted. In the next chapter, I will consider the developments that led to the shaping of the Bengal Pact—an arrangement that allowed for the governments of India and Pakistan to be legally accountable to one another over the welfare of minorities in Bengal. To some extent, the spirit of Khaliquzzaman's suggestions: that the sovereignty and jurisdiction of India and Pakistan not be defined in such exclusivist terms as to hurt the minority populations still within them, were heard in that situation. However, as I will also show, this was also heavily moderated by the presence of the separated government apparatus of India and Pakistan—minorities in Bengal were not told that their new nationalities did not matter, and that they were free to carry out their lives as if partition had not taken place. Instead, they were asked to work more closely with both governments. Participating within this exercise, however, did not always preclude the possibility of a closer collaboration between both governments.

The advent of the partition itself, had not necessarily predisposed the leadership and bureaucracy to be firmly committed to a single policy of bilateral hostility. After the fact of partition was established, the nature of the relationship between both sides could, for all three of these individuals, have just as well have been quite amicable, as it could veer towards hostility. Obviously, there was a diversity of opinion within the leadership and bureaucracy in India and Pakistan over how best to go about shaping bilateral relations, ranging from Zafarullah Khan's forceful denunciation of India's discriminatory policies towards minorities at the UN, or even to Sri Prakasa's jovial questioning of the merits of the two nation theory. But within this spectrum, those who advocated working within the implication of the partition, and accepting the necessity of a clear separation of two states that came into being as a consequence of this, had the greatest ability in getting their views across.

2

THE NEHRU–LIAQUAT PACT

In April 1950, Nehru and Liaquat Ali Khan met in New Delhi, and signed a declaration that their governments would protect the interests of minorities in both their countries. Both governments would now be accountable to each other on the issue of the protection of rights of minorities; and the declaration set out a variety of infrastructural elements by which its requirements would be implemented. In its definitions, scope and flexibilities, the Pact was amongst the more accommodative pieces of writing in the history of the bilateral relationship, but what was particularly interesting about it was that it was also in the political interests of both governments to sign to it, even in the midst of what seemed like catastrophic developments leading to war.

The Nehru–Liaquat Pact in fact represented something quite unusual: it was a joint agreement to extend the jurisdiction of their high commissions into the welfare of minority citizens across the border. To states as notoriously prickly about their sovereignty and jurisdiction as India and Pakistan, the signing of such an agreement by their prime ministers did represent a significant moment. Exactly why this pact should be entered into, therefore, requires a further analysis, and, in this chapter, I argue that it was a way of in fact bolstering their claims to a separated and viable statehood. This was an example of how, in the aftermath of partition, the necessity of solidifying the fact of the partition further, could also enable acts of greater cooperation between both states.

During the early 1950s, the question of migration and refugees represented a substantial threat to the political stability of both governments. As refugees and migrants streamed in in uncontrollable numbers in search of rehabilitation, employment and security, the issue also became politically charged, which could be hurled between the central and provincial governments in India and Pakistan as accusations of incompetence, corruption, and neglect.[1] In 1948, the ministry of Khuhro, Chief Minister in Sindh had collapsed over the refugee issue. Indeed, the politics of refugee rehabilitation in Sindh formed a mirror image to that of West Bengal, where the provincial government, while politically unable to form very hostile positions to the incoming refugees, attacked the central government for its lack of any wherewithal in being able to adequately address the problem, or the will to provide adequate resources from the centre.

The politics of the refugee question also played out particularly dramatically in the Bengal delta, where, unlike the relative quickness of the migrant movement across the Punjab, people crossed the border in fits and starts over a prolonged period.[2] Movement across the Bengal delta was in fact a more complicated phenomenon. Not all migrants, necessarily crossed with the intention of establishing a permanent home across the country—in many cases, this was about seasonal occupation, a temporary move, or simply of seeking short-term shelter until communal troubles at home blew over. Even more significantly to governments in the eastern provinces, the Bengal delta represented an extraordinarily dense set of economic, cultural and migratory networks, in which travel across what was to become the new boundary line had always been quite frequent. Migration patterns across this region—seasonal, vocational and habitual—were difficult to conclusively mould to the requirements of the two nation states. But the spectacle of thousands of migrants streaming in unchecked across their borders—and the conflation of this question with the tussle between central and provincial authority—represented a debilitating threat to the stability of both central governments.

As people traversed the complex, frequently bloodied distances between the categories of minorities, migrants, refugees and citizens, they discovered they had to negotiate with two governments who were determined to attach lasting meaning to the consequences of the partition.[3] Both governments were also determined to avoid circumstances that allowed for people to belong to 'both' countries—but the only way this could be achieved, paradoxically, was the collaborative construction of an infrastructure that could enter into these nether spaces of the effects of the partition. The inter-dominion conferences on the movement of minorities between India and Pakistan were aimed at staunching the numbers who were departing from or arriving into Bengal. The scale of the migration, its complexity, as well as the historical legacy of easy travel across the Bengal delta, had convinced both governments that their efforts had to be directed, not towards rehabilitation, but instead at persuading migrants to remain in place, or even better, to return, by providing for joint safeguards from both states for their protection.

Inter-Dominion Negotiations

Both governments also faced the formidable opposition put up by provincial premiers, who insistently argued that they were being dangerously inundated by the inflow of refugees across the border. The central governments therefore were confronted by a double dilemma: on the one hand, there was every requirement to maintain a semblance of symmetry and balance in terms of the numbers entering each country, which could only be secured by reassuring minorities of their future stability in the country; on the other hand, carrying this too far would unleash the potentially fatal wrath of chief ministers who would then use their muscle to oppose the agenda of the government.

B.C. Roy, for example, the Chief Minister of Bengal, and a powerful political figure who was quite well placed to pose a threat to the stability of Nehru's government, argued that the influx of migrants into the state of West Bengal was the result of 'a deliberate policy of the government of East Bengal to drive out the minorities.'[4] On 22 October 1948, while Nehru was away in Europe, Gopalaswami Ayyangar met with Syama Prasad Mookerjee, K.C. Neogy, Mohanlal Saxena, and B.C. Roy—a group of individuals who had been expressing dissatisfaction with the centre's policy towards Pakistan in an increasingly loud chorus. The feasibility of the option of holding a complete exchange of all minority populations of India and Pakistan was discussed, as a 'possible alternative for preventing uncontrolled migration on a large scale of non-Muslims from East Bengal'.[5] A few days later, Ayyangar reported to Nehru that 'the grave situation in West Bengal owing to the arrival of large numbers of Hindu refugees is daily worsening… West Bengal is faced with complete disruption of its economy.'[6] Moreover, Ayyangar warned, the cabinet was increasingly of the view that this migration was caused by deliberate policy on the part of Pakistan, and that 'we must decide soon on a strong policy on this issue'.[7] Politicians such as Syama Prasad Mookerjee, leader of the right-wing Hindu organisation the Jan Sangh, Dr Bidhan Roy, Chief Minister of West Bengal, as well as Vallabhbhai Patel were voicing their support for an 'outright solution', in terms of a wholesale exchange of minority population, or recourse to war, with the object of gaining more territory from Pakistan where these migrants could be settled.

Both Nehru and Liaquat Ali Khan worked quite hard to ensure that this suggestion was not put into place. Their unwillingness—to say nothing of the complete incapacity of the non-existent machinery for law and order in Bengal—to actually take this step forced them into a framework of collaboration on the refugee issue. The sizes of the minority populations in Bengal, for one thing, and the mutual unwillingness to enter into a war over the minorities question for another, meant that the only way the logic of partition could be 'sealed' and finalised was by putting in place a reciprocal structure of accountability for the minorities' issues.

The first inter-dominion conference on minorities was held in Calcutta in January 1948, in the sombre and imposing setting of the Writers Building. The head of the Pakistani delegation at this conference was Ghulam Muhammad, minister for finance; on the Indian side, the delegation was headed by K.C. Neogy, minister for rehabilitation. Discussion at the conference quickly focussed around the issue of the extent of, and reasons for, both governments being involved with the concerns of minority populations in the other country. H.M. Patel, a senior ICS official, who had been a member of the steering committee of the Partition Council, urged that the question not be addressed 'in terms of the prestige of either government', but rather as a 'big, human problem.'[8]

It was also clear to most politicians during the conferences that minority policies in both India and Pakistan had to be part of an interconnected process. Much of the discussion was in fact focussed on the nature of rights that minorities would enjoy in both countries—as Ghulam Muhammad pointed out at the Conference: 'When we are trying to work out the rights of minorities, if you want it I am quite prepared to have an identical thing for both the Dominions'.[9] If the flow of minorities across the border had to be curtailed, it was necessary for both governments to take action to ensure their security in their current situation. A joint declaration that undertook both governments' protection of minority rights was a possible solution. Muhammad continued, 'A great service would be provided for the minorities, wherever they are,' if the Conference could lay down machinery that both countries could impose for their protection of minorities.[10] While the machinery set up to do this would not necessarily lead to a complete halt in the movement, it would nonetheless provide both governments with means to address and contain the threats posed by it. Sri Prakasa, the High Commissioner of India in Karachi, also suggested that a joint undertaking on behalf of minorities across the subcontinent would 'clear the air'. The question of how minority populations across the border could look to the governments for protection and guidance therefore could be controlled by this means.

What was also unusual about these discussions was the acknowledgement that representatives of both governments were quite intimately connected with the concerns of minority communities across the border. Ghulam Muhammad, Pakistan's minister for minorities, pointed out that the Indian High Commissioner, Sri Prakasa was closely involved with the concerns of minorities in West Pakistan. 'Mr. Sri Prakasa looks after the interests of Hindus in Sind. My government gives him every facility to do so... Ask him if his house is not the beehive of lots of people.'[11] Indeed, added K. Shahbuddin, a part of the Pakistan delegation, his own government had every right to raise the issue of the treatment of Muslims throughout India, since it was also 'a question of principle, involving both the governments' concerns with minority welfare across the border.'[12]

Such density of these kinds of contacts with people who were, after all, citizens of another country, also represented an unusual innovation in the consequences of partition for Bengal. Part of what was going on during this process was an attempt by India and Pakistan to in fact bolster their claims to statehood further, by inserting themselves into a deeply inter-connected, and dense set of community patterns in Bengal. The bilateral machinery therefore also provided for the role of the two governments to protect the interests of minorities across the border, but paradoxically enough, this was only possible as a consequence of the process of partition, rather than a negation of it.

The proceedings of the Calcutta conference of 1948 also reveal the diversity of the set of actors who were involved in the crafting of policy with regard to inter-dominion movement. The governments of the provinces of the eastern boundary line—East Pakistan, West Bengal, Assam, and Tripura—thus became critical players in the question of how movement across the boundary line was to be defined, and in deciding who would constitute a migrant, or refugee. Mostly, however, the tone of inter-dominion negotiations over the late 1940s about the question of minority populations in Bengal was predominantly irate. Rather than piously declaring solidarity with all other co-religionists in South Asia, the inter-dominion conferences were often angry exchanges about who should have to foot the bill for the dispossessed migrants of Sindh, Bengal, and to some extent Punjab and Delhi. Their arguments were not about the necessity of welcoming their suffering brethren with open arms; instead, they were furious denials about exactly why India or Pakistan should not be saddled with the financial responsibility of migrants who were technically the responsibility of the other dominion.

Ghulam Muhammad, for instance, while arguing against charges of discrimination by the government of Pakistan for minorities in East Bengal, argued that the persecutions of Muslims in Uttar Pradesh and in north India was an equal threat. Attempting to bring these questions into the fold of the conference, Ghulam Muhammad argued that 'if you really want to purge the minds of hatred we must cover *all* those areas.'[13] The Indians however, were reluctant to bring other states into the discussions, arguing that the conference had 'met principally for East and West Bengal'[14]. The agreements signed were aimed specifically for the migrants across the Bengal basin, and were to be implemented mostly through the provincial ministries of the East and West Bengal government. Ghulam Muhammad's suggestions about a cross India arrangements were not met, but, in Bengal, a partial step towards these ideas was repeatedly taken by both governments.

Delegates at the Calcutta conference acknowledged that the stability of the minority populations on the eastern side of the subcontinent was important to secure, and would have to be accommodated. This was crucial to the economic viability of the region as a whole, which rested partly on the traditional networks of commerce and migration that criss-crossed over the region, and partly on the sheer size of the numbers involved in these transactions. The issue of migrants from East Bengal, minority communities in that province, and trade between East Bengal and India were all deeply connected with the politics and economics of the provinces of Assam, East and West Bengal. The delegates also agreed that the chief secretaries of East and West Bengal would meet every month to deal with issues relating to traffic between the two provinces, including the terms of transit and customs for goods.[15]

The Calcutta conference opened with an outburst from the chief minister of Assam, Gopinath Bardoloi, on the influx of migrants from East Pakistan into his state. Bardoloi, an increasingly shrill advocate of the policy of protecting the state of Assam from the influx of 'outsiders', complained to the conference that the policies of the East Bengal government were driving migrant cultivators—both Hindu and Muslim—into his state in increasingly large numbers. His government, Bardoloi continued, was entitled to evict those—mainly Muslim cultivators—who had migrated to the province after 1938, on the basis of an agreement reached that the government of Assam had entered into with the Muslim League in 1945.[16]

This, K. Shahbuddin, a member of the delegation from Pakistan countered, would only drive out minority cultivators into East Pakistan. Estimates for the numbers who made the crossings differ—they were the subject of notorious controversy between the two governments—but conservative estimates put the number crossing the border at 100,000 per week. The Government of Pakistan released figures that claimed the entry of more than three million migrants into East Bengal that year, though that estimate was not accepted by India.

The nuances of this dilemma were brought out particularly well in the confrontations between Nehru and the chief minister of Assam, Gopinath Bardoloi. In the years that followed 1947 they became an important theme in the bilateral relationship. In May 1950, Semiruddin Munshi, son of late Karipora Bogmari of Goalpara subdivision in Assam, filed an First Information Report (FIR) with the police for the death of his son, Azzan. Upon 'seeing some people armed with guns and [spears]', Semiruddin told his son to:

> fly west carrying a small case carrying valuables and jewellery. Upon seeing my son, 10-12 rioters armed with guns chased him, and fired him and stabbed with him with spears, thus killing him instantly, and took away his attach case. My houses were burnt and pulled down. My property and livestock was removed. Upon returning home with the police, I found nothing left.

A copy of Semiruddin's report was attached to a letter sent to Nehru, by a member of parliament from Assam, Wajed Ali. Ali warned in no uncertain terms that Muslims in this district were 'selling their cattle, goods, paddy etc., and leaving.' Furthermore, he warned, 'The District Congress Committee is inactive, and even we were refused cooperation by its president.'[17]

In the years following the partition, the government of Assam insistently pressed for a permit system to be imposed on the traffic between Assam and East Bengal.[18] Both the Ministry of External Affairs and Gopalaswami Ayyangar discouraged the idea, and repeatedly argued against setting up a permit system in the east. This was discussed in a meeting in Ayyangar's house, with Bardoloi, B.C. Roy, and K.C. Neogy in July 1949.[19] Bardoloi argued that a permit system was essential if the influx of migrants into Assam was to be controlled. He suggested that persons without permits attempting to enter Assam from the Goalpara checkpoint should be turned back. Yet Ayyangar pointed out this could only lead to reciprocal action from East Pakistan, and further controls would be imposed all along the Assam as well as West Bengal boundaries with Pakistan. Within the state of Assam, Ayyangar argued, the Khasi and Jaintia Hills would be adversely affected, in addition to upsetting what equilibrium had been achieved in West Bengal with regard to the arrival of Hindu migrants. B.C. Roy also voiced his disapproval, fearing that a similar retaliatory measure by East Pakistan against migrants from West Bengal would only lead to a further onslaught of Hindu migrants into their own state. Such a measure could also be disruptive to trade, and the flow of goods, cattle, as well as vital food supplies including fish, in that region, all of which were vital for the economic wellbeing of the state.[20]

Indeed, it was also difficult to cite legislation under which migrants could be expelled from the state of Assam: the provisions of various laws barring the entry of outsiders—such as the Influx from Pakistan (Control) Act of 1949, Assam maintenance of Public Order Act of 1947, Indian Passport Act and Foreigners Act—all lacked clauses which could specifically apply to migrants from East Pakistan in Assam being deported back.[21] This also reflected a dilemma on part of lawmakers regarding a pattern of migration which was well established in the east before the partition, and whether this could continue to remain permissible with partition having taken place. Drafting an ordinance especially for this purpose also carried the risk of attracting the attention of the Pakistan government, who would make retaliatory provisions in their own legislation for migrants.

In the end, however, Gopinath Bardoloi got his bill, and the Immigrants (Expulsion from Assam) Act was passed in 1949. The legislation in fact had several predecessors, owing to Assam's attractiveness for indentured migrants from Orissa, Bihar and East Bengal over the first half of the twentieth century. One example of this was the 'Line System' which was introduced in 1912, to distinguish the rights to purchase land between indigenous communities and outsiders. By 1949, however, Assam's decision to expel those who had arrived from East Bengal acquired additional connotations. The bill stipulated that those who had arrived in Assam after 1938 would be repatriated back to East Bengal, provoking a angry protest from the latter government. A press release from the government of East Bengal termed the introduction of this legislation 'unjustified' and 'unilateral', which could not 'but have the most undesirable results', and 'constrained [the government of East Bengal] to conclude that the intention of the government of Assam is to force a mass exodus of Muslims into East Bengal in an effort to disrupt this provincial economy'.[22] Indeed, as we saw above, the question of how minorities were treated across the border in the Bengal delta, was in fact the foremost task for the offices of the high commissions of both governments in Bengal.

While the question of migrants coming in from East Pakistan was the source of much discontent to the chief ministers of the eastern provinces in India, the delegations from Pakistan could also argue that the movement into Sindh had in turn crippled that government. The impact of partition migration transformed the demographics of Karachi, and threatened in fact to make for a split between the city of Karachi, increasingly filled with migrants, and the rest of the province. Just how the provincial ministry was to react to this was also ambivalent: the rapidly changing demographics meant that the chief minister had to toe a careful line between the outflow of Hindus—so that his city could retain some of its original composition, and not move into hands of the central government—and the inflow of refugees, whose arrival it was politically suicidal to block. Indeed, the 1951 census of Karachi placed the refugee population in Karachi at 51 per cent, the majority of whom had arrived from northern and north-western provinces in India.[23] In fact, if the policies of discrimination towards minorities in East Pakistan was a cause for complaint in the inter-dominion conferences, then the treatment of Muslims throughout India, in states like Bombay, Bihar, and Uttar Pradesh was also a valid cause for concern. Indeed, according to the 1951 census, about 700,000 had migrated from India to East Bengal, compared to some six and a half million to West Pakistan.[24]

Exercises in Defining Minorities Rights

The inter-dominion discussions were not aimed at devising solutions for forbidding migration across the eastern sector, but instead put in place a set of machinery that recognized the importance of this issue within the bilateral dialogue. The way it was addressed, moreover, was through an official discourse that further clarified, rather than diluted, the basis of the partition: indeed, because of the partition, minority rights in India or Pakistan could not be ignored, and had to be safeguarded by the state structures of India and Pakistan. The governments of East and West Bengal fashioned a series of administrative arrangements whereby, in order to improve the security of minority populations on either side of the boundary lines, representatives of both governments would be legally empowered to raise concerns about their welfare, and entitled to answers about what should be done to correct these.

Partly, this was also due to the fact, simply put, that there was no other way of getting around the problem—the size of the minority populations in Bengal were simply too large, and mostly too poor to be able to be easily transferred and rehabilitated.[25] In her study on the aftermath of partition in Bengal, Joya Chatterji outlines how the Nehru Liaquat Pact was an exercise in damage control by a government completely overwhelmed by the size and inflow of refugees, and being entirely unequipped to grapple with it. Srinath Raghavan, on the other hand, frames this episode as an example of how the tactic of coercive diplomacy could be used: in the face of a realistic threat of war, the pursuit of an agreement could also yield results.[26]

Nonetheless, it is also important to see why this particular solution—of all others—was adopted. Policy makers in Bengal, could after all, have just as well have declared that the movement of all minority populations should henceforth be barred altogether; or that incoming refugees would have to face even harsher penalties from the state; or even have endeavoured to continue with their spectacularly ill-thought out attempts at shipping them to the island of Dandakaranya.[27] The bilaterally constructed element in dealing with this question, reminiscent of multi-national solutions to the question of minority welfare in inter-war Europe, however, also suggests the pursuit of a slightly different model of statehood for India and Pakistan during the 1950s.

This kind of administrative device, moreover, represented an unusual arrangement, particularly given the state of bilateral relations at the time. Left to themselves, this kind of arrangement might not have seemed the most obvious course of action of embittered bureaucrats dealing with the consequences of the partition. In fact, it seems plausible to suggest that in negotiating the wording of the treaty, South Asian bureaucrats would have also cast around for similar administrative solutions fashioned in other parts of the world.[28] The League of Nations' deliberations on these questions would have formed a relevant precedent to policy makers in South Asia a few decades later, and appeared, in diluted extents, on their undertakings on minority rights.

The question of minorities, their rights and protection, has traditionally been a classic test of the paramountcy of the sovereign state, above that of all other source of law-giving. The issue served to crystallise particularly clearly the contestation of authority between the individual nation state's domestic jurisdiction on the one hand, with the limits on how to curb it by external forced due to its inability to protect its vulnerable on the other. The deliberations of the League of Nations and political developments in inter-war Europe seemed to settle these questions conclusively in favour of the nation state. One way of safeguarding the boundaries of the nation state, in fact, was to ensure that those communities who shared affinities with defining features of the nation, but who were outside of this boundary, were provided with adequate safeguards for their security.

Furthermore, the League's deliberations also developed conceptualisations of how minority rights ought to be defined, the markers through which they could be evaluated, and the standards they were to meet. The Polish Treaty on Minority Rights, for example, signed in 1919, stipulated that 'all inhabitants were to be entitled to the free exercise, whether public or private, of any creed or religious belief, whose practices were not inconsistent with public order or public beliefs'. Minorities, moreover, were to be able to 'establish, manage and control, charitable, religious and social institutions, schools, and other educational establishments, at their own expense, free from governmental interference, and to exercise their own language and religion freely therein'.[29] Violations of this clause were to be reported to the League of Nations Council by a member of the League, and, theoretically at least, the League was then entitled to seek answers and solutions from the concerned state. While the sovereignty of member states was accommodated within the League's ambit, what was also provided for was a degree of accountability by each of these states about the well-being of their minorities.

Indeed, Muhammad Iqbal—one of the earliest thinkers on the constitutional dilemmas of minorities in South Asia—had, not uncoincidentally, called for the formation of an 'Eastern League of Nations', which, would be differentiated from the European namesake, so as to assert South Asia's anti-colonial position against the imperialism of western powers, but also retain its fundamental logic. Indeed, he argued in favour of a similar arrangement in South Asia, saying, during the thirties that 'The possibilities of the Palestinian problem may eventually compel them [South Asian politicians] to seriously consider their position of that Anglo French institution called the League of Nations, and to explore practical means for an Eastern League of Nations'.[30] Furthermore, J.C. Coyajee, economist, academic, and delegate from India at the League of Nations in the 1930s commented that while 'it is true that the League cannot be appealed to for decision in the communal problems of India which are a domestic matter. But what is more important is the spirit in which the League works and it would be so much to the good if we could imbibe that spirit'.[31]

Interestingly enough, the Indian historian Beni Prasad, writing in 1940, also recognised the parallels of the question of Hindu–Muslim political representation in South Asia, with the issues faced while constructing the administrative architecture to try to contain the forces of nationalism in inter-war Europe. While critiquing the failure of what he termed the 'Guarantee System' in Europe, he warned, 'the deeper cause of the tragedy—a false idea of nationality, and a falser equation of nationality with statehood, was not adequately understood, in India, or elsewhere.' A striking parallel, Prasad found, was to be seen in the trajectory of Sudeten Germans in Czechoslovakia, with the situation in India during the 1940s. 'The Sudeten Germans demanding equality of legal status [with the Czechs], a guarantee of this equality by recognition of the Sudeten Germans as a unified legal personality, and full autonomy in every department of life'. Eventually, these conditions led to the secession of Sudetenland from the rest of Czechoslovakia, and also created, Prasad warned, conditions at present, expectations in Czech patriotism for the resurrection of Czech unity.[32]

While in some ways Prasad's anticipatory diagnosis of the contours of the problem were not incorrect, to South Asian bureaucrats immersed in the task of emulating European models of statehood, such demarcations would have served as a useful model for the nature of responsibilities that states being disentangled from a larger administrative entity should adopt.[33] For the League, these rights had to be vouchsafed firmly within the structure and inclinations of member states, and its ambit, in fact lay firmly within, accepting of, and even embracing, the limitations imposed by the state structures of the member states in its Council. At the same time, however, viable states, the League of Nation's trajectory demonstrated, might still emerge from administrative arrangements that extended the responsibility of minority communities to entities outside their boundaries. The Nehru Liaquat Pact represent a partial—if not necessarily completed—attempt at arriving at such ideals.

The outcome of the 1948 inter-dominion conference in Calcutta was a declaration between the Chief Ministers of East and West Bengal, B. C. Roy and Khwaja Nazimuddin, safeguarding the rights of minorities on either side of the boundary in Bengal. The agreement declared that both governments 'are determined to take every possible step to discourage such exodus and to create such conditions as would check mass exodus in either direction, and would encourage and facilitate as far as possible the return of evacuees to their ancestral homes'.[34] To this end, it 'guaranteed equality in rights, opportunities, privileges and obligations' to minorities, and, significantly, also stipulated that 'all tendencies towards an economic boycott of minorities or strangulation of their normal life should be curbed'.[35] Provincial and district minorities boards, with representation from members of the minority community who had been elected in the legislative assemblies, were moreover to be set up under the terms of this agreement, for the daily welfare of minority-related concerns.

Following the inter-dominion conference at Calcutta, a 'Branch Secretariat' of the Ministry of External Affairs was set up in Calcutta. Its primary purpose was dealing with the concerns of migrants on the eastern borders. The secretariats' files groaned with the sheer weight of the correspondence with the Foreign Ministry in Dhaka regarding the treatment of migrants at the border check-posts by the Pakistani government. The question of how close a hand the high commissions ought to take in the affairs of minorities across the border was not always clear-cut. Subimal Dutt, a senior official in the Indian Ministry of External Affairs, and for many years a key figure in the handling of questions relating to Pakistan in the ministry, has written that 'Nehru himself was not clear in his mind as to what the Government of India could do to assist those who were nationals of Pakistan and were still living in East Bengal'.[36] He also wished to instruct the deputy high commissioner in Dhaka not to go too far in getting involved with the problems of minorities in East Pakistan.

Dutt instructed the first deputy high commissioner at Dhaka, Surjit Bose, that 'in strict theory, minorities must seek the protection of their Government, and not of the Government of the neighbouring Dominion.' But in the same note, Dutt told Bose,

> You should advise the complainants accordingly, while at the same time keeping a note of the complaints so that at a suitable opportunity, either informally or on the occasion of the Chief Secretaries' or Premiers' Conference, you can point out that minorities are not being treated in the way provided by the Delhi Agreement.[37]

S. Sen, a chief secretary to the government of West Bengal pointed out 'If we want our High Commissioner or Deputy High Commissioner to pursue complaints from Hindus in East Bengal, a similar request from Pakistan is sure to come.'[38] Too close a relationship between the minority populations and the diplomatic missions would also lead to 'Muslims in India coming to regard the government of Pakistan as their protector' and which would 'be taken advantage of by Pakistan and will lead to embarrassing results in actual practice.' Moreover, the consequence of such a policy would also require the granting of facilities to the Pakistan deputy high commissioners to 'visit all parts of the Indian Union, since it is their contention that that Muslim migration has been taking place from all across the Indian Union.'

The activities of the Branch Secretariat, therefore, were not unquestioningly accepted in India. By 1952, an official in the secretariat noted, 'the Branch Secretariat had been reduced to a Secretariat of the Minorities Minister and the main part of its work is devoted to long range and often interminable correspondence on individual cases of harassment of non-Muslims in East Bengal'.[39] At the same time however, its existence in the first place—and the decision to not to simply terminate its activities—have to be explained further. Its purpose—a machinery that was designed to officiate over and intervene in the grievances of the citizens of another country—would seem, at first glance, to be an incongruous feature in the landscape of India–Pakistan relations, usually defined by stances that fastidiously protect the exclusiveness of their sovereignty and jurisdiction from any intervention from the other.

Even if the bilateral dialogue about the position of minorities was seen as 'lengthy and interminable', it was nonetheless important to perpetuate this structure of linkages, as a way, paradoxically, of cementing the basis of separation. Inter-governmental dialogues that synchronised and calibrated their position on minorities were in fact an important way of maintaining the principle of separation. Much like the League of Nations had envisioned, the security of the nation state would in fact be further buttressed by provisions to meet the requirements for the welfare of communities that shared its national features, but were outside its boundary lines.

Surjit Bose, the Indian deputy high commissioner in Dhaka from 1949–51, found that his duties predominantly related to the condition of the Hindu population in the province. He forwarded, almost daily, to the foreign office in Dhaka, complaints on unlawful requisition of land, harassment of Hindus by customs officials on the border, cases of abduction of women, seizure of cattle following raids from parties of peasants across the border, and a variety of complaints on different scales.[40]

Similarly, in November 1948, Surendranath Haldar, ex-Chairman of the Jessore municipality, met with B.C. Roy, the premier of West Bengal. Haldar presented a report on the situation of Hindus in the Jessore district of East Pakistan, and urged the minister to use his position to alleviate their position. His report concluded: 'The whole show of house searches, arrest warrants, and sealing of houses is to dub the individuals as enemies of the state, blackmail them in open public and strike terror into the hearts of the people.'[41] B.C. Roy promised that he would look into the matter, and instructed Indian officials in the high commission to raise the matter with the authorities in Jessore. A few months later, the Ministry of External Affairs in Delhi received a letter from the Pakistani deputy high commissioner in Calcutta, requesting that he be allowed to visit the town of Silchar in Assam, to enquire into disturbances that had taken place there recently. A disagreement between a Muslim shopkeeper and his Hindu customer had turned violent, and resulted in 'brickbats and stone chips freely thrown on the fixed shops and sheds in the bazaar'.[42] As a means of restoring peace in the neighbourhood, Abdul Hamid Chowdhry, the Pakistani deputy high commissioner in Calcutta, accompanied by D.M. Gupta, deputy secretary in the branch secretariat, went on a day long tour of Silchar, 'talked to eye-witnesses at the bazaar, and met local leaders, the chairman of the municipality board, and other state officials.'[43] After submitting a joint report on the situation on the ground, and assuring the locals of their continued assistance, the officials returned together to Calcutta.

Much like the unease that Indian officials had voiced about wading in too deep with the concerns of minorities across the boundary, such doubts about the process were also raised by Pakistani officials. One proposal from the Pakistan high commission, for example, suggested that such correspondence could be restricted to 'only major cases involving whole classes of people, breaches of clear rules, action designed to embarrass one of the two countries politically, e.g. pushing in refugees etc., and important individual cases'.[44] Azizuddin Ahmed, the Chief Secretary of East Pakistan, proposed, possibly with the intention of saving time, that the deputy high commissioners of both countries need not extend contributions to the monthly Chief Secretaries' meetings, about accusations against his government on violations of agreements on minority protection.

To this, however, B.K. Acharya, the deputy high commissioner of India in Dhaka, truculently replied that it was 'absurd that at conferences in which the deputy secretaries, secretaries, board of revenue etc. of the two provincial governments freely take part in the discussions without any objection being raised, objections should be taken only when the deputy high commissioners open their mouths.'[45] Moreover, he noted, 'the Pakistan deputy high commissioner has been speaking freely at these Conferences in connection with the desecration of mosques etc.'[46] The mission in Karachi was instructed that since complaints continued to be received from the government of Pakistan, it should therefore correspondingly present 'important cases' to the notice of the Foreign Ministry of Pakistan.

But this state of affairs was, in some ways, also responsible for some attempts, however halting and ineffective, at bringing about a measure of relief and security to the position of minorities in Bengal. In a sense, it was also responsible for moving the states forward in pushing for a better bilateral relationship. On his return from a tour in East Pakistan, J.N. Mandal—an even fiercer critic of Liaquat Ali Khan's policies on minorities, and Law Minister of Pakistan—met with the Indian Deputy High Commissioner in Karachi, M.K. Kirpalani. He argued that the exodus was taking place due to economic and not political reasons. Deteriorating economic conditions in East Pakistan, he warned, due to 'India's strangulation of East Pakistan', were responsible for the increasingly hostile environment for Hindus in East Bengal.[47] Furthermore, he counselled, the only course to be taken for minorities to have a stable existence in the place that they already were, was to ensure that the state of bilateral relations did not deteriorate beyond a certain point.

By August 1948, it was clear to Subimal Dutt noted that 'since the Calcutta Agreement... there has been no radical change... [and] the Pakistan Government have entered on an undeclared war against India'.[48] Complaints came in increasing numbers regarding the movement of food and other everyday commodities between East and West Bengal. The District Magistrate, West Dinajpur, reported 'In spite of the decision of the Inter-dominion conference, movement of eggs, fish vegetable, bamboo, fuel etc are not being allowed by the Pakistan officials and people.'[49] Dutt argued, India's implementation of the clauses in the Agreement, relating to the supply of coal and steel—which were 'materials that were essential to the prosecution of that war'—could be halted.[50] It was clear the situation in Bengal was fragile, and remedial steps would have to be taken to arrest the slide towards an even further deterioration of the position on inter-dominion migration and inter-communal rioting and unrest.

This sentiment was brought out particularly clearly, in the dire—and politically toxic—warnings of the then chief minister of Assam, who warned that 'Pakistan has evil designs on India', by attempting to choke it with refugees. These statements produced another round of strong condemnation from Pakistan: the Branch Secretariat in India was warned about 'a tendency noticed by the government of East Bengal on the part of Indian leaders in their statements to revive the exploded myth of persecution and exodus of East Bengal Hindus and that non official organisations, such as the Council for the Protection of Rights of Minorities have also indulged in such chorus of anti-

Pakistan propaganda with the tacit backing of the Indian authorities.' The Ministry of External Affairs also received an angry dispatch from East Bengal in February 1950, about the situation in the district of Karimganj in Assam. As a result of a conflagration there, the note charged, 'more than a thousand people streaming into East Bengal, with heart rending stories of discrimination and violence.'[51]

Nehru and Liaquat

In February, 1950, as the numbers of refugees moving across the Bengal boundary line reached levels that forced both governments to take stock of their options, Liaquat Ali Khan had written to Nehru suggesting that a declaration be made 'from the two Governments that all possible steps shall be taken to rehabilitate the minorities in their homes and to see that they are given full protection of life and property'.[52] In fact, Khan concluded bluntly: 'The responsibility which is now thrown on us is indeed great, and we have to work jointly to find a practical and lasting solution to this problem as early as possible.'[53]

According to the Nehru Liaquat Pact both governments would:

> solemnly agree that each shall ensure, to the minorities throughout its territory, complete equality of citizenship, irrespective of religion, a full sense of security in respect of life, culture, property and personal honour, freedom of movement within each country and freedom of occupation, speech and worship, subject to law and morality.[54]

The Pact also guaranteed safety of movement for migrants who were leaving areas which had seen communal tension, and stipulated that they not be harassed by customs officials at the border. Migrants across Bengal were entitled to continued ownership of their property while absent, and entitled to rehabilitation from their government, should restoration of property not take place.[55]

Secondly, minority commissions would be set up in East and West Bengal, and Assam. These would be chaired by the chief minister of the province, along with a Hindu and Muslim member, who were elected representatives of the state legislature. The commissions would have their own staff, and would supervise the implementation of the agreement in the province. Subsequent to the April agreement,

C.C. Biswas and Dr A.M. Malik, the ministers for minority welfare, met in August to review the steps taken to implement the agreement, and to put in place arrangements whereby cases of discrimination would be promptly investigated, and redressed. The annexure also called for the results of the enquiry, and action taken, to be communicated to the other government.[56] It was also decided that travellers between East and West Bengal, via the border stations of Darsana and Benapole in Pakistan, and Banpur and Bongaon in India, would be counted jointly by both sides of border officials. The agreement also specified that the figures released of inter-dominion travel would be mutually agreed upon by both sets of officials, although this was seldom true in practice.

In some ways, admittedly, the Nehru–Liaquat Pact represented something of a hastily improvised solution to a massive political predicament to the central leadership of both sides who wished to avoid the costs of escalating a refugee crisis in Bengal to the brink of war. It was also variously criticised from different sides in both India and Pakistan—for not going far enough, for not being effective enough, and for taking a dangerously conciliatory approach in the face of discriminatory policies of exclusion and marginalisation of the minority community by the neighbouring country. As Ghulam Muhammad pointed out in 1948, this was also not a complete solution to the plight of minorities all across the subcontinent. Nonetheless, its provisions do offer an interesting perspective about how the role of the Indian and Pakistani state was envisioned—and the extent to which their jurisdiction and sovereignty could also, in the pursuit of a finalised definition of state, be defined in ways that could meet the requirements of both.

Indeed, the only way that both governments could assert their final separation from one another had to be through a process that synchronised and calibrated their dialogues about the position of minorities across the border. In conceptualising the frameworks within which the rights of minorities affected by the partition were to be drawn, therefore, India and Pakistan took approaches that had remarkable affinities with one another—affinities which were based on drawing up a more exclusivist language of belonging and citizenship on the one hand, but also on recognizing that where these did not easily apply, the bilateral machinery was integral to maintaining a sense of balance, on the other.

The precedents which had led to the Pact, including negotiations at the interdominion conferences of the two previous years, themselves were undoubtedly heated, messy, and frequently inconclusive. But they were also were also, I argue, based on a realisation that the way towards a more amicable relationship between both countries lay in their abilities to acknowledge, and then further cement the basis of the partition, and, correspondingly, the basis of existence for both states. This offers an opportunity to study how the impact of partition also constitutes an opportunity to fashion new techniques of governance and administration in its wake: rather than only being a reason for the systematic and widespread displacement of people, it could, to some degree at least, also lead to mechanisms that provided for mixed communities to continue to exist side by side. The Pact itself had patchy degrees of success, though it did succeed in stabilising the flow of migrants across the Bengal delta for the time being. The consequences of the Pact, moreover, went some way to avoid the breakout of a war between the two countries over the question of the uncontrollable numbers of refugees flowing across the Bengal boundary line. Yet, for all its limitations, the agreement also represented nothing less than a signed statement by two prime ministers about the nature of their policies to their minorities being of concern to the other. In terms of measuring the motivation and intent of India and Pakistan towards one another, therefore, the Nehru–Liaquat Pact is as strong an indicator of the array of responses taken, as any other.

The Pact was quite specifically based on the acknowledgement and then implementation of the fact of partition. Migrants were not told that their new nationalities of Indian or Pakistani did not matter, or that they were free to conduct their lives as if the partition had not taken place—but rather, that the better prospects of their security lay in recognizing the finality of the partition, and then in working with the newly created state. Its logic lay in trying to finalise the partition—to recognize the authority of the states of India and Pakistan—rather than to let the looseness, or inadequacies of their existing definitions threaten both. The role of the governments, having now come into existence, lay in trying to protect the position of minorities in the other dominion—and not necessarily in trying to convince those minorities that they ought to come across the border. The bilateral machinery, therefore also provided for the role of the two governments to protect the interests of minorities across the border, but paradoxically enough, this was only possible as a consequence of the process of partition, rather than a negation of it.

Critics of the Pact

In India the Pact had caused a storm of opposition in Nehru's cabinet, and two members—K.C. Neogy and Syama Prasad Mookerjee—resigned in protest. Surprisingly enough, it was the support of India's Deputy Prime Minister and Home Minister, Sardar Patel, that allowed Nehru to weather these resignations and generate support in his cabinet and party for his Pact. Patel was certainly no stranger to religiously polarising rhetoric aimed at further heightening the bellicosity between India and Pakistan. As the political crisis around the refugee movement heightened, he had argued that the only way for India to support the burden of additional refugees coming in from East Pakistan was to secure a larger extent of territory from that country. In effect, this implied the military occupation of the districts of Khulna and Jessore in East Bengal. He argued 'the seriousness of the situation had to be conveyed to Pakistan', and that 'unless we take concrete steps to solve the problem, India would be crushed under their weight.'[57]

Nonetheless, Patel also argued that the wiser course of action was to support Nehru and the Pact. In a speech in Calcutta, where he campaigned extensively to generate support for the pact, Patel asked:

> The question before West Bengal is not so much whether the Agreement is good or bad, beneficial or harmful, but whether in the face of the stark reality of a partitioned Bengal under two independent Governments and placed in the present set of circumstances, any other peaceful means is open to it to bring hope and faith and succour and relief to the unfortunate victims of the recent disturbances on both sides of the border. I have asked, and looked in vain, for an alternative...[58]

Concluding, Patel added, 'On the basis of past remissness, to accept future bad faith as an unalterable fact denotes a lack of faith in the basic goodness of human nature which constitutes the very elements of our philosophy'.[59]

In the weeks and months that followed the agreement, the numbers of refugees crossing the Bengal boundary-line stabilised to a substantial degree.[60] The return of Hindus from West Bengal back to East Bengal, meanwhile, also rose in the months after the Delhi Pact had been signed. For example, the last week of March 1950 had seen a net influx of approximately 100,000 Hindus from across the border into West Bengal. In July, the government of West Bengal estimated that it had rehabilitated some 7,907 Muslim families of returned migrants.[61] Similarly, the government of Assam also reported that 15,727 families of displaced Muslims had been provided for by the state.[62] The agreement brought about temporary relief in the scale of migration across the border, but more importantly, its terms validated and replenished a structure whereby such a flow could be addressed and regulated.

In October 1950, J.N. Mandal sent a brutally worded letter of resignation to the cabinet, subsequently published in both the *Dawn* and *Anand Bazaar Patrika*. Castigating the government of Pakistan for being unsympathetic to the position of the minorities, Mandal asserted that the recently concluded Minorities Pact was 'treated as a mere scrap of paper alike by the East Bengal Government and the Muslim League', and that in fact the future of Hindus in East Bengal as a result of the Delhi Agreement 'is not only unsatisfactory but absolutely hopeless.'[63] Liaquat responded to these allegations in a speech to the Constituent Assembly of Pakistan. He pointed out that the Pact had been signed as a means of preventing a situation of war, since the alternatives to this step, which Mandal now seemed to be advocating, were an exchange of the minority populations of both countries. But this scenario, warned Liaquat, could only culminate in outright war between the two countries, and 'would bring anarchy and chaos to this whole subcontinent'. He added that the 'Delhi Agreement… is the only path of sanity and peace', and that, furthermore, 'whatever resentment might be felt at the conduct of an individual, it should never be allowed to affect our national policy and our duty towards the minorities.'[64] The success of the Pact may well have been short-lived, but the argument that Liaquat Ali Khan was making was that a greater amount of bilateral stability would come from pushing policies towards this direction further, rather than not entertaining the prospect of the Pact at all.

Also consistent with how dialogue and summitry in India–Pakistan relations has always played out was the preoccupation with how the Nehru–Liaquat Pact would be covered by the press. The two governments embarked on fairly substantial exercises for publicising their peace-making overtures. The aftermath of the Pact saw a flurry of activity on both sides to utilize the improvement in the atmosphere to bring about some lasting changes in media portrayals of each other. A dispatch in the second half of April 1950 from the Indian deputy high commissioner in Lahore wrote of an 'an almost unbelievable change' that came around with 'open and enthusiastic talk of close and cordial relations between India and Pakistan on every side'.[65] What also comes across strongly is the impulse to utilise the limited machinery of the government in highlighting the achievements of the Nehru–Liaquat pact:

> The following further action has been undertaken: One lakh copies in Bengali and 50,000 copies each in Urdu and Hindi of a booklet containing the Agreement as well as extracts from the speeches of the Prime Minister in Parliament and his broadcast to the Nation, and of the Prime Minister of Pakistan's speech in Pakistan Parliament and his broadcast have been issued for wide distribution. State governments have also been requested to bring out regional language editions of this booklet.[66]

A delegation of editors from Pakistan was invited to visit India in the aftermath of the Nehru-Liaquat declaration. After his interaction with the president of the Pakistan Newspapers Editors Conference Nehru noted delightedly that 'It is evident that the Pakistan Editors have been powerfully affected by their visit to Delhi. Their old conceptions have changed and they are going back full of the determination to preach peace and cooperation. I have no doubt of the sincerity of their present feeling'.[67] The *Dawn*, then in return, enthusiastically described the Nehru–Liaquat Pact 'as a breath of fresh air in these tumultuous times'.[68]

To the leadership in India and Pakistan, it was also apparent that the perception of how matters stood in India–Pakistan affairs was as important as the 'on-the-ground' situation itself. Press releases and talking points were thus hastily circulated on both sides, in the attempt to tone down the vitriol in many publications. When attempts were made to improve relations, both states moved to tackle image and perception issues. This was done as a way of acquiring a greater measure of stability in their domestic politics as well as bolstering the claims to international standing.

Clearly, and as any superficial glance at the statistics about the developmental indices of minority communities in South Asia shows, the reality of the position of minorities on the ground in South Asia remained unaffected. Yet, the ways in which this was carried out, also suggest that the prospect of giving a viable and practicable shape to the meaning of partition was entertained realistically by both governments, who did not see a certain extent of diluted sovereignty as a negation of that principle, since it had also been attempted in other parts of the world. A collaborative arrangement between the states of India and Pakistan, had thus been arrived at, in order to further bolster their foundations, arising out of a difficult partition. In fact, if the partition had been entered into by India and Pakistan, it was also done so in the expectation that some of the dilemmas in its wake would be mutually reconciled. Looking at the structure in which the bilateral negotiations over the position of minority populations in Bengal—the definitions used, and the tactics deployed by both states—is also an exercise in understanding how South Asian states were attempting evolve structures of statehood and its demands, on their own mutually constituted terms—both regionally, as well as globally defined.

3

EVACUEE PROPERTY

At heart, South Asia's partition story is about property—about the sin of breaking the sacrosanct bond with ones' land. In the novel *Sunlight on a Broken Column*, Attia Hossain, a member of a prominent *Taluqdar* family from Awudh, the first woman of her clan to graduate from Lucknow University, and a member of a divided family, dwelt on the impossibility of going home again.[1] One afternoon, fourteen years after partition, Laila, the protagonist, returns to India and goes to her childhood house, Ashiana, in Lucknow, where 'My eyes saw with the complex vision of my nostalgia and sadness the loved arches and domes and finials…'.

Upon arrival, however, Laila finds outsiders are living in her house: 'strangers who were names in Government files balancing Saleem's name against theirs—he labelled "evacuee", they "refugee". Their presence here, and Saleem's in their erstwhile homeland, was part of a statistical calculation in the bargaining of bureaucrats and politicians, in which millions of uprooted human beings became just numerical figures.' The house, Ashiana, eventually had to be sold, and Laila's aunt had wept, recalling the 'ifs, buts and might-have-beens'. Laila, herself, however, realises she cannot undo what has happened, and so tells her husband, when he comes to look for her that evening: 'I'm ready to leave'. Eventually, Hosain, the author, worked in the BBC's eastern division in London, broadcasting a weekly program on politics, current affairs, and gender.

The Ministry of External Affairs was an instrumental institution in shaping the debate about how these rules ought to be fashioned on the basis of a reciprocity. In this chapter, I look at the various stages of the negotiations—how definitions hardened, and when, and the reasons why this was so. I track the changing ways in which this question was conceptualised, and the extent to which the role played by the foreign ministries and inter-dominion conferences on the question impacted the process. I argue that it was the principle of reciprocity that in the end was the pin that held up the structure of evacuee property legislation. In carrying out this exercise, the ministry was also adhering to a formulation that a more fruitful outcome would be where the question of property appropriation was more closely informed by similar pieces of legislation across the border.

The terminologies that Hosain referred to—refugees, displaced persons and migrants—would, at the time, have reverberated around the world. In South Asia, delegates from India and Pakistan at the Evacuee Property conferences based their discussions on the assumption that property which had been 'abandoned', or, in many cases forcibly taken away from evacuees, would be used by the state for the incoming refugees. The land left behind by migrants who had crossed the border—for a variety of reasons, and not all of them permanent—was, according to the Inter-Dominion agreement of 1947, to be maintained by a 'Custodian of Evacuee Property' in India and Pakistan, until, a lasting settlement arrived at. In both countries, the Custodians' control over the property had all the rights of the owner: to collect rents; to lease out; as well as to arbitrate disputes. As more and more migrants swept into both countries in search of resettlement, the Offices of the Custodian of Evacuee Property were under increasing pressure to allot vacated land to displaced incoming refugees. In both countries, thus the Custodian of Evacuee Property went about distributing allotments to refugees, often in decisions that proved to be notoriously controversial. The manner in which this was conducted—and the speed with which these exercises were completed—in both countries was coordinated and choreographed in a series of evacuee property conferences in the period 1947–55.

Inter-dominion conferences on evacuee property were held in quick succession over 1948 and 1949. They were attended by a diverse cast of characters, who came from across the political spectrum in both countries, including Gopalaswami Ayyangar, the Indian Minister without Portfolio, Mehr Chand Khanna, Indian minister for rehabilitation, and the Pakistani ministers for rehabilitation, Khwaja Shahbuddin, and Mian Iftikaruddin. Indeed, negotiations at the conferences were based on a consistent kind of arithmetic: the total value of property left on either side, as against the numbers of claimants for rehabilitation. Decisions about enacting the legislation were based between two kinds of arguments: those in favour of the need for resources for rehabilitation or refugees, as against those who cautioned against the stringent application of evacuee property laws. These included several inter-ministerial and prime-ministerial conferences, held at frequent intervals immediately after partition; in Delhi in December 1947; in Lahore in March 1948; Dhaka in April 1948; Lahore in July 1948, and Karachi in January 1949, May 1949 and April 1950.

The conferences reveal two parallel processes: while one of these was simply about a brutal tussle about control over more property; the other was the joint desire by India and Pakistan to emulate systems of governance that had been established elsewhere in the world. These decisions, moreover, were made at the same time as the constituent assemblies of both governments were seated, and the links between nationality, citizenship, and the right to own land, were discussed and debated, and then defined in lasting ways, by both governments. But the overriding feature of a great deal of debate and discussion around evacuee property legislation was the concern with reciprocity. The problem with declaring pieces of property as 'evacuee property' in unchecked numbers, was that this could also be copied across the border. This concern with reciprocity, therefore, shaped the evacuee property legislations in particular ways. While it was not directed at keeping a more pluralist profile for the ownership of land in either country, what it did do was to calibrate the speed at which the legislations were drawn up.

The scholarship on evacuee property legislations in India and Pakistan is a relatively crowded field, and several scholars have drawn attention to the process through which the basis of defining the right to citizenship as well as access to evacuee property, are inter-related. In 'The Long Partition', Vazira Zamindar argued that the tussle over evacuee property was one of the lengthy—and unresolved—shadows that partition left behind. [2] Zamindar demonstrates how the hierarchy of prioritisation of who could own land took shape after the partition: in India, Hindu males were ideally placed, while Muslim property owners struggled to retain control over their lands. The rehabilitation of refugees was critical in fashioning the narrative of legitimacy to both nation states. These questions manifested themselves particularly clearly, for example in the Sindh province, whose politics were shaped by the tussle between the *muhajir* population and those who had belonged there prior to the partition. [3]

Joya Chatterji has shown how the evacuee property legislations were mirrored on both sides of the border, and argues that this was a key component in the shaping of the nation states of India and Pakistan. These decisions on the right to own land were also part of an attempt in both countries to make this an exclusive decision: it was not possible to own land in both countries. In this sense, cooperation on the issue of evacuee property was a most essential task, since it entailed the clear assertion of the directions that both governments wanted to adopt, on the question of laws on the ownership of property.

However, the reasons for the mutual inter-referentiality between the two governments in fashioning the rules around the control over evacuee property has been studied in less detail. [4] The legislations about evacuee property that both India and Pakistan enacted were consistently, almost mirror images of one another, leading the *Civil and Military Gazette* of May 1950 commented:

> The constantly growing mass of increasingly complicated rules and regulations, which the two governments have formulated for the control of evacuee property, apparently in keen competition with each other has caused H. E. the Governor of the Punjab to remark that government policy seems chiefly concerned with safeguarding this property against its rightful owners. [5]

Indeed, the evacuee property conferences between India and Pakistan, reveal two parallel processes: partly simply a ugly exercise about land-grabbing and ownership, but also an attempt at emulating current definitions about nationhood and state-making, were, in many senses a collaborative exercise between India and Pakistan.

The concept of evacuee property as an administrative tool migrated from different parts of the world, and varying political contexts. Evacuee property—a quintessentially war-time concept—and entailing debates as to how it should be compensated for—had a lasting impact on the post- colonial political practises of several regions of the British Empire. As a response to the financial demands of the Second World War, Allied nations had also enacted different versions of 'Enemy Property' Acts, through which they could appropriate the incomes and properties of establishments that were deemed to have ties with hostile nations. Indeed, as Alexandre Kedar shows, how the Evacuee Property legislations in India and Pakistan drew substantially from the Trading with the Enemy Acts passed in the United Kingdom, during the Second World War. A year after these acts were passed in India and Pakistan, moreover, the state of Israel used a similar model to pass the 'abandoned property' legislations with regard to Arab lands.[6] After the 1948 Palestine war, for instance, the cabinet of the Government of Israel had sat down in January 1949 to hammer out policy on how 'refugee' policy ought to be framed.

The ways in which these approaches did—and did not—manifest themselves in South Asia are interesting. In fact, it is important to see how they fit with—intentionally, and otherwise—with patterns of what constituted acceptable definitions of state behaviour, in the aftermath of partitions in the twentieth century. While carrying out such administrative post-partition measures, however, both countries were also further entrenching definitions of which sets of people had a stronger claim to citizenship and the ownership of property. What is also interesting to track here, is how these sets of people given prioritisation in this process—those that the states of India and Pakistan were more concerned over than others—were usually those who possessed land. The legislations adopted in India and Pakistan, thus, effectively aimed at cutting off all connection to erstwhile land, had been crafted with these objectives in mind. In a sense, therefore, the evacuee property legislations are also a parallel process of a further entrenching of the system of a land-owning oligarchy in India and Pakistan. The ownership of property was always an important consideration of the assessment of an individual's importance in India and Pakistan—the evacuee property legislations offered a further opportunity for defining exactly who these individuals were to be.

But a broader study of the comparative effects of population transfer across the world is instructive for several reasons, not least of which are an understanding of how the commonalities in the politics of the post-war state, which to some extent, transcend the particularities of the South Asian refugee regime: including, for instance, concerns about 'over-crowding' in urban areas due to refugees, the arrival of, and hostility towards, destitute, parasitic 'new-comers', the active use of the rehabilitated population to shape a new narrative about the state, as well as, finally, the lingering resentment amongst other, often equally destitute, communities who had been ignored in the rehabilitation project.

The formal creation of Israel by the United Nations occurred in 1948, but the precedents for the role of the state in the event of the division of land on the basis of ethnicity was in fact well established during the inter-war years. In the 1920s, an erstwhile ICS official, and later a politician with the British Liberal Party, Sir John Hope Simpson, had outlined a plan for land resettlement in Palestine. Given the high rates of migration by Jews into Palestine—a mandate territory roughly the size of Wales in the United Kingdom—Simpson warned that the government had to work closely with both Arab and Jewish landholding properties to bring about development that could eventually help in absorbing the high rates of settlers into the region. The basis of the classification of land, moreover, and the use of these categories in determining what should be fair compensation for either community, moreover, was also, in the context of our discussion below, interestingly. The basis of distributing land, Simpson argued, was to be organised along 'Agricultural' and 'Urban' properties, and compensation schema had to be drawn up accordingly. In a lecture at Chatham House, on the problem of refugees, moreover, Simpson—like many others in this period—pointed to the apparent benefits of a final population transfer he pointed to three case studies: between the change of Greek and Turkey, and the transfer of Greco-descent Bulgarians to Greece. Noting that 'refugees are no problem... We have known them ourselves during and since the war', he argued that the optimal solution was one that was mediated by the government in terms of negotiating exchanges.

The way in which the role of the state in dispersing resources—and deciding who ought to be prioritised in this process—had magnified exponentially in the post-war decades. As the historian Matthew Franks has shown, war time displacement and the subsequent exercises in repatriation became one more instrument to achieve the further ethnic homogenisation of post war European nation states.[7] In many ways, therefore, the decisions of the governments of India and Pakistan in the aftermath of partition were also shaped by precedents set in the inter-war and post-war years in Europe: these were the standards of statehood that they were both attempting to emulate.

In this chapter, I argue that the Indian and Pakistani attempts at grappling with the question of evacuee property must also be placed within this context—as a way of emulating the behaviour of other recently fashioned, and viable states. These attempts at fitting in with such requirements, moreover, also aligned with the shaping of a hierarchy of who constituted the 'model' citizen in India and Pakistan—but these definitions, I argue were collaboratively arrived at. Finally, I show how the Ministry of External Affairs' participation in this process affected the progression of evacuee property laws, which, I show, were also part of the daily concerns of high commissions for both countries. This chapter will, therefore highlight how the element of bilateral cooperation was necessary in the making of evacuee laws, since not only was the acquisition of assets for rehabilitating refugees crucial to both governments, it was also necessarily to effectively sever the trans-dominion ownership of property.

Evacuee Property Conferences

The office of the Custodian of Evacuee Property had initially been envisioned as simply as an interim, caretaker arrangement until better conditions prevailed, so that evacuees would be allowed to dispose of their properties. As the conferences progressed, moreover, a series of proposals were also examined, which would allow evacuees to be able to receive fair settlements, or rents from their properties. While the progression of the evacuee property conferences over 1947–53 points mostly to the trends of how both governments were about tightening their grip over property left behind by evacuees, it is also interesting to examine how, in the months that followed the partition, this was not always the intention.

The evacuee property conferences are not a story about inclusivity, or even driven by a particularly powerful sense of making amends to the many who had lost everything. Many decisions made at the bilateral level about this issue merely reinforced the structures of class, political influence, and a differentiated rights of citizens—structures, moreover, that both governments had profound stakes in upholding. The insertion of the state into the process of evacuee compensation (and lack thereof) reinforced the need of both governments to assert themselves, define themselves against the other, and further ground the basis of the partition. But they are, nonetheless, a story about how the states of India and Pakistan tried to come to a calibrated agreement about exactly who should receive which state's resources. They also thus reveal the assumptions, held by both sets of delegations about which sets of people were the most 'meritorious' for receiving compensation. These assumptions, moreover, were clearly biased on both sides towards class, and the desire to protect those with property. If there was a unifying concern for both Indian and Pakistani delegates at the conferences, it was that the rights of property owners in their states had to be to the extent possible, defended first.

In the last week of August, in a meeting of the Joint Defence Council—which itself was to be disbanded within a few weeks, Nehru, Mountbatten and Liaquat Ali Khan agreed to the appointment of a Custodian of Evacuee Property on both sides.[8] Ordinances issued by both the governments of the Punjab were again exact mirror images of each other—but were aimed at stopping illegal seizures and the looting of vacant properties. On 3 September, Nehru and Liaquat Ali Khan starkly warned the people of both sides of Punjab that 'illegal seizures of property will not be recognised.'[9] This was followed up on in the next couple of months, and ordinances were issued in East and West Punjab to the effect that the Custodian would 'take such measures as he considers necessary or expedient for preserving such property or effects' of those who had had to flee from their home without having made arrangements for its protections.

The Protection of Evacuee Property Ordinance of Pakistan, passed in 1948 provided for the 'appointment of one or more Custodians of

Evacuee Property in such areas as may be specified by a notification.' Moreover, in these areas, the Custodian was entitled to examine, and if necessary, revoke, leases for agricultural land granted after the 1 August 1947.[10] In case the owner had, in fact, made arrangements for the temporary transfer of his property in the wake of the Punjab rioting, then the custodian would also respect those measures, and his authority would not extend to these properties. The tenor, in short, was about preserving the rights of the owner: the custodian's office would prioritise his claims, over those of others.

In 1948, for example, delegates considered sanctioning the disposal of evacuee property through the assessment of a 'Joint Valuation Board', whose members would fairly assess the value of agricultural property, and, on this basis, have refugees pay rent to the custodian. The agreements of 1948, for instance, provided for 'individual exchange' of private property within the 'agreed areas' in India and Pakistan. The possibility of exchange of urban property on either side of the border between individual owners was also examined, and generally accepted, at this conference.[11] But this proved to be a narrow window of opportunity for property owners. Nonetheless, the question of receiving income from evacuee land continued to be discussed at successive conferences, and, at a conference held in June 1949, in Lahore, it was also agreed that 'an officer of the other dominion should be associated with the custodians of evacuee property of each dominion with a view to ensuring equitable management and early payments of rents due to evacuee owners'.[12]

Provincial and central governments also agreed to work fairly closely together on the issue of movable property: that is, financial assets, bank deposits, bonds and annuities. For example, a Secretariat level inter-dominion meeting in December 1947, agreed that 'Insurance Companies, in particular General Insurance companies will be accorded all reasonable facilities by the Pakistani government in respect of protection and investigation of claims... the Govt. of India will accord reciprocal facilities'.[13] Dealing with the question of evacuee property also brought about a growth in the size of machinery to facilitate dialogue at various bilateral levels. The infrastructure to deal with claims relating property allotment, verification of abandoned land, and channels of revenue collection were instituted by both governments from an early stage. The governments of both East and West Punjab, exchanged copious amounts of records relating to rent collection and methods of revenue calculation for the evacuee property in their territories. Work on the exchange of revenue records (*jamabandis*) began as early as July 1947, when the Rehabilitation Secretariat in Jullundar started to receive copies of the land ownership details of evacuees who were coming in from West Punjab.[14] It was decided that agricultural evacuees from West Punjab would be resettled in East Punjab and the PEPSU [Patiala and East Punjab States Union]. Indeed, the volume of this work called for the increase in manpower at the Secretariat, which peaked at some 7,000 officials for carrying out the work of re-allotment of land.[15] This kind of work was particularly hectic on both sides of the Punjab border in the months that followed partition, and the avenues of bilateral cooperation, especially in terms of exchange of information on refugees, was thus well established, and fairly dense.

Much of the exchange at the early Inter-dominion Conferences on Evacuee Property was, in fact, constructive dialogue on how this problem could be handled. Land revenue records and income assessments had to be made by both governments before settlements could be made. But, within a year or so of the partition, arguments about the Custodian's rights on the property shifted quite drastically on both sides. Its premise had increasingly shifted towards the understanding that considerations of ownership on land in the other dominion were unviable.

This was also due to an arithmetical calculation. It was soon clear—though the figures, as in often the case in India–Pakistan relations, are contested—that India could make a larger claim for compensation based on the valuations of property left behind in West Pakistan. The Indian side put forward a claim that 'Hindu and Sikh urban evacuee property in West Pakistan at Rs. 525 crores and Muslim urban evacuee property in India at Rs. 125 crores.'[16] It was argued that the value of the land left behind by those who had left Pakistan was some five times as that of land left behind in India.[17] Yet, the nature of such a claim also reveals the extent of dialogue there was between the two sides regarding this question, and how it was to be settled. These calculations also led to its increasingly rejecting Pakistan's proposals for evacuees being allowed to swap pieces of property by agreeing to 'individual exchanges'.

By the next conference, Nehru decided, that it would be more beneficial if a collective pool of property was to remain in fact under the control of the Custodian: he wrote, 'If a few, valuable pieces of property were to be removed from this pool, refugees as a whole would feel that the value of their stake in evacuee property had gone down.' Instead, India asked for a 'government to government' exchange, whereby the two governments would estimate the value of the property in their territories, and then settle the difference.[18] Like J. Simpson had suggested for Palestine, negotiations on evacuee property concerned three kinds of property: that of agricultural property, urban immovable property, and finally movable property. The custodian's jurisdiction would only operate within 'Agreed Areas' in both India and Pakistan. In the two years that followed the partition, the 'agreed areas' were selected on the basis of those localities from which mass migration had taken place, and, for the most part were concentrated along the Punjab and north India.

The government of Pakistan pointed out in 1955 that 'that almost every conference or discussion since held on the subject has broken down on account of the Government of India's insistence to settle the problem only on the basis of Govt.-to-Government liability.' Sardar Amir Azam, Minister for Rehabilitation in the Pakistan Government, argued that this could only be explained by the 'desire of the government of India to obtain as large a compensation for the evacuee properties in Pakistan as possible in the course of what may be protracted negotiation spread over several years'. The agreement of January 1949, moreover had been consistently disregarded by India by their permitting the extension of the rights of the Custodian of Evacuee Property.[19] Finally, Amir Azam concluded, that in view of the actions of the Indian government already taken with regard to the evacuee property in their territory, and their subsequent invitation to Pakistan to 'settle the manner in which compensation could be distributed as if the govt. of Pakistan have been party to or had approved the expropriatory action taken by the Government of India in utter violation of the Agreement of January 1949', discussions on this basis could only be fruitless.[20]

Agreeing on 'Agreed Areas'

But what is also consistently noticeable throughout the course of the evacuee property conferences is the importance that both sides placed on reciprocity. Indeed, many of the critiques of the Indian or Pakistani governments' positions on evacuee property reflect the assumption of a mutual reciprocity: the reason the criticism was being levelled, was because the principle of reciprocity was not being observed. In 1949, at the Constituent Assembly in Pakistan, for example, I.H. Quereshi declared that Pakistan was being cheated over the evacuee property negotiations, because '[a]gainst our law and the Agreement, India has been encouraging exchange between non-evacuee property in India with evacuee property in Pakistan.[21]

At a conference in Lahore on 22 July 1948, Indian and Pakistani delegates considered the expansion of areas where land could be declared 'evacuee property', and which would, in India's case extend the arrangement to Ajmer Merwara, Malerkotla State, the Matsya and Rajasthan Unions, Saurashtra, the States of Jaipur and Jodhpur, and Western Districts of United Provinces.[22] In Pakistan, these included Sind, West Punjab, North West Frontier and Baluchistan. Agreed areas connoted those from which evacuees had fled from under duress; and so were entitled to compensation from the government. In these areas, the custodian's jurisdiction could apply; refugees could be settled in the property of the custodian.

Indeed, argued Ishtiaq H. Qureshi, 'this obsession of the Indian Dominion that much more evacuee property lay within the bounds of Pakistan ... is at the root of a large number of difficulties with regard to evacuee property'.[23] Qureshi's diagnosis, however, was not wrong. Sucheta Kripalani, a member of the constituent assembly, for instance argued that provisions related to remittances being sent across the border were too lenient:

> We know of cases where the head of the family has remained here, while his son or his nephew or his relations went over there; they bought Hindu or Sikh property for a song and carried on business there; gradually he liquidated his property here and smuggled all the money out to the other territory.[24]

Possibilities for long-term agreements on evacuee property, though conceivable, were not easy to put into motion. Nor were they necessarily politically desirable: while frequently disagreeing with the individual decisions made by the offices of the custodian—the famous instance of a businessman from Bombay having gone abroad on work, only to return to find his house sealed up by the Custodian had, for instance, provoked a particularly incensed letter to the rehabilitation ministry—nonetheless, the process as a whole, its institutions and frameworks, were mostly given leeway to continue. For instance, he was also clear that, although fairer solutions were not difficult to construct, the 'main difficulty will be to carry our large population of displaced persons with us in any agreement we may come to with Pakistan.'[25] In a letter to Nehru, a senior Indian refugee politician, Mehr Chand Khanna wrote, that as far as the evacuee property question was concerned 'The average displaced person... though he may acknowledge that something has been done for him, he feels that his ultimate rehabilitation is largely dependent upon the liquidation of his own assets in Pakistan'.[26]

Yet, the coordination of these areas had to be calibrated carefully; expansion of rehabilitation into 'non agreed areas' was consistently resisted by both sides. Moreover, provincial governments in both countries protested vehemently against having to rehabilitate refugees from 'non agreed' areas, as this would further stretch their already slim purse strings. Ilyas Chatta, for instance also shows how Pakistan's minister for rehabilitation, Mian Iftikaruddin, had to eventually resign over this question.[27] At a discussion between Nehru and Khwaja Shahbuddin, which took place at the same time as the inter-dominion conference of 1950, the possible means of finally resolving the evacuee property dispute were examined, although it would take a few years yet for this to in fact 'complete'. Later, in May 1950, Ayyangar despatched a telegram to the Pakistani minister for rehabilitation, Khwaja Shahbuddin, and stated 'We are determined to solve this evacuee property problem on the basis of the very friendly relations between the two governments brought about by the Nehru–Laiquat Pact'.[28] One option was that all declarations of evacuee property could cease as of 8 April 1950. The possibility was repeatedly examined by officials on both sides. Subimal Dutt, for instance, a key official in the shaping of Nehru's Pakistan's policy listed out the merits of the suggestion of the Pakistani prime minister that declarations of evacuee property cease after a certain date. Dutt pointed out that if this provision were to be accepted, the urge towards pushing out members of the minority committee in order to claim their properties might reduce.[29]

Indeed, Subimal Dutt also advised that both governments should facilitate the process of sales and exchange of evacuee property where these could take place. He felt the proposal for setting up a joint agency for the collection of income tax from immovable agricultural property, was, however, unfeasible. The joint collection of revenue from evacuee property would have implied prolonging the uncertainty of ownership over this land. Dutt's main concern in all of this—while endorsing some aspects of Pakistan's positions on this question—was about settling the question of ownership once and for all. Property, he argued—channelling Locke—ought to firmly belong to one person—and certainly not, to sets of people on both sides of the border.

At the same time, concerns about reciprocity also acted as a kind of check on the decision-making process on evacuee property. The long term disadvantages of the forceful requisitioning of land were thus clearly recognised even at the time itself. In 1953, the question arose as to whether the titles of land-holdings of Muslim evacuees could simply be unilaterally quashed, as a means of simplifying issues of current land ownership. Badruddin Tyabji argued that the option of quashing the titles of Muslim evacuees who owned land in India, so that refugees from West Pakistan could be rehabilitated, was short sighted. He pointed out that to do so, would go against the International Court of Justice, which had ruled that a government could not, by means of its internal legislation, deprive a foreign citizen of their proprietary rights. On the particular issue of evacuee property, moreover, it was calculated that India had a better leg to stand on, and the minister for rehabilitation, Ajit Prasad Jain, had gone so far as to threaten to take the whole question to the international court. Several arguments were therefore made, that to flout its rulings would not be beneficial. Tyabji thus argued that quashing all evacuee property titles once and for all would leave India vulnerable to action taken against it by the government of Pakistan in the International Court of Justice. Furthermore, he argued such an action would 'necessarily equate the claims of India and Pakistan to property left behind by their citizens, even though India's claims to property in Pakistan is larger.'[30] These objections were echoed in a note drafted by Sir B. N. Rau on the contemplated action on Evacuee Property, although he also noted that the prospects of Pakistan in fact raising this issue at the International Court of Justice, given that the proportion of Evacuee Property was greater in Pakistan, was uncertain.[31]

Furthermore, while frequently cloaked in terms like 'deadlocked' and 'reneging', the conversation was nonetheless choreographed: As an editorial of the *Economic and Political Weekly* pointed out in 1954,

> On immovable evacuee property, there has been deadlock from the beginning...though this problem has solved itself through the policies of both governments relating to quasi permanent allotment of evacuee agricultural land to the respective displaced persons.[32]

Yet, the process through which these decisions were enacted in both countries was remarkably consistent. Although the legislations passed with regard to evacuee property were not necessarily aimed at enabling a greater control of evacuees over the properties they left behind, it was nonetheless important to both governments to discuss the nature of these legislations, and to attempt their calibration.

Shaping the Intending Evacuee Clause

At a Conference in July 1948, the Pakistan delegation proposed that migrants who moved from India to Pakistan after a certain date—30 September 1948—should not be declared as Evacuees by India.[33] Gopalaswami Ayyangar had rejected this proposal, arguing that it would be unfair to those who had already migrated. The decision to migrate to Pakistan—even if temporarily, or having left other members of the family behind—was seized on by the government as a way of acquiring their land.

In August 1949, T. B. Coeh, an official at the Ministry of Foreign Affairs in Karachi wrote to the Ministry of External Affairs protesting against 'discriminatory laws affecting Muslims are enforced in areas in India in contravention of an Inter-dominion Agreement, and in a spirit of revenge against Muslims'.[34] The office of the Custodian placed increasing restrictions in the way of the individual transfer, sale, or exchange of land. The role of the Custodian's Office, a circular noted in 1949, would include informing its officers of 'all instructions, directives, copies of all inter-dominion agreements'; and, moreover, 'all instructions having a bearing on policy or inter-dominion relations shall be issued only in consultation with the ministry of rehabilitation.'[35] Increasingly, the notion of 'evacuee property' became synonymous with that of rehabilitation, and the acquisition of more property by the Custodian became a legitimate pursuit by that office, frequently regardless of the current location of the owner.

One particularly insidious piece of legislation over evacuee property concerned the term 'intending evacuee'. The 'intending evacuee' was defined comprehensively:

> Persons who have transferred their assets wholly or in part, or have acquired either personally or through any dependent relative any right to, interest in, or benefit from any evacuee or abandoned property in Pakistan or by the execution of any document, or any other document in writing sought to effect exchange of the whole or part of the property in India with property in Pakistan can be declared as an intending evacuee.[36]

In effect, this legislation was aimed at sealing the first right of the custodian over the property of Muslims and Hindus who were deemed to be contemplating a move across the border—specifically, at members of divided families who were thought to be consolidating their interests on the other side of the border. The government of Pakistan enacted legislation, again with uncannily similar wording, in April 1951.

Yet, what evacuees attempting to re-establish control over their property quickly discovered, were the growing tentacles of the office of the custodian of evacuee property, and the restriction placed in the way of their individual transfer, sale, or exchange of the land. The concerns about reciprocity in these endeavours, however, also led to a kind of cooperation between India and Pakistan: both governments were in fact quite anxious to define their rights to the ownership of property quite tightly in the aftermath of the partition. Yet, the definitions of 'intending evacuees' were also being discussed in India, and introduced in the legislations on evacuee property in provinces such as West Bengal and United Provinces.

In India, the issue of how the writ of Evacuee Property Law was to be extended, and, if it were centrally enacted, it could apply to the state governments of Bihar, Uttar Pradesh, and, subsequently, Hyderabad, were also repeatedly considered. By July 1949, less than a year after the police annexation of the state, discussions to extend the Evacuee Property Law in Hyderabad were underway. Extension of central legislation on administering evacuee property entailed that provisions of previous State law on the subject would no longer apply. The issue arose as to how an evacuee would be defined in the case of Hyderabad, where large scale migration had recently taken place as a result of the police action. In July 1949, a meeting of representatives from the Ministries of Rehabilitation, external affairs, and various state governments was held to discuss this question. The question of migration as a result of the police action should bear on a person being declared an evacuee was discussed. However this did not alter the definition of an evacuee, since 'It was pointed out that the police action itself was a result of the setting up of the two Dominions and that the migration to Pakistan was also a corollary of that event'.[37]

Legislation passed by the government of East Bengal in 1952, to the effect that the rights of refugees who did not possess sale or exchange deeds for the property they currently resided on, would not be recognised. This however, ran counter to a declaration made a few months ago by the Ministers for Minorities for India and Pakistan which recognised that land transactions made during the disturbances may well have been unfair. By 1952, however, the state governments of Assam, Tripura and West Bengal were asked to consider the merits of passing similar legislation in their own states. The West Bengal government argued that there was need for central legislation on this issue, although this ran counter to the view of the central minister, who argued 'any legislation should be enacted for the purpose of validating the transactions only if it appears that the sale or exchange had been on a fair basis. Otherwise the transactions ought to be set aside, and the parties should be put back in possession of their respective properties, with profits to each for interim occupation.'

In September 1952, a conference was held at the Central Secretariat Office in New Delhi, where the machinery for implementing such a re-distribution was held.[38] The Ministry of Rehabilitation was contemplating the ways in which the claims of displaced persons from West Pakistan could be compensated.[39] One option was that the 'titles of evacuee owners would be extinguished by enacting special legislation so that permanent titles may be conferred on the buyers and allottees of evacuee property'.[40] If such a course were to be taken, the matter would have to be handled carefully, and a meeting of the Cabinet took place on 19 August 1952 to consider its various dimensions. Those present included Nehru, Gopalaswami Ayyangar, at that point Minister of Defence, and Ajit Prasad Jain, the Minister for Rehabilitation. Since a great deal of evacuee land was falling into disrepair and incurring unsustainable expenditure to the government it was argued, the best course would therefore be to formally hand over such properties to refugees, and quash the titles that evacuees held over this land. At this meeting, it was decided that the ministry of rehabilitation would dispatch a note to the government of Pakistan stating that the Indian government would be happy to accept arbitration on the matter by a group of people agreed to by both governments, or by reference to an international court. Subsequently, the Indian prime minister could write to the Pakistan prime minister over this matter. At the same time, the ministry of rehabilitation would prepare a draft bill along the lines of their proposed measures with regard to Evacuee property. In his opening address at the conference for redistributing evacuee property, the Indian minister for relief and rehabilitation stated 'While we are approaching the Pakistan government for a settlement of the evacuee property question, as you know, we cannot expect much from Pakistan. Perhaps, there may be some counter-accusations.'.[41]

This process had striking similarities in East Pakistan. The East Bengal State Acquisition Bill, by which the government would be entitled to convert into evacuee property those who had left for India, was fiercely opposed by Hindu MLAs, as the debate raged in the assembly in the 1949 and 1950 sessions. They were also a powerful opposition of the Bengal Zamindari Bill. These debates, and the State Requisitioning and Tenancy Act in particular, became very acrimonious, and was fought clause by clause by the Hindu MLAs of the assembly in sessions from 1947–53. The State Requisitioning Act effectively transferred the interests of the—substantially Hindu—rent-receiving classes to the government. Nurul Amin had accused the MLAs of directing their speeches to an 'international' audience as the MLAs protested that the measure would further deteriorate the security of the minority community in the province.[42]

Moreover, the process of passing legislation in favour of more requisitioning by the state of evacuee property was given similar justifications. Tafazzal Ali, a member of the legislative assembly who proposed a motion in favour of greater requisitioning argued:

> A house on Sri Ramakrishna Road has been sold by the Hindu owner to a Muslim gentleman who now occupies it. Now the tactics adopted by that particular gentleman were merely a subterfuge in order to defy the requisition of that house so that he may make some gain by selling his house privately.[43]

Brushing aside the objections of his opposition, who argued that places of religious worship or private charitable institutions ought to be exempt from this bill, Tafazzal Ali went on to argue that:

> There may be cases where, even though a particular place is dubbed as a place of charitable institution or as a place of educational activities, it may be found on enquiry that this institution or place does not really serve any useful purpose, and so in the larger interest of the State, even though it may cause inconvenience to some, is to requisition.[44]

N.G. Gopalaswami Ayyangar led the Indian delegation at the inter-dominion conference in Karachi in June 1949. Upon his return to Delhi, he called a press conference on 27th June. The latest conference he said, had 'resulted in nothing but an exchange of complaints' for several reasons. Pakistan had argued that India's enactment of legislation providing for the uniform administration of evacuee property throughout the country was a breach of the previous agreement. In particular, the Pakistani delegation had argued, the application of the evacuee property laws to Bombay, where considerable, and valuable, swathes of evacuee land were situated, was an infringement on the rights of Muslims in that province.

But, for many officials in both governments, the idea of simply taking away land which had belonged to someone else was inherently uncomfortable, and the evolving frameworks for putting these decision into motion also allowed for several qualifiers along the way. In fact, it is also worth emphasising, that evacuee property matters were rarely straightforward in either government: there was also consistently an articulate critique made against the unnecessarily zealous activities of the custodian. In a report compiled on this issue, Mridula Sarabhai argued that the evacuee property problem did not elicit a uniform reaction among either refugees nor, indeed, evacuees.[45] Her report noted that the Muslim community in India was ambivalent about the idea of a government to government exchange, as this 'would only lead nowhere, and to the perpetuation and increment in the scope of partition.'[46] One feature of refugees' sentiments on this problem, she argued, was that in the event of their being allowed to return in large numbers to their own properties in Pakistan, the two governments should not have snatched away their rights over their properties. At the same time, she noted, there was a great deal of support for the notion of 'nationalising' the evacuee properties within India, failing, or even accompanying, a government-to-government settlement of the issue.[47] At the most extreme end of this spectrum, she noted, the Hindu right-wing organisation the Rashtriya Swayamsevak Sangh was 'advocating their extreme theory of "Every penny from Pakistan/ Every penny to the Refugees"'.[48] But it would be rash, she argued, to force through a uniform legislation on evacuee property, since the question was so complex, and elicited so many reactions. While the rehabilitation of refugees was certainly a priority, the option of whole-scale requisitioning of evacuee land needed to be carefully considered.

The question of how this process could become more efficient became a foremost concern at the Ministry of Rehabilitation. For example, in July 1949, one proposal from the Ministry of Rehabilitation argued that it would be more efficient to make the administration of Evacuee Property into a central (rather than provincial) subject. This, argued V.D. Dantyagi, joint secretary at that ministry, would ensure uniformity of legislation relating to Evacuee Property in all areas of the country, as well as enable quick action in a matter that was a subject of discussion with a foreign country.[49] The issue of the expansion of lands under the control of the Custodian of Evacuee Property also entered into the dialogue between the two countries. Indian delegates pressed for the expansion of the area in which the writ of the Custodian would apply. This would imply that the amount of land under the control of the custodian—and therefore more removed from complete ownership by evacuees—could increase. This became increasingly central in the negotiations at the inter-dominion conferences.

But there were also strong reasons why this could not be done in a wholesale manner. In a note on the forthcoming inter-dominion negotiations on this issue, Nehru stressed 'The fact is, that in our application of evacuee property laws and rules, we have to be exceedingly careful in future and take up only special cases, which must be borne in mind by all the Custodians. Justice is to be done in all the cases, and where there is the slightest doubt, it has to be in favour of the person concerned'.[50] Similarly, in September 1949, C.N. Chandra, a secretary to the government of India, wrote to the chief secretaries of the states, cautioning them that the indiscriminate application of evacuee property laws would be undesirable. He argued that:

> it seems imperative for the officers charged with the duty of administering the law to realise that these powers must be exercised with the utmost care and circumspection... [and] it must be always kept in mind that the evacuee legislation is an extraordinary piece of legislation which has been forced on us by circumstances altogether beyond our control.[51]

The results of this kind of attempt at a calibration of the speed at which property ownership could be transferred, were also, to some extent at least, visible in Bengal. Absent in the evacuee property legislations on either side, from 1947–51—and again as a result of coordination over the exercises—was the extension of the Evacuee Property Ordinance into Bengal. In fact, given the incessant feuding that accompanied all conversations about Evacuee Property at all the levels of both governments, it is particularly striking how any mention of Bengal—by a wide margin, the most vexed site for the urgent need of refugee rehabilitation of all provinces—was studiously avoided until a few years later, in 1951, and even then in a relatively diluted form. Part of the reason that evacuee property legislation was introduced in stages in India, were to do with the dynamics of the migration. In the months after the partition, migration across the eastern sector was—compared to what was to come—relatively muted. Yet, it was with the desperate air of staving off this eventuality that the Inter-Dominion Conference of 1948 in Calcutta, drafted a joint declaration that 'Evacuee Property Management Boards shall be set up in the localities where these are deemed to be necessary. The Boards shall consist only of members of the Minority Community. The Boards shall come into action only when it is established there is specific demand for their decision'. The vocabulary of this declaration was one that was designed to attempt a staunching of minority movement across the Bengal boundary. For all the tussle over expensive pieces of property in north India and Punjab, where Bengal was concerned, the two governments were working with a very different set of calculations. For one thing, the vast majority of those who crossed the border in search of refuge would bring very little material wealth with them—either in money, or in fixed assets that could be reclaimed. For another, actually bringing in evacuee property legislation into this notoriously fluid province would only give rise to subsequent flows of inter-dominion migration—as opposed to the case in Punjab, where to a greater extent, the legislations were enacted post-facto massive movements of population.

In a fortnightly report in August 1949 S. K. Banerji noted 'the promulgation of the Evacuee Property Ordinance in different provinces of India has worried many Muslim gentleman... They are making anxious enquiries from us in this respect, and enquiring whether there is any likelihood of the Ordinance being promulgated in West Bengal also'.[52] Similarly, the Branch Secretariat of the Ministry of External Affairs in Calcutta often dealt with complaints from Pakistani citizens about the requisition of their land by the East Pakistan government. The Office of the Deputy High Commission in Dhaka also routinely forwarded complaints of forcible occupation of land, or land not being restored to returning Hindu migrants, to the Government of East Bengal.

Yet, in India, the office of the Custodian became increasingly concerned with limiting the sales of Muslim property holders, of what was potentially evacuee land. A letter from the Ministry of Relief and Rehabilitation to the provincial governments included within the 'Agreed Areas' of the Evacuee Property agreement, urged that they take suitable steps to 'prevent the frittering away of Muslim property by sale, especially to non refugees'.[53] The Ministry of Relief and Rehabilitation went to considerable lengths to ensure that the avenues of privately selling property by Muslims in India were restricted. A note from the Ministry of Rehabilitation to state governments stated 'the government of India are anxious to have all available information regarding any attempts by Muslims to remove their property or its sale proceeds to Pakistan.' To this end, it continued, 'censoring communications between India and Pakistan, we have been able to secure very valuable information leading to the property of Muslims, which had previously escaped undetected.'[54]

Conclusions—The House of Chamba

A particularly fascinating set of questions came to the forefront over the position of properties owned by princely estate of Chamba, in Himachal Pradesh, in Lahore. The property, not far from Lahore's Mall Road, consisting of an enormous bungalow and the grounds stretching along Golf Roads, with 'antique furniture, silverware and other articles worth around Rs. 5000'. When the issue of its maintenance arrived at the Ministry of External Affairs, an accompanying note from the Rehabilitation ministry—no stranger to the worth of real estate in post partition south Asia—immediately pounced on the claim, stating '[Since] Chamba along with the other hill states of Shimla have merged, and all the assets and liabilities of the state are now assets and liabilities of the Government of India.'[55] The house had thus far been maintained by 'some long serving Hindu retainers, who have run away owing to the recent disturbances.' The family itself had also requested 'A retired PCS officer of the Punjab Government, who was Chief Judge of the State to contact local officers in Lahore with a view to securing adequate protection for the property, but could not get any adequate assurances'.

The whys and wherefores of this question produced fascinating contortions. One option was to examine whether Pakistan's evacuee property laws could be circumvented in this particular case, as the property now technically belonged to the government of India, not a particular person. Since the evacuee property laws, it was argued, could not apply to the entire governments and not to a particular person, it might be possible to petition the government of Pakistan for its release. The opinion from the Ministry of Law, however, was the crucial: the matter simply boiled down to whether the government of Pakistan had claim to any similar pieces of property in India. Bahawalpur House, on Sikander Road in Delhi had belonged to the erstwhile ruler of Bahawalpur, whose kingdom had them acceded to Pakistan. The house had been taken over by the Custodian General, who had supervised its sale to the American Embassy. The proceeds of the payment, had been split, between the Raja and the government of India—unevenly, in the latter's favour.

In the successive years, the rehabilitation ministry put up a determined effort to persuade the Indian government to further pursue its case with regard to Chamba House. In 1956, when asked by the legal ministry why the custodian should have seen fit to dispose of Bahawalpur House, it came up with the truly inspired statement that 'Bahawalpur House was declared as an evacuee property under a Notification which covered only the superstructure which belonged to the Nawab, and not the land, belonging to the government'.[56] The slightly bizarre legalities of the case concerned precisely who owned the property. Officials in the ministry of rehabilitation and the provincial governments of Himachal Pradesh busied themselves with poring over revenue records from the state in the 1920s, to decipher if taxes on the property had been paid personally by the family, or whether they had drawn from the state exchequer. If it could be proved that the property had belonged to the state, and used for state purposes, then the government of India, the rehabilitation ministry persevered, might have a stronger case for laying claim to the property. Attaching a copy of a tax receipt from the 1920s, thus, in 1953, S.K. Banerji, the Indian deputy high commissioner in Lahore, optimistically wrote to the Chief Secretary of Western Punjab, arguing that:

> Under Evacuee Property Law of Pakistan only a *person* can be declared an evacuee. As we have shown, however, these properties belong to the government of India, and therefore cannot be treated as evacuee property. Therefore, I am to request you to kindly release the house and grounds in favour of the government of India.[57]

On the other hand, the government of Pakistan firmly held to the position that in the municipal records, the property had been listed under the name of an individual—the Raja himself—and was thus liable to be treated as evacuee property. In any event, the consensus between the law ministry and that of external affairs was this: this was purely a matter of reciprocity. Since Pakistan could cite the case of Bahawalpur house in India as a precedent, any amount of tinkering over title deeds was likely to be fruitless. A note from the Law ministry flatly stated: 'It is not desirable to raise this issue unless the Indian government in turn are treating State properties of Pakistan states in India as not being evacuee properties.'[58] After all, the note pointed out, the position of the Rehabilitation Ministry over the evacuee property laws was insurmountable in both countries: 'Even in India, the heir of an evacuee would not be legally entitled to the restoration of the property unless he could produce adequate certification from the government, or from authorised agencies recognising that the applicant is entitled to this.' The same, the Law Ministry warned, would hold true in Pakistan. Similarly, Y. K. Puri, the MEA's official in charge of Pakistan in 1952, also flatly noted: 'It is not very clear how we can claim exemption for these properties from the Evacuee Property Law in Pakistan, when we have held as Evacuee Property the personal property of the Nawab of Bahawalpur in India.'[59] What this also shows is the importance of the principle of reciprocity in determining the actions on evacuee property on either side. Unless the case could be made that Pakistan was violating a principle that was not jointly held, then there was no realistic basis for the government's actions.

But, thanks mainly to the dogged attempts by the Ministry of Rehabilitation, the case was still open in 1959. It transpired that there was another weakness in the government of India's case on Chamba House: the Raja of Chamba had in fact applied for grants under the displaced persons Act of 1950, and was to receive Rs. 8 lakhs from the settlements commissioner. The Rehabilitation ministry pointed out that finally giving this sum to the Raja of Chamba would, in fact, legally make him into an evacuee, and therefore give the government of Pakistan further grounds to justify their decision about Chamba House. In his statement, Raja Lakshman Singh deposed that the property—built by his father in 1920—did not belong to the state, but was the personal property of the ruler. The regional settlement commissioner in Jullunder was directed not to actually release the compensation to the Raja's family until the matter could be verified—yet again—for legal loopholes.

Indeed, in many ways the evacuee property conferences, along with the lofty ambitions of completing enormous rehabilitation exercises, were also part of an unseemly exercise of two governments muscling out their claims into very expensive pieces of land. But there was consistently an articulate critique against the perils of excessive appropriation of evacuee land. The two governments wrangled extensively on who an evacuee was—and therefore whose land could be appropriated by the Custodian of Evacuee Property—and thus shaped, not only the contours of their own debates on citizenship, but also the measures adopted by both governments simply to acquire more land.

Ideas about ownership suddenly, and frighteningly, became much less certain. The assumptions about what it meant to really own property were dramatically shaken in the years that followed the partition: classical definitions of the ownership of private property—that an individual owner's right to his property was absolute—were considerably qualified; these rules were no longer unconditional, and were also shaped by realities based on reciprocal definitions of ownership across the border. Property-owning individuals from the minority community were consistently dogged with the question: could their claims to ownership be conclusive enough in the light of the new realities after partition? Definitions changed rapidly and increasingly shifted from the basis of having just inherited the property, or earned it, or acquired it, to requirements about residence and, even more problematically, to the perception of rightfully belonging in the residence. Indeed, as Rohit De points out, the journey of the evacuee property legislations—how they were drafted, who they benefitted, and how they conceptualised the definitions of ownership—also reveal the new political economy of the aftermath of partition. The ways in which the legislations were shaped show how partition created a new relationship between the sets of ownership rights that the state would enforce, and the sorts of people whom it would primarily do this for.[60] But in entering into this process India and Pakistan were also vouchsafing their claim to statehood vis-à-vis one another. Their actions were aimed at consolidating the effects of partition, and at sealing the benefits that it brought for the additional control over land.

4

NO WAR PACT

'ALL MEN OF GOOD WILL'?

The No War Pact correspondence between Jawaharlal Nehru and Liaquat Ali Khan is interesting for several reasons: its timing, the personalities, the possibilities it seemed to offer for the relationship ship, and the glimpses it offered into the world views of India and Pakistan during the 1950s. The Evacuee Property Conferences, as well as the refugee crisis in Bengal formed the immediate context in which Liaquat Ali Khan and Nehru opened negotiations on a possible No War Pact. In many ways, moreover, the correspondence also shows how deeply connected the shaping of foreign policy was with domestic politics—India's and Pakistan's international relations were shaped out of the domestic concerns of both nation. One reason that the correspondence was taking place at all was that it could offer the possibility of some movement on the questions of water and evacuee property. The correspondence offered an opportunity for India and Pakistan to clarify their positions internationally as mutually exclusive entities: at the same time, it was also for progress in leading to more accommodative outcomes for talks around the agenda of separation.

In fact, this chapter shows that the business of going about disentangling oneself from the other did not in fact necessarily mandate international stances that had to be hostile to one another: they could also be built upon an attempt at dialogue. The reason that a refugee crisis in Bengal, that took place some seventy years ago, is worth considering in great detail, is that it offers us a glimpse of why, in the midst of an increasingly hostile confrontation, the two governments were looking for means to effect a drawback. In this chapter, I will outline the progress of the No War Pact correspondence—undertaken between Nehru and Liaquat Ali Khan, during the period of the refugee crisis—to illustrate the importance of atmospherics in the conduct of India–Pakistan relations. Furthermore, I will also show that what the two countries wishes to project to the world was first and foremost their shared desire to seek a settlement to the tension.

The 'No War' declaration was intended to guarantee that neither India nor Pakistan would declare war on the other in the first instance, and the possibility of reaching such an agreement was explored by Nehru and Liaquat through a correspondence that spanned over eleven months, comprising more than a hundred letters and telegrams. I begin by offering an account of the correspondence, and suggest reasons for its initiation, as well as eventual failure. I then explore how the 'Frontier of Public Opinion' was seen as being the most crucial in most matters of India–Pakistan relations, and how it was often the appearance of trying to create a sense of stability and cooperation that was considered as vital as the specific actions of either government in this direction.

But an analysis of the progress of the No War Pact negotiations also offers several other interesting conclusions. For one thing, it offers us a glimpse into the decision making process on India–Pakistan relations, and enables us to appreciate of the benefits, as well as hindrances to the shaping of a better climate in the relationship. Secondly, it also allows us to examine just how the possibilities of improving bilateral ties were conceptualised within the two governments, and what paths when the situation necessitated it, the foreign ministries of both governments chose to embark on. The correspondence also shows that, contrary to the assumption of a default position that was based on an instinctive need to propagate a hostile relationship, decision making also included a keen appreciation of the political dividends of an improvement in bilateral ties. The No War Pact correspondence failed—Nehru and Liaquat could not agree to the terms in which the Agreement should be made. But the very reasons for undertaking it at all have to be further incorporated into the analysis of the India–Pakistan dynamic. Moreover, I will argue, these impulses for dialogue and reconciliation, were not merely fleeting or whimsical, but drew on concrete imperatives which were in the political interests of both governments.

Towards a Pact: Domestic and International Considerations

During his six-week tour of the United States in the winter of 1949, at a press conference in San Francisco, Nehru was asked a question about the future of India–Pakistan relations. In his reply, Nehru gave voice to an idea he had been toying with for some time. He stated that his government would like to work within a framework in which outstanding issues between India and Pakistan, including canal waters and evacuee property could be peacefully resolved. To that end, a declaration jointly made with Pakistan, committing both to the position that neither would declare war on the other in the first instance, was one option. According to this, the governments of India and Pakistan would resolve all their disputes by negotiations, arbitration, and mediation, and renounce the use of war as an instrument of state policy. His answer immediately prompted breathless speculation in the media about what the next development in this story would be. Others disapproved. The *Times of India* sceptically sniffed, 'At a time when the cold war interferes violently with the independence of judgement of most nations, India... cannot afford to surrender its vital interests to third party judgement.'[1] Nonetheless, the question of how Nehru would pursue his No War Pact gained substantial currency in the media, and its progress was closely tracked in both countries.

Back in Delhi by December 1949, Nehru began to consider means by which this could be secured. In his recent speeches, Prime Minister Liaquat Ali Khan had shown he was definitely not averse to talking about such a pact, and publicly declared his eagerness for it. He said this could provide an opportunity for '[a] fair and just settlement of causes that led to the breach of peace'.[2] In November 1949, Nehru wrote to Liaquat formally suggesting such a declaration, stating that both governments were committed to 'maintain good relations between the two countries, and advance the cause of world peace.' This could, he wrote, 'lessen the unfortunate tension that exists between our two governments, and produce an atmosphere which is more favourable to the consideration and settlement of particular disputes.'[3] The two prime ministers then embarked on a lengthy and voluminous correspondence—more than two hundred letters and telegrams were exchanged—on what the exact terms should be set into the text of such a declaration, and which procedures of arbitration could be used to settle the outstanding disputes between the two countries. The correspondence then spanned across the Bengal crisis, and the subsequent signing of a Nehru Liaquat Pact in April 1950, which made both governments accountable to one another for the protection of their minority populations.

Nor was war at all an unlikely event in the foreseeable future. Indeed, in February 1950, Nehru chose not to immediately reject the possibility of resorting to war with Pakistan over the question of swelling numbers of migrants flowing across the border. He ordered the movement of divisions of the Indian army closer to the West Pakistan borders, and for a heavier concentration of war related stores and equipment in militarily important areas like Ferozepur, Jullunder and Ludhiana.[4] In a letter to C. Rajagopalachari, he noted 'The situation is so complex and difficult that even I, with all my abhorrence of war and my appreciation of its consequences cannot rule it out completely.'[5] This was also reflected in some furious epistolary exchanges between Nehru and Liaquat at the time, asserting that the persecution of minorities in Bengal had to end, and both governments had to come to clear conclusions as to how the security of minority populations should be ensured. In Parliament, Nehru had to state: 'we owe it to those in East Bengal who may be in danger to give them protection in our territory, or to give them protection in their own territory if circumstances demand it.'[6] Moreover, Sir Girija informed the UK High Commissioner, Sir Archibald Nye that unless the situation of the influx of refugees across the Bengal borders were redressed, Indian military actions against Pakistan were inevitable.[7] Yet, as the inter-dominion correspondence on the No War Pact during this period shows, neither government was actually predisposed to a belligerent position, and critically engaged with the possibility of signing a declaration that renounced the use of war. As I hope to show through my discussion of the correspondence on the No War Pact, relations between India and

Pakistan were not necessarily confined to hostile exchanges, and both governments also repeatedly engaged with each other to attempt to find spaces of agreement and compromise.

As the refugee crisis became more acute, Liaquat despatched a telegram to the British Prime Minister Clement Attlee, urging that the Commonwealth intervene on behalf of Pakistan. Liaquat pointed out, 'thousands of Muslims are being driven out of India and are pouring into Pakistan to seek asylum'.[8] This was exacerbated, he added, by a 'systematic and organised campaign in the Indian press and by some Indian leaders that India should declare war on Pakistan to avenge the ill treatment of Hindus across the border.' He concluded:

> When I am confronted with an enormous concentration of men, armours and stores so close to the Frontiers of Pakistan, you will no doubt agree with me that I cannot but treat the situation as extremely anxious... We have, despite the gravest of provocations, kept our heads cool. We still believe that the difficulties between India and Pakistan can be settled by negotiation and arbitration.

He also stated that his government was considering allowing Sir Zafrullah Khan, Pakistan's representative at the United Nations, to raise the issue of the refugee crisis at the General Assembly.

Matters, as we saw in a previous chapter, came to a head in the early months of 1950, when an influx of migrants across the Bengal borders in swelling numbers drew forth furious protests from provincial governments on both sides, unwilling to support the additional burden of incoming refugees. The scale of this migration threatened the stability of both governments. The government of Pakistan released figures that claimed the entry of more than three million migrants into East Bengal, though estimates for the scale of migration differed on either side of the border. Nonetheless, in the midst of this context, avenues for dialogue about a No War Pact were explored.

By January 1950, Sir Girija Shankar Bajpai, had summoned the Pakistani High Commissioner to India, and opened negotiations on the exact wording of a No War declaration. The High Commissioner, Zahid Hussain, replied that existing disputes relating to Kashmir, Junagadh, the canal waters, and evacuee property ought to be settled first, but promised to explore the matter further with his government.[9] It was recognised from the outset that the real question in the proceedings was not that of persuading the other of the wrongs in using force as a tactic, so much as the extent to which agreement could actually be secured on the kinds of means to be employed for resolving outstanding disputes. However, it is also important to note that in neither country was the possibility of such a pact rejected out of hand because of a reflexive hostility to the other. It was also immediately recognized that in fact closing such a deal could bring huge advantages for India's and Pakistan's international standing. The idea was critically thought through on both sides, and its pros and cons were carefully weighed.

The crux of the correspondence concerned the methods of arbitration and mediation on the prevailing differences between India and Pakistan. While Pakistan argued for more detailed processes of mediation to be clearly incorporated into the text, India preferred a more general declaration which renounced war, but which left the methods of mediation unspecified. In Pakistan the possibilities in the declaration were quickly pared down to its concrete implications. Five main issues were listed as needing to be resolved in the Indo–Pakistan relationship: evacuee property, the canal waters, division of assets, Junagadh, and Kashmir. One key implication from such a deal was that Pakistan would de facto have formally acquiesced on paper to the existing cease-fire line in Kashmir. Liaquat wrote to Nehru saying that his government could accept a No War agreement with India, but that it had to contain in its wording specific bodies of arbitrators in the disputes, whose decisions would be binding, and a time frame within which they could settle the disputes. Liaquat pointed out that both India and Pakistan were members of the United Nations, which in itself implied that they had renounced war as means for the settlement of disputes. For a declaration to have any weight, argued Liaquat, it would need to contain 'concrete and precise suggestions regarding the procedure to be followed in the settlement of disputes.'[10] Liaquat declared on the floor of the National Assembly that 'even if these disputes could not themselves be settled at least the procedure for settling them could be laid down by agreement in precise terms so that both parties entered into firm commitments which would in the course of time definitely lead to resolution of disputes.'[11] What the Pakistani Foreign Ministry argued for in the No War negotiations was for a commitment to a standing position on these issues; such a declaration would, Liaquat argued, be welcomed in Pakistan, as well as in the United States.[12]

In India, meanwhile, the advantages of how much a No War declaration would shift from the ground already ceded to Pakistan was carefully scoped out. Nehru was initially unequivocal in his advocacy of signing such a declaration, and felt that Liaquat's terms for a more detailed text in the agreement about methods of settling outstanding disputes were at least worth examining. He was willing to pursue the statement further and, in a note to the Secretary General of the Ministry of External Affairs, Sir G. S. Bajpai, argued that the outstanding disputes between India and Pakistan should not 'come in the way of the declaration. If the questions could be decided without the declaration, no need for the declaration arises. It is in order to ease the situation between the two countries and help in creating an atmosphere of peaceful settlement of disputes, that we have made our proposal.'[13] He went even further with his cabinet and pointed out that the No War declaration would coincide with principles that 'we have already accepted, although we have avoided saying this with clarity.'[14] Secondly, he pointed out such a declaration would receive a positive reception in the United States, and the banking authorities there with regard to loans to India. In a press conference, he stated that a declaration of No War, would allow the possibilities of direct negotiation, and failing that, reference of that problem to a judicial tribunal could be applied in the various Indo Pakistani disputes.[15] A No War Pact, moreover, might help in framing a more favourable setting for dealing with issues in the bilateral relationship, such as the terms of inter-dominion trade and the canal waters issue. He concluded: 'This would be a further step which would be difficult for the Pakistan government to refuse to take... [and] in any event, will be helpful to us in different ways.'[16] With these incentives, Nehru urged his cabinet to consider accepting arbitration by external bodies on the question of the evacuee property and canal waters disputes.

The idea behind the No War Pact was also modelled on the Briand Kellogg Pact. Subimal Dutt, had also furnished a copy of the Pact to Nehru, as they were preparing for drafting their correspondence to Pakistan.[17] Sections from the text of the Briand Kellogg agreement, Dutt noted, might be relevant for purposes of the diplomatic dialogue. 'As I informed the Hon. Minister for Transport [Goapalaswami Ayyangar], the intention is that after a final draft is ready, it is to serve as a basis of discussion between us and the High Commissioner for Pakistan, before it is formally communicated to the Pakistan government.'[18]

The Kellogg agreement had been signed in Paris, in August 1928 between fifteen states, including the United States, Germany, and France, the United Kingdom, including its dominion members, such as Ireland, Canada, Australia and New Zealand, as well as Poland and Czechoslovakia. It enabled the neutralising of the mutual hostility between Germany and France, through the structuring of a delicate agreement of balance, guaranteed by the United States. This had mainly been envisioned as a pre-emptive measure, according to which all the signatories of this Pact agreed to outlaw war as an instrument of national policy and to settle their dispute by peaceful means. The clauses of the Pact had stipulated that all the contracting parties 'denounced the recourse to war for the solution of international controversies', and moreover that 'settlement of all disputes shall never be sought except by pacific means.'[19]

In applying such a concept to their bilateral relations, Nehru and Liaquat were defining the Indo–Pakistani relationship as one that was admittedly tense, but one that could also be negotiated in inherited frameworks of international relations, and the emphasis they placed on the paramount capacity of the nation state. Although the correspondence eventually failed, it is interesting that the representatives of both India and Pakistan, when they went about seeking peaceful solutions to their bilateral disputes, groped for ideas in the international precedents that had been set during the inter-war period, in Europe. The 'idealised' versions of how states ought to behave, and what should be done in order to improve relations, therefore, were mutually held and shaped by a common experience of the interwar decades.

But bringing these ideas into fruition also involved navigating fairly treacherous political landmines. By February and March that year, in Delhi—as the political landscape deteriorated in Bengal—the thinking about the No War Pact rapidly honed in to two different versions, and a debate arose about which should be forwarded to Liaquat Ali Khan. Nehru instructed Bajpai to draw up a draft incorporating Pakistan's demands for a more detailed statement about outstanding disputes, and which included a time frame for settling these differences. This Sir Girija did, but recorded in an accompanying note the grave misgivings he felt about letting this be sent out. 'I am not sure whether the draft prepared by me does not, in regard to certain matters, go too far.' For instance, he warned, 'the current version accepts Pakistan's demand for ultimate reference to the International Court of Justice over the dispute over canal waters'. He added, 'Another point about which I am in doubt is the inclusion, in points of difference to be settled by arbitration, of differences relating to the procedure for arbitration. Arbitration on arbitration, as it were, seems to me to carry arbitration too far.' Sir Girija argued that a more generalised draft which included none of the specifics Pakistan had mentioned, be forwarded instead. 'Another criticism of the draft declaration that I submit now is that it goes into too much detail. I should have preferred something briefer and more general.'[20] Something, he felt, to the effect of the governments of Pakistan and India would hereby declare that neither would declare war in the first instance, ought to be sufficient—it was unwise to commit in writing to a detailed declaration on the methods of arbitration.

Yet what is also interesting in this exchange is the way in which avenues for a more peaceful relationship were conceptualised. In Sir Girija's view, the course of improving the bilateral relationship could, at best, be a generalised declaration of No War. These deliberations also offer insights into how the bureaucracy were consolidating their position on the decision-making process on India–Pakistan relations. The Indian bureaucracy distrusted the implications of the pact since it loosened their ability to control the outcomes of the relationship. A stable but hostile and separated existence, with the ministry firmly in control of the proceedings in the relationship, seemed preferable to Sir Girija, than the unpredictable prospect of ceding away authority by the government to an outside authority. Nonetheless, the spaces within this for compromise and dialogue were also carefully considered, and occasionally, expanded.

Sardar Patel's condemnation of the No War correspondence was even stronger. When the proposed draft so reluctantly prepared by G. S. Bajpai was forwarded to him, his reply on 25 February, he flatly stated '[t]o me, the whole matter seems to be so unrealistic in the present circumstances that I wonder if we cannot put an end to this talk, at least for the time being.'[21] Patel said that his 'reading of Liaqat's letter is that he is cleverly trying to commit us to a line of procedure both in regard to outstanding and future disputes which would give Pakistan... a perpetual advantage over us. While everything binds us, nothing seems to bind them'. The idea of ceding so much ground with regard to arbitration was unacceptable. 'The only result of going to arbitration in such circumstances would be that we would lose what we have got under the (current) agreements, and the whole question which was settled as a result of a joint agreement of partition will be opened afresh with results which are unpredictable.' His belief was that the India–Pakistan dialogue had to be conducted through far tougher postures. 'I sometimes wonder, having regard to the present situation, whether we could really talk of peace with Pakistan when it is quite clear that it is thinking and preparing in terms of war and is doing everything possible to cast us on a burden which would break our back.' Nehru's proposal, Patel continued, had been a 'fairly simple one... whatever differences may exist between us, we would never resolve them by resort to war'. But Liaqat's attitude, 'is fundamentally different... First you provide a machinery for settling disputes, and then I shall see, in the light of that machinery, whether I can agree to outlaw war.' He then pointedly hinted that there was a relatively simple way out:

> If you feel it is not possible to confine ourselves to a simple declaration of no war, then the best course would be to get out of the whole business by pointing out this fundamental difference in approach and indicating to Pakistan that this approach is suggestive of their having mental reservations on this simple issue.[22]

Patel then detailed his specific objections. Kashmir, he said, was already before the Security Council and having 'invoked a forum of settlement of disputes open to both India and Pakistan, as members of the United Nations Organization, nothing further need to be done... than to leave matters to be adjusted through that forum'. On Junagadh, 'our position is well known to Pakistan and we cannot modify it'. On canal waters or evacuee properly, 'the position is fundamentally different from other international disputes' since these partitions 'do not arise between two nations or countries. They arise as a result of the partition of an undivided India'. On canal waters agreements already existed between India and Pakistan: 'The Pakistan Government is not only going back on those agreements but is also giving the whole dispute a wider significance and making the whole controversy more comprehensive.' The consequence of moving away from bilateralism would be 'that the whole question which was settled as a result of a joint agreement will be opened afresh with results that are unpredictable.' In sum any other approach than the 'simple issue of outlawry of war without any mental reservations' would land India in entanglements from which it would be difficult to 'extricate ourselves, except by prejudicing whatever advantages we have gained.'[23]

These tussles illustrate how Nehru was not always an omnipotent figure in the making of Indian foreign policy.[24] Interestingly enough, the No War Pact correspondence also coincides with a period when Nehru had threatened to resign over the issue of communal troubles in Bengal. To Krishna Menon he lamented, 'There is far too much intrigue and fraction and pulling in different directions.' He had had a detailed discussion with Sardar Patel on this question, and had argued that their approaches to Pakistan and on minority issues were too wide to bridge: 'There is a constant cry for retaliation and of vicarious punishment of the Muslims of India, because the Pakistanis punish Hindus. That argument does not appeal to me in the slightest. I am sure that this policy of retaliation and vicarious punishment will ruin India as well as Pakistan.'[25] The initiation of the correspondence by Nehru thus also simply reveals his attempts at regaining control over the making of policy with Pakistan—something that was frequently challenged by a variety of actors within and outside the government. However, its introduction into the bilateral conversation in the first place also shows to us the political room available for politicians to seek a more stable bilateral relationship.

For the Commonwealth High Commissioners in India, however, it made more sense to wait for the outcome of a meeting between Nehru and Liaquat in the near future, before making definite predictions about war in the subcontinent that summer. In fact—given the widespread concern about the imminence of war during these weeks—the temperateness of their suggestions for response over the build-up of troops in the Indian side is striking. Sir Archibald Nye, the British High Commissioner in India advised his government not to make formal contact with Nehru for the moment over the East Pakistan question. In a memo to Attlee's cabinet, he argued that they should wait longer for events to unfold, rather than many any direct interventions for the moment. The two prime ministers themselves were already in close touch, he added, and Liaquat Ali Khan was due to arrive in Delhi in a few weeks. Moreover, attempts at direct intervention by the British in the past had yielded limited results. When the High Commissioners of Canada, Australia and the American Ambassadors to New Delhi met with Archibald Nye for lunch at his Lutyens bungalow in King George's Avenue (present day Rajaji Marg) in Delhi's leafy Diplomatic Enclave to discuss the build-up of tension over minorities in East Pakistan, their consensus was to send a tempered account of the political developments in South Asia, to their respective governments. 'Our joint impression was that there is unlikely to be any substantial amplification of Indian troop dispositions before Liaquat arrives to Delhi'.[26]

Similarly, Loy Henderson, US Ambassador in Delhi at the time, while responding to the questions raised on this issue by Zafrullah Khan, the Pakistani representative at the United Nations, also advised his government to take no formal action over the troop movement. Although he would convey to Bajpai the concerns expressed by Pakistan to the American government, and urge them towards signing the joint declaration, his telegram also noted, 'If either the Indian and Pakistani Prime Ministers were to actually refuse to a meeting, this would then bring much to the fore whether the situation should be brought before the Security Council.'[27] This was also endorsed by the United Kingdom. The Commonwealth Relations Office, in a telegram to the Australian Foreign Ministry, pointed out that 'while the tension between the two countries may be extremely grave, we do not think we should be precipitate in deciding to refer yet a further dispute to the Security Council.'[28]

The Commonwealth high commissioners' diagnosis of only an illusionary brittleness in the current state of bilateral relations was justified, and on 1st April 1950, the Nehru–Liaquat Pact was signed.

According to this, both governments agreed to protect the interests of the minority populations living within their territories, and would be accountable to one another over their welfare. This was aimed primarily at reassuring minority populations of their security within the country, and to discourage them from migrating. This agreement was greeted with great fanfare in both countries, and seen as a significant step towards better relations between the two governments.

When the pressure of the East Bengal refugee movement had somewhat abated in May 1950, Liaquat met with the British Secretary of State for Commonwealth Relations, Gordon Walker to argue that in the event of such a military build-up again, the Commonwealth should pledge to give concrete assurances of support against the aggressor. Indeed, in his despatches, the British High Commissioner to Pakistan, Sir Lawrence Grafftey-Smith, had advocated that the United Kingdom support a guarantee to maintain the territorial integrity of India and Pakistan; and moreover, and that the Commonwealth pledge their support for defence against the aggressor in the event of an Indo–Pakistani war. But, for the moment, these recommendations were rejected in London. In his reply Gordon Walker told Liaquat that it would be difficult to make such a pledge, and it was difficult for Britain to decide who the aggressor was.[29] Yet, what was also implicitly recognised was that descent into outright war between the two countries was not, in fact, a headlong and impulsive calculation. The challenge in understanding the relationship was not the analysis of the reasons behind the hostility, but rather in gauging the potential of different frameworks for dialogue and reconciliation to bear fruit.

Achieving a Partial Truce: The Frontier of Public Opinion

To shrewder observers, however, it had been clear from fairly early on in the No War Pact correspondence that this declaration would not materialise. While a Minorities Agreement could be signed to fend off the rising numbers of incoming refugees that neither government could afford to absorb, the No War Pact lacked requisite backing in either government, whatever their public protestations had been. The No War proposition was examined, and then unravelled, quickly, within the space of three months.[30] By August 1950, the tone of

Nehru's letters in the correspondence had altered, and the possibilities of having methods of arbitration included in the text were withdrawn. Nehru wrote to Liaquat, saying that although his government had given careful consideration to the matter of having a detailed plan of arbitration in the text of the agreement, it was felt that such a plan would not work. He maintained that a straightforward declaration stating that neither would resort to war would be sufficient.

Ultimately, the Indian government had balked on counting the potential cost of Liaquat's suggestions for the No War declaration and, on the whole, felt it was unwise to commit to these provisions. Recognizing the role of other mediators in the canal waters and evacuee property dispute was not a position that the Ministry of External Affairs in Delhi felt comfortable with. Losing an exclusively bilateral footing with Pakistan would be a disadvantage, and a declaration that officially committed them to accepting the awards of international mediators—that may well not be in their favour—was therefore not acceptable. There was no need to give up as much ground on the various outstanding disputes; a commitment to arbitration, argued many, including Sir Girija, would only limit options. Moreover formally ceding so much ground on the issue of arbitration would not necessarily yield correspondingly positive results, particularly when there were a number of potentially serious problems that could later arise in the relationship anyway. Counting the cost of the No War declaration, therefore, took the ministry further away from consenting to sign it. The *Times of India* was approving. An editorial in December 1950 noted that the failure of the correspondence in producing a declaration should 'leave no more room for wishful thinking in New Delhi.'[31]

By October 1950, although the No War correspondence still continued, its urgency had been lost. In a letter to Nehru, Liaquat noted that the course of the No War correspondence had shown that 'the crux of the difficulty is the reluctance of your government to substitute on any issue, impartial arbitration for threatened and actual use of force.'[32] Nehru denied this, and argued that the mechanisms for resolving outstanding conflicts were in fact already in place. The correspondence ended with the two briskly trading allegations over the various failures in reaching a settlement on the canal waters dispute, evacuee property and Kashmir. However, in a speech to parliament in November 1950, by which time hopes for such a declaration materialising had been shelved, Nehru maintained that every attempt had been made by his ministry to persuade Pakistan of the benefits of the pact. 'India's will to peace', he continued 'is no less than that of Pakistan's, and I can give a common assurance that we shall continue to work for peace with our neighbour.'[33]

What is also significant about the progress of the No War Pact correspondence is its very public nature: the objective of having the correspondence was to be able to declare loudly that it had taken place. In itself, a general statement renouncing war was no guarantee of India and Pakistan never again going to war—as Liaquat had shrewdly observed, as far as the legality was concerned, both countries were already signatories of the UN, which forbade them from resorting to war in the first instance. Instead, the question of projecting the right image became a central concern as the correspondence continued. Once in motion, it was thoroughly publicised by both governments. In India, Sir Girija had already told Vijaya Lakshmi Pandit and Krishna Menon in London and Washington to make sure that these governments 'confidentially' knew of the proposals under consideration.[34] It attracted a great deal of speculation in the press, its substance was widely leaked, and was shortly compiled into a white paper publication by both governments.[35]

Both Nehru and Liaquat, moreover, stood in their Constituent Assemblies to report on the progress of the exchanges, and weathered questions from sceptical political opponents on its outcome. It was important for both governments to show that they had made genuine efforts towards lasting peace, and that failure towards this object was not due to a lack of flexibility on their part. In India, it became necessary for 'our line to be communicated to individual press correspondents', since, 'unless we release our own proposals, the Indian press as well as the world outside would only know of Pakistan's counter proposals.'[36] Indeed, even when Pakistan's proposals for a detailed plan of arbitration being included in the text had been rejected, Nehru felt that the correspondence ought to be publicised. To Liaquat he wrote: 'As our previous correspondence has already been placed before Parliament here, and your Constitutional Assembly I think this letter should be placed before Parliament. Indeed, I gave an assurance to this effect to Members of the House. If you like you can publish it on the same day'.[37] This was confirmed by Liaquat in his next telegram: 'I enclose a list of papers which may be published… and would suggest that simultaneous release be made in New Delhi as well as Karachi.'[38]

The progress of the correspondence in 1950 reveals a variety of agendas being pursued under complicated circumstances. A joint declaration renouncing the use of war never materialised from this correspondence. Yet, what is significant about the No War correspondence was that it acknowledged, and vocalised the possibility that India and Pakistan could have a stable coexistence. Although the ways in which the two could gain a stronger position vis-à-vis the other were consistently explored, the India–Pakistan dynamic was also based on the necessity of asserting the possibility of a future amity. Such a situation allowed for a fairly elaborate smoke and mirrors game being played in both countries, although an examination of the concrete decisions made with regard to one another does reveal very pragmatic calculated, and inherently stable approaches on the positions to be adopted. While it never materialised, the possibility of having such a declaration made did need to be articulated. It offered a powerful incentive, as a way to try and change the political moment, as well as the advantages of the international, as well as domestic, approval this could bring.

Although the correspondence failed to result in a declaration in 1950, this was not the only time that such a possibility would be examined. The political potential of such a declaration tempted the leadership of both countries at various junctures in the India–Pakistan relationship. Nehru would renew his offer again in 1956, and 1962. In 1959, Pakistan made a 'joint defence proposal' to India, and, some twenty years later, a 'No War' offer was made by President Zia.[39] None of these proposals were rejected in instinctive and hasty reaction to the idea of compromising with Pakistan or vice versa.

This had also, for example, been taken note of in a shrewd editorial in the *Dawn* in September 1950, which pointed out 'the Pakistan Prime Minister's oft repeated views that a war between India and Pakistan would be disastrous to both is echoed by everyone; and an intransigent attitude by the government of India may not impress impartial observers about Bharat's earnestness in first seeking an agreement with Pakistan.'[40]

The possibilities of international mediation have often been dismissed in many writings on India–Pakistan relations, as being improbable and remote. It is argued that pressure from international mediators is ineffective in deterring India from exercising its size and strength maintaining its hold on the state. For instance, the author and diplomat Shahid M. Amin squarely charges India as being responsible for international mediators not being able to play a larger role in the Kashmir dispute: 'its [India's] larger size, its greater attraction for trade and investment purposes, as also its military prowess have tilted the balance in its favour.'[41] Thus, Pakistan's attempts in multilateral forums is seen in terms of attempting to reduce such advantages: 'Pakistan's multilateral diplomacy has stemmed from its security anxieties, particularly with India, and the expectation that the UN and the world bodies in general would insist on the principle of self-determination for the people of Jammu and Kashmir.'[42]

The reasons that the correspondence failed in 1950 were not, in the end, particularly surprising—indeed, they were structural: for Pakistan, signing to such a declaration would have implied its formal acquiescence to the status quo in Kashmir. In India, Nehru's bureaucracy cautioned implacably against the future risks of committing to the correspondence. But a closer reading of the justifications offered by either side during the correspondence, also offers insights about how the appraisals of the merits of all the different aspects of mediation were not always fashioned so that they could be adhered to in hard and fast terms. Furthermore, the extent of disagreement and contingency in the decision making process also did not allow for a consistent adherence to a given position on mediation. And what also does come across from the debates about the drafting of the No War Pact in India is the extent to which options for the mechanisms for resolving disputes were quite carefully considered—they were not instinctively rejected out of hand. There was an evaluation of what various options for mediation could potentially offer, and whether there could be a plausible case that could be made for pursuing any of these channels.

This is relevant, for what emerges from these discussions are in fact not the contours of a policy of the paramountcy of self-preservation against the other—which was immediately grasped and pursued by implacable statesmen for the benefit of their own countries—but rather a more uncertain, tenuous and fragmented set of policies, often flexible, and sometimes discarded. By the close of 1950, Nehru himself had also reached a similar conclusion—during the year, one major agreement with Pakistan on minorities had been reached, another had failed. To parliament, in response to a question aimed at criticising his approach to India's foreign policy, he argued: 'We have to deal with matters as they come up. In matters of foreign policy especially, one has to decide almost every hour what has to be done.' Idealism could also play a role in the shaping of foreign policy, since it was merely, he insisted, perhaps even somewhat problematically, 'the capacity to know what is good for the day after tomorrow or for the next year, and to fashion yourself accordingly'.[43]

5

INDUS WATERS

In this chapter, I wish to offer a pre-history to the Indus Water Treaty of 1960. Since the period that this book covers ends at 1952, and since I wish to situate the discussions around the treaty as a means of implementing the partition, it becomes particularly important to understand the considerations that affected the early stages of the Indus negotiations. I argue that although the Indus Waters Treaty, negotiated under the auspices of the World Bank, was signed only in 1960, over a decade after the partition, many of its clauses had built upon the assumptions that had been formed by 1950. Indeed, by 1951, both the source of the problem—the fear that enough water would not be allowed to flow in to Pakistan from the canals that had been built before the partition—as well as its solution—that new canal networks would have to be developed in a way that would satisfy the separate requirements of both India and Pakistan—were already apparent. The discussions around Indus waters in the years that immediately followed the partition, offer valuable insights into how the implementation of the partition was conceptualised.

In particular, I will concentrate on a specific slice of the early history of the negotiations: those in 1950, about whether or not the agreement on water sharing in 1948 ought to be registered with the United Nations; and a set of discussions between India and Pakistan that followed, about the setting up of a joint technical mission to study the potential for irrigation supply to both India and Pakistan from the Indus river system. This registration—and, indeed, the 1948 agreement itself—was bitterly contested by the government of Pakistan. Yet, the terms of the discussions between the two governments on this issue, also reveal the way in which arguments about sovereignty and the role of the state, were conceptualised—and then pursued—by both governments. Although the question of irrigation from the Indus canals obviously concerned the provincial governments the most closely, it was the considerations based on what would best solidify the centre's position that ultimately drove much of the negotiations on the Indus rivers.

Moreover, the early stages of the water negotiations also reveal an interesting pattern about which kinds of notions of territorial integrity—whether it was the princely state, or the nation, or the undivided province, or the river delta—India and Pakistan were most willing to give precedence to. The way in which these agendas were rebranded, as part of an exercise about defining the concerns of India and Pakistan, was an equally integral part of the process of the negotiations. The Indus waters negotiations were also about imposing a new set of timelines onto an older dispute. In many ways, both governments were simply carrying forward the complaints that had been made to the government of India by the provincial governments of Sindh, Patiala and Punjab, during the 1920s and 30s. Above all, what the Indus Waters Treaty of 1960 affirmed, in fact, was about strengthening the right of the governments of India and Pakistan to speak on concerns of water. These questions are relevant to our study here, since they help in illuminating further our own concern about how the practicalities of implementing the partition served as a complex basis of a partnership between India and Pakistan.

As I have argued across the book, most importantly held were the considerations of how any agreement arising out of the partition would further bolster the claims to a viable statehood of India and Pakistan. These considerations were also impacted by the prevailing notions of what constituted authority and legitimate government in the international context, and India's and Pakistan's behaviour with one another was as much a statement of their differences about pre-partition patterns of water flow in the Indus, as their attempts to fit in with these considerations. Furthermore, I also dwell on which notions of arbitration India and Pakistan found to be acceptable. In India, many of the early discussions relating to water, for instance, were deliberating on, and not always easily discounting, the possibility of mediation by the International Court of Justice on this issue. My argument is that entering into this terrain was in fact done in a way that furthered the argument about why India and Pakistan were possessors of a legitimate claim to statehood.

If, in the immediate aftermath of the partition it was clear that the boundary line was one of the most important ways in which the existence of the state structures could be demonstrated, then this process was highlighted particularly clearly with regard to the administration of the Indus canal networks. To give a broad overview, the Indus waters treaty had provided for a plan for the development of the Indus basin which would allow for the separate utilisation of irrigation networks for the development of India and Pakistan.[1] The negotiating teams from the World Bank, India and Pakistan had examined the options for the 'joint' development of the river basin for all of three weeks before deciding that exploring methods of India and Pakistan separately utilising the irrigation networks would be a more profitable course of action. From 1952 onwards, the Indus waters negotiations at the World Bank had therefore focussed on exactly how plans could be devised for the development of the Indus basin, which would cater to both India's and Pakistan's separate requirements. In this chapter, I argue that the groundwork for many of these ideas had in fact been laid out in the bilateral negotiations between India and Pakistan, over 1949 and 1950. The basis for cooperation on the Indus Waters Treaty, therefore, arose out of a desire to finalise the repercussions of partition. It was when this premise could be worked out to its fullest extent, so that the requirements for the validity of both nation states as viably separated entities were met, that the Indus treaty could be signed.

Princely Claims

N.D. Gulhati, an official who had been retained in an advisory capacity to the Ministry of Science and Power, headed by Gopalaswami

Ayyangar, made a critical reference to the process of the finalisation of partition in a 1951 letter. Complaining about the lack of aid from the United States for the building of the Bhakra Nangal Dam in 1950, Gulhati stated:

> This ministry is surprised by at the attitude taken by the US Government to deny technical advice and even to refuse equipment being tested for Bhakra Dam, because of their desire to steer clear of all possible complications connection with the Canal Waters Dispute between India and Pakistan... [But] it may also be remembered that the work on the Bhakra Dam was taken in hand by the United Punjab Government long before the Partition of the country was thought of.[2]

Indeed, the United States had initially refused to lend technical assistance for the development of the Bhakra Dam, on the grounds that it may further inflame the India–Pakistan dispute. Its reasoning was not as surprising as Gulhati had made it out to be: water being channelled for the development of the Bhakra Dam would have been diverted at the expense of the irrigation supplies flowing into western Punjab. But for Gulhati and other officials in East Punjab, the partition had in fact represented a clear opportunity to establish control over the headworks in more or less exclusive terms. All negotiations on the canal waters between East and West Punjab were also carried out with the intent of establishing this principle in the most unambiguous terms possible. Nehru was not unwilling to support them in this agenda, being, in any case unable, as he told Ghulam Muhmmad, unable to effectively oppose it.

Indeed—regardless of the inherent value in his arguments—it makes sense to chart out the trajectory of the Indus Waters Treaty via the career of N.D. Gulhati, who was closely associated with the decisions of the East Punjab government in 1948, was present at the signing of the 1948 agreement, and who, in the end, got his way with how the clauses of the Indus Waters Treaty were crafted. Ultimately the terms of the Indus Waters Treaty, which specified a division of the Eastern and Western Rivers, with separate linkages being made in Pakistan to supply west Punjab with alternative sources of irrigation, were those that Gulhati had advocated, and which would also ensure that India's own irrigation plans, such as the Bhakra canal, could continue uninterrupted. The ways in which Gulhati tackled the issue of the canal waters, therefore, are indicative of the processes of the implementation and finalisation of the partition, and which also included, eventually, the signing of the Indus Waters Treaty.

The Arbitral Tribunal—which had been put in place to decide arrangements about allocating resources to India and Pakistan in the period immediately after the partition—had decided that the canal systems would be valued, and that both the provinces of Eastern and Western Punjab would pay a proportionate share of interest for its benefits. It ruled that the government of West Punjab pay a tax for the waters received from the Indus canals, since the development from this irrigation had taken place mainly in areas that now fell in Pakistan.[3] The ratio upon which the financial settlement could be worked out was however disputed between the two sides, with the East Punjab side trying to secure a greater sum of compensation from Pakistan, with a view to discouraging it from establishing any basis for the argument that the control over the headworks could be jointly shared, or that Pakistan was in any way legally entitled to control over the headworks. That partition would have to represent a change in the terms of engagement on the issue of water was certainly understood by all parties: much of the correspondence and debate on this question rested on exactly how the rhetoric of the nation state could be superimposed onto the previous conflict relating to the canals.

A day after the Partition Council's ratified Standstill Agreement lapsed, India unilaterally cut off the water supplies to Pakistan. On 1 April 1948, a day after the term of the Arbitral Tribunal expired, the government of East Punjab cut off the supply of water going into West Punjab, on the grounds that in order for the water to continue to flow, the agreement would need to be formally extended. The event sent shockwaves through the rickety apparatus of the state structures of both India and Pakistan, and, within a week, a team was dispatched from Pakistan to work out a settlement for continuing water supply from the Upper Bari Doab Canals (UBDC) and other canal systems. This included the Finance Minister of Pakistan, Ghulam Muhammad, and two ministers of West Punjab, Shaukat Hayat Khan, and Mumtaz Daultana. An agreement was signed, on 4th May 1948, according to which Pakistan would have access to the water flow, and water was restored to the Dipalpur and UBDC canals. However, the agreement also specified that the West Punjab government would have to pay a fee to the government of India for the cost of maintaining the flow of canal water into Pakistan. In addition, India would gradually diminish water supplies flowing into Pakistan, so West Punjab would have to tap alternative sources eventually. This agreement was fiercely criticized in Pakistan. Chaudhry Muhammad Ali asserted that the country's delegates had been forced to sign it because of the urgency of the circumstance, but it was not in Pakistan's favour. The agreement, Muhammad Ali continued, was laid out in front of Ghulam Muhammad, who was 'asked to sign without changing a word or comma'.[4] This treaty was repudiated within a year.

Most significantly, however, Nehru's point of criticism of the actions of the government of East Punjab was that 'This would hurt us in the eyes of the international community.'[5] Moreover, he pointed out, such an action was, after all in the short term quite futile, since 'water will have to be allowed in future because such stoppages cannot occur normally unless there is actual war'.[6] The East Punjab government argued that their actions were intended to clarify their exclusive ownership of the Upper Bari Doab Canal. They argued that, in the absence of any formal agreement, if East Punjab had not closed the water supply, at least temporarily, this might have led to West Punjab acquiring legal rights on the UBDC, for the benefit of the lower section of the canal, now in Pakistan.[7]

Pakistan's arguments about the Indus canals, had rested on the supplies that it had made for irrigation in West Punjab prior to the partition. Zafarullah Khan had therefore argued that if the government of Pakistan was to pay its share for the maintenance of the canal headworks, then the government of Pakistan would also be entitled to the water supply that it would provide. After all, Zafarullah Khan argued, the Arbitral Tribunal had ruled that the award of the headworks in India's favour was also contingent on the maintenance of Pakistan's pre-partition rights to irrigation. Therefore, Zafarullah argued, Pakistan was fully entitled to its existing irrigation supply having completed the payments for the maintenance of the canal headworks.

Despite Nehru's stated disapproval of Bhargava's government, the provincial government's action was not unequivocally condemned by Delhi. Although it was generally accepted that although the water flow could not be stopped to Pakistan, such access would need to be determined on the basis of an agreement. While Nehru, and many of his officials were frequently irritated at the East Punjab government's initiatives with regard to the Indus canals, what is worth highlighting is that Nehru himself was not in fact fundamentally in opposition to their positions. In fact, the source of irritation related to the Punjab's non-acknowledgement of the national project. The government of India's position with regard to the Indus waters question, was developed not as a way of dampening down provincial positions, but rather to adopt them within their own state-building agendas.

In their justifications for exactly why East Punjab deserved more water than west Punjab, the argument Gulhati and other bureaucrats in the provincial government had been one that highlighted the contributions of the princely state under the Maharaja of Patiala to the building of the canal. It was as descendants of that tradition of governance—rather than as a member of a central government—that East Punjab drew up arguments about the justified nature of their course. But rather than disagreeing with the substance of East Punjab's demands with regard to water, it was the way in which they were couched, that particularly irked Nehru and the Ministry of External Affairs. The water question, as with a whole host of other items on the bilateral agenda, had to be seen as an opportunity to strengthen the nation state first, and then secondarily be the source of more water in East Punjab.

The construction of a dam in Bhakra-Nangal was amongst the foremost priorities of the government of East Punjab, and was, moreover a project that Nehru was keen to promote. A key spectacle designed to promote greater faith in the capacity of the Indian nation making project was that of the Bhakra dam, famously described by Nehru as the temple to modern India. At a speech at the dam site in 1954, Nehru also pointed out that 'This is a work that does not belong only to Punjab or PEPSU or the neighbouring states, but to the whole of India'.[8] Yet the construction of the Bhakra dam, funnelling water away from the headworks in the Sutlej, would alter the course of irrigation from what had been the pattern prior to the partition.

Indeed, the complaint about the proposed construction from regions that were now in Pakistan were not new. In 1942, the government of Sindh had argued that 'that the effects of the Bhakra Dam Project and other projects contemplated by the Punjab, when superimposed upon the full effects of the Thal and Haveli projects and of certain older projects already executed, will be to cause such lowering of water levels both in upper and lower Sindh during the months of May to October, inclusive as will seriously affect the efficient working of Sindh's inundation canals.'[9] This issue remained unresolved until 1947, and along with other debates about the canals were best to be developed, were in effect carried forward by India and Pakistan.

The government of Pakistan's assertion that the building of the Bhakra dam would affect Pakistan's pre-partition rights to the water was warranted. But more importantly for our purposes, how this situation was addressed also offers additional insights into the way in which the partition was implemented into the decision-making apparatus of South Asia. Gulhati insisted that 'the construction of the Bhakra Dam will not therefore throw any area in Pakistan out of cultivation, although Pakistan will have to spend some money in these areas. This additional expenditure is a necessary consequences of partition based on Muslim League ideology.'[10]

But for Pakistan, the project constituted all the elements of the breach of a legal contract: west Punjab had relied on water flowing out of the Sutlej for its irrigation. The government of Pakistan had made payments for this to be continued, and the Arbitral Tribunal (and, arguably, the International Court of Justice, should it be broached) would agree that it had rights towards the water. For it to be shut off, and diverted for different purposes, while being potentially calamitous for the province, also offered grounds on which a legal challenge could be credibly mounted by the state of Pakistan, cementing, in a sense, its international personality. The Civil and Military Gazette reported the 'brutal and aggressive design by India found practical shape on Thursday when the water supply in the Sutlej Valley Canals reached their lowest ebb yet, having been reduced to about 9,500 cusecs from a normal supply of 25,000 cusacs to Pakistan'.[11] This act, the gazette warned would 'turn barren, hitherto green and irrigated areas of Kasur, parts of Montgomery and Multan districts and the whole of Bahawalpur State', along with a 33 per cent decrease in annual grain production of the province.[12]

In September 1950, C. M. Trivedi wrote to Nehru on the issue of the upcoming inter-dominion conference to discuss the Indus Waters. He argued that Pakistan's proposals that no further irrigation works be embarked on pending further arbitration on the matter would not be satisfactory to India. This would imply that the work on the Harike and Bhakra Projects would be halted.[13] He argued that it was essential for the conference to come to the understanding that 'there can be no question whatever of stopping the works at Bhakra or Nangal.'[14] The question, for our purposes, that the Indus Waters negotiations were trying to grapple with was how to implement the process of partition by creating two self-sufficient and viable entities. It was to the extent that this broader question was being answered, that the negotiations were productive.

The 4 May Agreement

So the engineers in East Punjab, and Nehru with them, were determined to build their dam. But going about this task also involved navigating a tricky set of provincial, national, and international commitments—all of which were important to India's and Pakistan's attempts at asserting a definition of legal statehood. Ghulam Muhammad, who in 1948 had come to Delhi as a delegate for the conference regarding the Indus waters, visited Nehru. It was clear that the agreement discussed was not to Pakistan's satisfaction. Ghulam Muhammad pressed that 'provisional agreement might be arrived at so that water should be paid for by the East Punjab government, and supplied by the West Punjab government.'[15] With Ghulam Muhammad, Nehru was uncompromising: 'After the provisional agreement which ended on 31 March, and the Arbitral Award, the rights in the canal head-works and the water vested completely in East Punjab.'[16]

In September 1948, the chief engineers of both sides met at Wagah to further elaborate the arrangements by which irrigation supplies should be distributed. This agreement—technically unrecognized by both central governments—allowed for a certain fixed quota of water share for both the provinces[17]. The amount that the West Punjab government was liable to pay for the irrigation waters was in dispute. Water continued to be supplied, however, on the condition that the disputed payment continue to be made to an 'escrow' account—one which could not be used for India's purposes.[18] Indeed, when a letter of complaint arrived from M. R. Sachdev, Chief Secretary of East Punjab, at the Ministry of External Affairs, arguing that 'Pakistan has refused to make any 'disputed' payments... even though it continues to enjoy the benefits of canal water', Y.K. Puri at the Ministry replied saying that, in strictly legal terms, 'a mere denial of the validity of the agreement, and refusal to deposit the disputed sums are not in themselves enough to invalidate the Agreement of 1948.'[19]

The agreement of 4 May also exacted from Pakistan the promise to pay India for the supplies of water to be let out into the fields of West Punjab. Part of the payment for this was agreed to by both, but there also existed, the government of East Punjab pointed out, another component of the payment, consisting of 'disputed' charges. In sum, this boiled down to Rs. 9,645 in the year 1951, Upon non-payment of this sum, the Indian government elected to complain to Pakistan about not having received this sum. The real matter at stake, as Gulhati pointed out, was that the recognition of this non-payment could be construed as an admission by India of not having the right to dispense the waters according only to its own terms.[20]

Officials in Pakistan, meanwhile, wrote back saying that they would be more than happy to pay for the disputed charges, if a verdict from a court of arbitration—such as the International Court of Justice—deemed that this should be so. Indeed, they reminded India, that the question of arbitration on those very matters was precisely what Pakistan had been arguing for all along: 'The parties should submit their contentions immediately to a tribunal that is already established and functioning... Until the rights of the parties are established by such adjudication, each must respect the share of water authorised to the other before the dispute began'.[21]

The build-up of pressure tactics to achieve the ends of being able to utilise the canal networks for their own purposes continued unabated in East Punjab. One option was to register the May 1948 Agreement with the United Nations, thereby formalising it into an international treaty. This debate, however, opened up a further dilemma. The main advantage for registering the agreement was so that it could later be cited as justification, when, as was widely expected, Pakistan would bring its case on the canal waters dispute, to the International Court of Justice.[22] Nehru had, however, been against this. He argued:

> it is exceedingly doubtful whether such interim agreements can be considered international agreements of the kind referred to Article 102 of the UN Charter. It is certainly not a treaty... I see no particular good coming from registration, and it may well result in complications and needless troubles for us.[23]

The problem, he continued, was its interim nature. 'It is essentially a preliminary agreement to be followed up by a more definite and formal agreement'.[24] The main problem of registering the treaty was that the terms of the water sharing agreement as a consequence of partition had not been adequately settled. He also argued that by this logic, all the scores of inter-dominion, and inter-provincial agreements—from those about evacuee property, abducted women, and refugees—that had thus far been signed, would have to also be registered by the United Nations.

In point of fact, as the Law Ministry argued, only those agreements that actually placed 'on-going obligations' onto both nation states should be considered for registration at the United Nations. Several of the inter-dominion agreements—those that had merely provided for the immediate exchange of assets, for instance—were, in the view of the Indian law ministry at least, not suitable for legal enforcement by the United Nations. Although they purport to be Agreements and impose continuing obligations, it should be seen whether the agreements recorded therein were really accepted as binding by the two governments.[25]

Subimal Dutt then helpfully pointed out that in order to avoid the appearance of having this particular treaty introduced into the United Nations at the last minute, he could draw up a list of interim agreements reached with Pakistan that could be simultaneously registered.[26] But, he argued, 'Our case in diminishing the existing supply of water to West Punjab lands is by no means a fool proof one. That is why para 4 of the agreement is so important, and, if the matter goes before a UN tribunal, it would be of considerable value in supporting our case.' Moreover, the 1948 agreement also put obligations onto Pakistan, which could be made legally enforceable. In the 1948 agreement

'Pakistan had agreed, apart from the question of the law involved, to approach the problem in a practical spirit on the basis of East Punjab progressively diminishing its supply to the canals now irrigating land in West Punjab in order to give reasonable time to enable the West Pakistan government to tap alternative sources.'[27]

For its part, Pakistan pointed out, as far as a finally binding treaty was concerned, the decisions of the Arbitral Tribunal ought to be given greater weight as a legally binding agreement, over that of the 4 May Agreement. The Tribunal's decisions, had suggested that the 'various awards that rested on the premise that the uses and allocations then existing would continue to be respected.'[28] Moreover, as far as the 4 May Agreement had been concerned, the Prime Minister of India himself, a mere two months after the agreement was signed, had expressed his wish in a telegram that the agreement would not be lasting. Therefore, the representative continued that Pakistan's disagreement with the treaty in question be listed under the record of the United Nations.

The problem with this, though, Gopalaswami Ayyangar pointed out frankly—while not disagreeing with the fact that the agreement itself did not necessarily have the same qualities as an international treaty—was the nature of the concessions that had been secured from the West Punjab government in 1948, which would not be easily recoverable again. In any case, he suggested, while it might not be possible to have it declared as the final word between two sovereign governments, the Indus case, however, was seen as tactically useful:

> The point is that if we do not register this interim Canal Agreement, we should be disabled from invoking the contents of this agreement in our favour in any proceedings before any organ of the UN. The dispute as regards the division of the river waters between the two Punjabs may have to come up before an international tribunal connected with the United Nations unless Pakistan and we agree to refer it to an ad hoc arbitral tribunal.

Deciding on the Arena

What was evident from India's calculations was its preference for solutions that would uphold the national structures of governance, as opposed to those that might try to undermine it. Dr Frederich Berber, an

East German refugee into West Germany, and, somewhat startlingly, an advisor to the Nazi government in an earlier professional role, wandered into the circle of people who had advised Nehru on the Indus waters question. Berber's routes towards the circle of Nehruvian foreign policy is interesting, since it also reveals the reshaping and contestations within definitions of international order and law during the interwar period.[29] As Katherina Reizler points out, during the 1920s and 30s, Berber was well positioned to develop a critique of the existing hierarchies of international law: as a German legal theorist, particularly deeply impacted by the post-First World War status quo, and able to perceive its inequality in favour of the 'traditional' colonial powers, Berber, along with an influential generation of theorists of international politics, were committed to developing a theory of international order that would accommodate a more 'state-centric' approach to international politics. These arguments had a close resonance with India's requirements after the second world war, and, in 1951, he was appointed as an advisor to Nehru on the river waters dispute. He worked closely with the government of East Punjab, was the author of several pamphlets published by the government of India on the Indus question, and a close associate of N.D. Gulhati on the legalities of the water question.

Berber's own suggestions about what India might do, however, were only met with limited success. One suggestion of Berber's that was aimed at achieving these ends, was for India to approach the Permanent Court of Arbitration to devise a solution to the Water dispute. Berber's arguments to India was based on the selection of particular judges who sat on courts who would be more amenable to India's own position. Indeed, the advantage of pushing ahead at the Hague would be that India would even have the right to appoint one of its own nationals as Arbitrators. Accordingly, he advised Nehru's governments on the various platforms through which it could voice its complaints with regard to the Indus waters issue. Berber argued that Pakistan's offer on the International Court of Justice could be countered with a different proposal. He was also closely involved in the question of whether or not India ought to accept Pakistan's proposals about taking the dispute to the ICJ.

Broadly, therefore, his advice to India was also about crafting a legal position that would tap into arguments about challenging the status quo in favour of colonial powers, and the paramountcy of the nation state. Berber was therefore tasked to find out whether or not India and Pakistan were signatories of the Barcelona Convention of 1920 on waterways. The Agreement had been signed under the auspices of the League of Nations, and the government of India had been represented—while in its capacity as a colony—in its proceedings. Theoretically, India and Pakistan had inherited the international obligations that had been undertaken by the government of India before 1947, unless they were territorially restricted to applying to one or another region. The arrangement that was now therefore being followed was that 'all rights and obligations to which India is a party immediately before the appointed day, will devolve upon the Dominion of India and the Dominion of Pakistan, and, if necessary, be apportioned between them'.[30] In 1950, however, it seemed to Dr Berber that if this agreement continued to be binding onto both India and Pakistan, an argument about the legal rights of India and Pakistan towards the water might be developed.

In the ministry, however, his recommendations failed to find much favour: engagement from Pakistan for this exercise was unlikely to be forthcoming, and it was important to be active in those contexts where this was more likely to be present. Simply choosing an arena which Pakistan would not recognize, was not a sufficient condition for the Ministry of External Affairs: it was only with the active engagement of the government of Pakistan could a viable strategy of shaping an international position actually be carried out. Subimal Dutt argued in his own note to the Ministry in 1952:

> We cannot take our canal water dispute to the Permanent Court of Arbitration without Pakistan's consent, and Pakistan is bound to withhold consent if it knows—as it must in due course—that our adherence has given us the advantage of choosing one of our own nationals as an Arbitrator. On the other hand, it would be difficult to justify our willingness to take the case to the International Court of Arbitration in preference to the International Court of Justice.[31]

Despite their differences with Frederich Berber, however, it was also of paramount importance to Nehru and his foreign ministry to locate platforms of international law that would further bolster India's claim to legitimate statehood. The ways in which this was conducted, moreover were often in calibration with Pakistan's own calculations about how to go about securing a very similar objective.

A Joint Basin?

In this section, I try to lay out exactly how any proposals about the joint development of the Indus basin came to nought. Six months before Eugene Black, the President of the World Bank sent his letter to Nehru and Liaquat Ali Khan, the foreign ministries of both countries were carrying out a preliminary set of negotiations about how the capacity of the Indus Waters to irrigate both India and Pakistan could be judged. A note from the foreign ministry in Pakistan suggested 'a negotiating committee meet to explore the possibilities of settling the dispute, including agreement as to the terms of reference of a commission to investigate and report upon the facts affecting an equitable apportionment of the waters of the Indus Basin common to India and Pakistan.'[32] M.R. Sachdev, and G.D. Khosla—author of the piercing *Stern Reckoning*—were thus put on the task force to represent India.

Arbitration in this matter was not necessarily dismissed out of hand. Pakistan had suggested approaching the International Court of Justice in July 1949, with a view to finding a solution to the Indus problem once and for all. The proposal, moreover, had also seemed a fairly tempting one to Nehru. In the government of India, the attitude towards outside arbitration, and intervention from the International Court of Justice was mixed. Some quarters within India, Nehru noted, seemed to feel apprehension. For his part, however:

> I do not understand this fear of arbitration, which some of us feel... surely this depends on the nature of the arbitration, and the kind of arbiters that might be appointed. I think there should be three and all of them foreign judges of international repute. The position that arose in connection with the Radcliffe Award, that is of the Indian and Pakistani representatives cancelling each other, and Radcliffe having the final say should not arise, when three independent foreign judges of repute are appointed.[33]

But, in his reply to Zafarullah, Nehru's recommendation was that the process undertaken by the International Court were likely to be lengthy, and also likely to ask both parties to explore methods by which their requirements could be met. With this in mind he asked Pakistan to send representatives to a taskforce which could carry out the research on exactly what the requirement across the Indus basin were. A letter from the government of Pakistan in 1949 signaled that it was not unwilling to go along with this for the time being. The letter allowed for an investigation of the basin, while keeping in mind that 'no attempt will be made to confine the proposed studies to the accomplishment of a rearrangement of the supply of the Dipalpur and Central Bari Doab Canals or to the accomplishment of any similar preconceived result.' While allowing for the possibility that alternative sources of irrigation might be found, it left the options for how to proceed on this question mostly open:

> It might appear in the course of a general investigation that by rearrangement of the source of supply for the Dipalpur and Central Bari Doab Canals optimum utilization of the water resources of the basin would or would not be promoted. The result which we appear to be in agreement in desiring is an equitable apportionment with optimum utilization.

Finally, the letter also enabled the engineers to explore the capacities of all six of the rivers, while maintaining that, as things currently stood, the bulk of the irrigation supply had to be acquired from those flowing out of the headworks in India:

> It would appear from the note of 5th October that the negotiators for India will be instructed to ask for the investigation of the requirements of areas that lie outside of the basin. Pakistan will interpose no objection to thus extending the studies so long as this extension does not delay or prejudice the study of the requirements of the basin itself.

For the time being, however, in 1949, there was no question that the existing methods of irrigation had to continue to be used:

> It is the position of Pakistan that the basin should in no event be called upon to sacrifice its water resources, to the extent that they are needed in the basin, for the purpose of developing areas outside of the basin. It may well appear in the course of the studies that the apparent divergence in the views of Pakistan and India respecting the area entitled to share in the Indus Basin waters has little practical importance.

If an agreement should be arrived at in an inter-dominion conference, Pakistan asked that:

> During the currency of such an agreement, the quantum of the present rights of user and enjoyment of the waters by all areas within Pakistan must be maintained intact on the same basis on which it had existed before partition, subject to any modification agreed upon as a consequence of the coming into operation of alternative sources of supply for UBDC and Dipalpur canals.[34]

Work also began in Pakistan on the Mangla Dam on the Jhelum River, as part of the effort to have a secure water supply.[35] While Nehru had dispatched cables to Liaquat and Zafarullah Khan, on 18 May, warning that this would adversely affect the supply of water in India, the reply from Zafarullah Khan on this was unapologetic. In view of their recent experience, Zafarullah asserted, 'you will agree that the government of West Punjab are fully justified in taking precautionary measures.'[36] What these exchanges also allow for, however, was the condoning of alternative arrangements after the partition.

A letter from the Pakistan foreign ministry in August 1949 suggested that a conference be called for thrashing this issue out once and for all, and included Zafarullah Khan and Gopalaswami Ayyangar—a reliable trouble-shooter and safe pair of hands for the execution of Nehru's decisions—as delegates. Nehru, for his part, was willing to signal his willingness to approach the International Court of Justice, once the dimensions of the problem had been agreed upon by India and Pakistan.

Pakistan's proposals in 1949 also reveal that the argument that Pakistan had been entitled to its pre-partition status of water supplies had also acted as a point of departure. At an inter-dominion conference on water, called at the instance of the Pakistan government, Zafarullah Khan had suggested that a 'fact finding team' be assembled, consisting of both Indians and Pakistanis, who would go to ascertain the capacity of the Indus basin for supplying water for irrigation. Indeed, in many ways, the premise of negotiations followed by the World Bank from 1952, were laid down in 1949. The consensus was that a 'joint Technical Mission' be formed, consisting of experts from India and Pakistan. Their task would be to find out how there would be an adequate supply of irrigation water into both India and Pakistan, starting out from the premise that there was more than adequate supply of water across the entire river basin, to meet the requirements of both countries.

Ultimately, then, the negotiations faltered on whether alternative methods of irrigation were to be built in Pakistan as a consequence of partition. Pakistan's case was that paying for the charges for the maintenance of the canal headworks ought to have been sufficient basis for it to be legally entitled to its sovereign rights; while India's case was that alternative canals would have to be built in Pakistan to supply it with irrigation. The reason that the Joint Technical Mission in fact met with delays related to precisely this problem: either the western rivers ought to be part of the resources that had to be tapped into for irrigation, or they could not. It was the ability to build further canals within Pakistan, therefore, that Gulhati and his team were trying to push through during their negotiations.

Zafarullah Khan and Gopalaswami Ayyangar then engaged in a protracted set of disagreements about exactly how the Indus basin should be defined, and whether or not the western rivers should be defined as irrigable. But essentially, as Gulhati had surmised, this was a question of convincing the government of Pakistan to construct additional canals, and of mounting a persuasive campaign against allowing their continuing use of the channels coming in from the Sutlej. It was at this stage that the negotiations between the two countries had deadlocked: fundamentally, the question was whether or not additional routes of irrigation were possible to construct in Pakistan, which would be able to replace its dependence on the canal networks flowing from the Sutlej. But, if there could be no agreement between them, then they would 'submit the dispute to the International Court of Justice whose opinion shall be binding on the two Governments and shall be given full effect to by them.'

But an exchange between Nehru and Gulzarilal Nanda, the new Minister of Power in 1953, is also illustrative of the dimensions of the problem, and Gulhati's sense of its solution.[37] In a letter to Nanda, Nehru complained about the lack of supervision over the activities of the Punjab engineers:

> We are told that some local people in charge of the head-works were responsible for reducing supplies for Pakistan. It is hinted also that,

> possibly, some Punjab Ministers encouraged them to do so. Even accepting this, the fact remains how and why our central supervision was so slack that this could have happened for any length of time, more especially when there was a loud agitation going on in Pakistan, and I was constantly asking for facts.

But more pointedly, Nehru also directly blamed ND Gulhati for his lack of cooperation in this question: 'I gather that Gulhati has been intimately connected with this problem and knows all about it. Why then should he not have known [what] was happening or not, and intervened as soon as his attention was drawn to it?'[38]

More troubling still, for Nehru, was Gulhati's portrayals of the extent to which replacement works for irrigation had been built in Pakistan. Gulhati, said Nehru may have 'ceased to be objective', and was displaying a tendency to 'emphasise some aspects and to ignore the others'. Most significant of these assertions included 'Gulhati's answers at our conference today, where he said that the new canals in Pakistan had been dug and could have been used to supply the water deficiency'. Immediately grasping that this statement went to the nub of the matter, Gulhati was closely questioned by others in attendance at the conference, but was not able to produce satisfactory justification. This, complained Nehru to Gulzarilal, made him uncertain about the comments of the Punjabi engineers who seemed to him to be speaking 'rather casually, regardless of their implications, financial or other'.[39] The argument that Gulhati would have been making would have been about the legitimacy of India being able to develop the canal networks within the country for its own exclusive purposes, since Pakistan had embarked on alternative methods of irrigation. But while, in 1953, Nehru would not have been able to vouchsafe if this was in fact true or not, in 1960, the Treaty itself was largely drafted along these lines.

But, despite appearances, in 1949 and 1950, the disagreements in the positions of India and Pakistan also kept in play a number of other moving parts in the same puzzle. In 1951, Eugene Black broached the possibility of a World Bank-mediated solution to the Indus problem. Black, on the basis of observations made by the Chairman of the Tennessee Valley Authority, David Lilienthal, was convinced that the Indus waters problem could be addressed.[40] In a letter to the prime ministers of India and Pakistan, Eugene Black, offered his offices for mediating in the dispute, involving solutions which would 'meet... the requirements of both countries for expanded irrigation though cooperative construction and operation of storage dams and other facilities [would] be financed in part, perhaps by this Bank'. In part, this was also due to the sense that both the banker and the engineer had, that the Indus waters issue was also a fixable problem—with costs. If it was merely a question of building something, after all, then there was no reason why the offices of the Bank should not be offered.

The argument may well have been one about exactly who would have to change the course of their developmental plans in the aftermath of partition in order to secure the best supply of water, but, given the adequate resources and manpower, there was no reason why this could not in fact be achieved. Exactly how this ought to be done, moreover, had also been the subject of fairly extensive consideration in both India and Pakistan. One of the questions that the Indus waters negotiations had revolved around was exactly who would commit to the expense of the right sequencing of canals being built so that there would flow enough water into west Punjab and Pakistan.

Conclusions

Ultimately, then, the signing of the Indus waters treaty, as well as the laying out of the principles on which it was based during the early 1950s, was one of the innovations of partition: this was an instance of how the fact of partition led to new methods of governance and administration being evolved. The treaty was not, however, hailed on either side as a success: for Pakistan, it effectively formalised the separation from the water that it had had access to prior to the partition, and was therefore legally entitled to after the partition. Yet, the principles of the treaty had also provided Pakistan with a legally secure access to water on the basis of its statehood. So, Ayub Khan wrote in his memoirs, 'The only sensible thing to do was to try and get a settlement, even though it might be second best, because if we did not, we stood to lose everything... while there was no cause for rejoicing at the signing of the treaty, there was certainly cause for satisfaction that a possibly very ugly situation had been averted'.[41]

The Indus Waters Treaty was not hailed in either country as a triumphant success. Pakistani critics of the treaty argued that she 'sold' the waters of the Eastern Rivers to India, and had received inadequate compensation in return. Accepting it meant that possibilities for the optimal development of the Indus basin were given up by both sides. Had the initial proposals of the World Bank for joint usage of the Indus canals been accepted, benefits immensely valuable to two poverty-stricken countries, such as the development of hydro-electric projects, would not have been foregone.[42] Indeed, the argument that it had been fostered mainly for the interest of the East Punjab government, and at the expense of all other beneficiaries of the water was, as this chapter shows, not unjustified. Those in favour of the treaty felt that it presented the best outcome possible under the circumstances. This argument is echoed in an article by Jagat Mehta, who had argued that while the opportunity costs that were given up in terms of a joint development of the Indus Basin were immense, the Indus Treaty was the best solution under the circumstances.[43] The nature of the negotiations on the Indus Waters shared characteristics with all of the most fruitful exchanges in the bilateral relationship: they were clothed, not with the overall aim of improving the relationship itself, but rather with the intention of securing aims that were essential to both. This was as much an attempt to hold up the authority of the state, as it was about the more equitable division of water resources.

The solution that both sides chose to grasp at, moreover—not unlike their instincts over the Punjab Boundary Force—was one that provided a lasting division of the water supplies, and prospects for the perusal of divergent policy directions with respect to the development of the Indus Basin.[44] The completed agreement, finally signed in September 1960, would be successfully implemented only when both countries would receive massive funds, not only from the World Bank, but other aid-giving countries, to be able to fulfil their sides of the promises. The terms of the treaty provided for the setting up of an 'Indus Basin Development Fund' to which the World Bank, as well as other countries would contribute a sum of some 640 million dollars to construct replacement works in Pakistan, as well as additional water resource development projects in India. Above all, as Dan Haines shows, the agreement on the canal waters was also therefore an act of border demarcation: of a division which had been recognized in practice over a considerable length of time, and the agreement was a means by which this was officially recognized. If a treaty could be signed at all between India and Pakistan, it would have to acknowledge, and then best and most fairly accommodate the fact of partition, and the viable coexistence of both countries.

6

SHAPING INTERNATIONAL PERSONALITIES

The fifties, author David Halberstam remarks, were a decade in which 'one did not lightly challenge a system that seemed, on the whole, to be working so well'.[1] What was consistently evident was the desire of the governments of both Pakistan and India to retain the administrative machinery they had inherited, and to further consolidate the benefits available from the opportunities they afforded. Much of the paraphernalia of the relationship—inter-dominion conferences, summitry, the modes of communication, and even the technology—owed itself to what had been used by the Foreign Office of the United Kingdom, and the organisation of the Commonwealth. In order to understand the pattern that the relationship took, it is also critical to contextualise the setting of the relationship within the patterns of internationalist thought and inter-state relationship that India and Pakistan were used to. The patterns that India and Pakistan chose to replicate in the making of their bilateral relationship were not drawn from scratch: they originated in the methodology followed in other parts of the world when inter-state relations were being defined.

In this chapter I wish to consider the patterns of statehood that India and Pakistan chose to emulate, and to enquire deeper into their provenance. In many ways, their approaches to determining the course of their international behaviour look remarkably similar: informed by the same objectives, and tempered by the same considerations. What also comes across is the fact that both India and Pakistan accepted a common set of rules about how states ought to behave—their pursuits within these frameworks might have occasionally varied, but their objectives were defined by a common set of concerns.

At the same time, what also becomes evident from a study of the early bilateral relationship is the extent to which the international context in which Nehru and Liaquat Ali Khan found themselves also fundamentally shaped their political behaviour. The leadership of both India and Pakistan had witnessed the steady ascent of the state as becoming the critical unit of consideration in international relations, over the inter-war years. In 1947, the two countries entered a world order which was evolving, and being reconfigured in the aftermath of two world wars; and one in which, moreover, London was acquiring a different, and diminished, political capacity. Such identities were also critically impacted in what Erez Manela has called the 'Wilsonian Moment', during which the articulation of an anti-colonial, and anti-empire based frame of reference gained credence. What India and Pakistan were also working with, therefore, was an international system in the process of reconfiguration; but one that recognised the integrity of the state as a fundamental premise.

What also comes across is the importance of solutions to disputes during the interwar years—in fact, several innovations for conciliation between India and Pakistan during this time were reminiscent of models that had been tried out in Europe over the 1920s and 30s. The kinds of models of statehood that India and Pakistan thus adopted were heavily influenced by their experience of colonialism, most particularly, perhaps, by their experiences of inter-state politics in the inter-war decades. But these also provide for a set of networks whose sheer density also held India and Pakistan in international proximity, rather than at an oppositional distance. Partly, these were due to the continuation of the same set of personnel: not only within India's and Pakistan's governments, but also in the ambit of global politics. More importantly, however, this was also due to the decisions of both countries to tap into and further develop a set of networks which were part of a mutual inheritance of a colonised past.

Despite the outbreak of a small war in Kashmir within a few months of their independence—and the subsequent and active discussion of the issue at the United Nations from 1948–51, the territorial dispute between India and Pakistan did not become the sole arbiter of their international relations. Several major foreign policy dilemmas of the late 1940s and early 1950s, moreover, had India and Pakistan on the same page. On South Africa, as well as the UN Refugee convention, Indian and Pakistani delegates at the United Nations dutifully trooped in their votes to the same sides. Furthermore, both India and Pakistan made full use of their connections with the Commonwealth in cementing the international standing of their state structures, while cultivating a relationship with the United States.

In the coming sections, I offer an overview of these decisions in the early foreign policy-making of India and Pakistan, and then explore what these suggest. The imperative of holding up—and, sometimes, if need be, just conjuring up—the appearance of a validated state structure was the primary motivator behind most of India's and Pakistan's foreign policy decisions of the 1940s and 50s. By highlighting the similarities in how India and Pakistan went about cementing their claims to nationhood in the international arena, this chapter also shows how the hostility between India and Pakistan in international affairs always had a curiously muted quality: an primarily ideological opposition at the visceral level was not possible for two countries whose existences owed themselves to a common process.

'Old Hands'

The historian of the Commonwealth and decolonisation, Nicholas Mansergh, reflected in 1958 that despite the tensions between the newly decolonised states of South and Southeast Asia in the wake of the ending of the empire, 'the sense of an underlying unity of interest of Asian peoples long subject to Western rule was something that survived its passing.'[2] But the value of old commonwealth linkages also comes across during the visits of Nehru and Liaquat Ali Khan, within a year of one another, to the United States. The United States' assessment of the geopolitical significance of the South Asian region as a whole was formed mainly due to the influence of the United Kingdom—particularly in the period of our study—and neither India or Pakistan was unwilling to participate in the shaping of these assumptions. Both, in fact, traded heavily on these connections in 1949, when Nehru and Liaquat Ali Khan were in Truman's White House.

The process of decolonization in South Asia was also accompanied by the assumption of a continued role of British inputs in the defence and foreign policy decisions of the region. As several historians of the Anglo-American relationship during the 1940s point out, including, for instance Wm. Roger Louise in the case of the international crisis in the middle east during the 1950s, the US sought consistently to enhance the capabilities of the British rather than discourage them.[3] The United Kingdom's conceptualization of the South Asian region was a crucial factor in how the United States approached South Asia, and analysed its potential in the global Cold War. The assessment of what constituted the balance of power in South Asia and how it could be maintained was a product of the long shadows of the empire, which continued to linger in the region. For their part, both India and Pakistan actively adopted—in practice, if not always in speech—a 'continualist' approach to their foreign relations, and their dealings with each other may therefore be contextualised into this approach.

Indeed, despite a great deal of internal opposition within his own party, including several heavy-weights who would need to be placated such as C. Rajagopalachari—and, it might be added, regardless of Pakistan's arguments about how India's inherited right to the Commonwealth was not correct—Nehru, for his part, lobbied fairly hard to ensure that India did remain a part of the Commonwealth on his terms. To his cabinet, he noted that entry into the Commonwealth offered a host of opportunities that India could avail of:

> On the whole, I feel convinced that we have every reason to be gratified at the result of this meeting... Apart from the obvious advantages gained by us, I think India will have the opportunity to progress more rapidly now, industrially and otherwise, and at the same time to play a much more definite role in Asian and World Affairs.

His assessment of the desirability of colonial linkages were quite unambiguous. In a letter to Ernest Bevin, for instance he stipulated clearly: 'We earnestly desire association in the Commonwealth and we feel it is feasible and likely to survive legal and other challenges'.[4]

Retaining India within the Commonwealth was, it was broadly felt, a mutually advantageous step.

The decision to retain India within the Commonwealth—in itself anachronistic, given the fierce resistance from sections within the Congress to the continuation of the British Empire in South Asia—was envisioned as a means of fashioning the Commonwealth to be the 'Third Force' in a world dominated by two conflicting power blocs. These assumptions may not have entirely played out according to plan—less than a decade later, these aspirations received a body blow with the Suez crisis—but the way this thinking proceeded, nonetheless allowed for a vital role of the British in global affairs. With decolonization, what the British effectively had in mind was a tactical retreat: they planned to continue their influence over the strategic affairs of the subcontinent in effect, if not in name.[5] The major global foreign policy crisis of the 1950's, therefore, saw the British attempt to utilize their power as a colonial, or recently colonial power. One important implication from membership in the Commonwealth was the advantage of some preferential treatment on trade from other member countries. Both India and Pakistan recognised the importance of this, and were keen to use this network in their foreign trade, developmental requirements, and, where possible, military needs.

By many accounts, Nehru's visit to the United States in the winter of 1949 was successful, and, amongst other things, Nehru used the occasion to renew India's request for one million tons of wheat from the United States. Nehru was accompanied on this visit by G.S. Bajpai, India's foreign secretary, M.O. Mathai, Indira Gandhi, and C.D. Deshmukh, his minister of finance. He was also followed by a retinue of newspapermen—K. Rama Rau from the *Hindustan Times* and D.R. Mankekar from the *Times of India*. In his joint address at the House of Representatives, Nehru, while pointing out that his government had just passed major land-reform legislation which could bring about improvements in India's agricultural economy, was blunt in his request for developmental aid and financial assistance for India: 'Though our economic potential is great, its conversion into finished wealth will need much technical and mechanical aid'.[6] Moreover, he argued, that such cooperation would be of immense value, not just for India, but also for the United States, due to India's pivotal position in Asia: 'Whichever region you take [while talking about Asia's geography], India inevitably comes into the picture… It has a great deal to do with the Middle Eastern World, with the Chinese World, and with South East Asia'.[7]

Liaquat Ali Khan had been accompanied by Rana Liaquat Ali Khan, M.A.H. Ispahani, Pakistan's ambassador in the US, and M. Ikramullah, his Foreign Secretary. During his visits, like Nehru, Liaquat Ali Khan made a speech at the US House of Representatives, and the Senate, and also visited the joint chiefs of staff at the Pentagon. Liaquat's visit was also choreographed carefully to present the United States' unbiasedness with respect to either India and Pakistan. Indeed, Dean Acheson pointed out to Truman, 'Out of consideration for the sensibilities of the Pakistanis, it would be tend to counteract any effect his visit to Moscow would have on the latter'.[8] His trip was long—over two weeks, and he visited businessmen, journalists, traders, military personnel, and students across Chicago, California, Boston and Washington.

Not only was Pakistan situated along an important position in the Middle East, he argued, its eastern flank also overlapped with Burma and South East Asia. Both these regions were in need of a stabilizing influence to counter the threat from communism, and, the argument was, Pakistan was a good country to establish this. This potential opening for a strategic partnership with the United States was certainly felt in Pakistan in the years that followed the transfer of power. Hussain Haqqani charts out how Pakistan's relations with the United States was from the beginning an energetic campaign about its utility in the region against the spread of Soviet influence. Successive governments of Pakistan insistently reminded the United States of its usefulness in the region, including, for instance, the uninterrupted use of an air force base in Badaber, from which Soviet activities could be monitored. During his own three-week tour of the United States, moreover, Liaquat Ali Khan, the first Prime Minister of Pakistan, repeatedly touted 'the fighting qualities of [Pakistan's] anti- communist Muslim warriors'.[9] He added that Pakistan's western wing, bordering as it did Iran and Afghanistan, could be an important locations for 'communications to and from the old bearing areas of the Middle East.'[10] When evaluating Pakistan's potential for trading relations, arguments about its strategic positioning seemed particularly encouraging. Liaquat Ali Khan also made vigorous appeals for the potential in Pakistan's economy in almost every single one of his speeches in the United States: 'Its economy is sound, its successive budgets have been balanced, and it has a favourable trade balance with the dollar area. It is fast educating itself, sending its men and women abroad for training and utilizing the help of technical experts from abroad'.[11]

One particularly influential character in the United States' early machinations in South Asia was Olaf Caroe—until 1946, the governor of the North Western Frontier Provinces, and had been foreign secretary to the government of India during the Second World War. Indeed, several commentators laid the thinking behind the Baghdad Pact squarely at the door of Olaf Caroe. In his 1951 book, *The Wells of Power*, Caroe had correctly argued that the big international struggles in the coming decades would be based on the search for oil. In addition to the North Atlantic Treaty Organization, the question of how to shore up Anglo American defences in the Middle East was a live one by the early 1950s. It was more or less evident by the end of the Second World War that the new global conflict would revolve around oil, and the best strategies to ensure access to it. After the transfer of power, Sir Caroe became a key advisor to the US State Department on its policies on South Asia.[12] Pakistan, Caroe pointed out, was located particularly favourably for a struggle over the security of the 'wells of power'—the oil resources of the middle east, the Gulf and Arabian peninsula. Pakistan, in fact, was particularly well suited to this function, as the operations to secure Iran and Iraq during the Second World War had been based out of the North Western Frontier region of the subcontinent.

In fact, all things considered, Caroe wrote, 'Pakistan had succeeded much of undivided India's responsibility in guarding its interests in the Indian subcontinent, the Persian and Arabian gulf, as well as the Middle East.'[13] So it would be sensible, Caroe pressed, if Pakistan were to be made into an integral part of the United States' strategies in South Asia, as well as the Middle East. In fact, in many ways, the deliberations about the Middle Eastern Defence Pact, along with the later Central Treaty Organisation (CENTO) and Southeast Asia Treaty Organisation (SEATO) treaties, were actually a continuation of the

Great Game: the tactics used by the British against the Russians in Asia in the nineteenth century, as Susanne and Rudolph Lloyd, amongst others, have pointed out, were continued in the twentieth, although the players would be replaced. The dynamics of the struggle to contain the influence of Tsarist Russia by the British would, in many ways, be replicated in the succeeding century by the United States, Pakistan, and the Soviet Union.[14]

Yet a 'continualist' set of assumptions about Pakistan's future use to the United States was not limited to Caroe's appraisals alone. For Chester Bowles, the American Ambassador in Delhi during the early 1950s, and a famously ardent advocate of closer ties between India and Pakistan, the argument about the United States extending further aid to India was also partly based on its geographical location—and its territorial proximity to Communist spheres of influence. Indeed, he noted in a letter to the university leader Raymond Allen, 'In effect, we have taken over the traditional foreign policy which the British had maintained since the war of the Spanish succession.'[15] Bowles, for his part, also became anxious on behalf of the rampant communism in student wings across the country—leaving them, he feared, 'directionless and dazed'. For instance, he wrote:

> Today Indo-China is on fire and we are spending some $500 million annually... If India was in an equally desperate situation, a panicky Congress could undoubtedly spend even greater amounts of money to save the situation there. However by that time not only does the cost multiply many times over, but the chances of success are greatly demised.[16]

What is particularly striking in State Department cables about South Asia is the way in which the region was still conceptualised as a whole. That the US had to increase economic incentives for India's and Pakistan's international support—to whatever degree—was also recognised with regard to its trade policies. Despite a substantial amount of trade that both India and Pakistan had carried out with the Soviet Union, closing its own trading links with these two countries could not serve anyone's objectives.

A report of the National Security Council in 1951 noted that the Soviet bloc was in fact one of the largest importer of Pakistan's goods, only to be succeeded, in the following quarter, by communist China.

In fact, the report pointed out, Pakistan had in fact violated a US law prohibiting trade with countries that had traded with the Soviet bloc during a period of hostility.[17] In the period of April to December 1950, 6.1 per cent of Pakistan's total exports went to the Soviet Union. The rest of its international trade, however, was firmly in the ambit of the free world. For the time being, the report concluded, it was best to give Pakistan the benefit of the doubt. Furthermore, it was indisputable that Pakistan was a strategically significant nation: 'Located on the East and West of the subcontinent of South Asia', the report noted, echoing Sir Caroe's assessments,

> it occupies two flanks of one of the largest non- communist areas of Asia and controls one of the routes from Sinkiang, and one of the major routes from Tibet. Eastern Pakistan, lying relatively near to Communist China, has importance in relation to possible Communist China expansionist tendencies. Western Pakistan has inherited the primary responsibilities of the defence of the North Western Frontier Province.[18]

All in all, then, it would not make sense to cut off trade contacts with Pakistan—even if it had established diplomatic missions with many nations in Eastern Europe, including Hungary and Poland. 'Pakistan's military manpower would enable it to make a significant contribution to the Middle East's capacity to resist Soviet aggression'.

A State Department cable on the eve of Nehru's visit noted that commercial exchange with India was tricky, but not impossible. 'Government leaders, particularly the Prime Minister have become acutely aware of the need for foreign investment, but, due to political reasons to defer to the popular attitude, and have accordingly not taken a firm stand in welcoming an inflow of capital.'[19] Nonetheless, this was not an insurmountable hurdle. 'Responsible members of the cabinet have assured our High Commissioner that the government is prepared to enter into individual agreements with United States investors which would guarantee practically all of the safeguards which we hoped to obtain by a general treaty.'[20] Furthermore, the US also assisted India in acquiring hefty loans from the International Bank: during the course of his visit, the bank approved $34 million to be granted to India for the maintenance of its railways, and a further $10 million for the purchase of agricultural technology.

Indeed, the set of contacts that the government of India cultivated within Harry Truman's, and then Eisenhower's governments were also wide-ranging, and highly influential. G.S Bajpai, for instance, definitely worked hard to achieve a more secure footing for India in the United States' considerations. Following a meeting with the Indian finance minister, C. D. Deshmukh ('a conservative, thoughtful individual'), Bowles pressed the State Department into action on the matter of expediting food and developmental loans to India. For its part, by the early 1950s the State Department did make some efforts towards securing a larger amount of loans for the Indian government. Deshmukh told Bowles in 1952, that it would be impossible for India to carry out her minimum economic plans without substantial aid from the United States.[21]

Following his meeting with Nehru and Bajpai at the White House, Truman himself campaigned energetically to push through legislation that would enable India to procure wheat from the United States at reduced rates, arguing that 'We must counter the false promises of communist imperialism with constructive action for human betterment.' Securing this legislation, moreover, was the only way to keep India stable and democratic, an objective which would always be in the United States' interest.[22] During a meeting with Acheson, Nehru expressed his intention to try to reduce the price of wheat in India by 10 per cent. Legislation would need to be passed accordingly in the United States, to permit sales of government wheat at lowered prices.

Nor was this the only piece of business between India and the United States that took place over the course of Nehru's visit. In 1951, President Truman announced to Congress that he would pass a bill that would enable emergency aid to be sent to India. Bowles was a strong advocate of greater American aid to India, along the lines of what had been done in the Marshall Plan, and pointed out that this strategy could only yield dividends:

> The Indian Government quite often fails to do what we would like, but there is no question of its devotion to democracy, nor is there any question as to what side it will fall on once it has built a solid economic foundation and developed the full confidence and support of its people.[23]

Bowles therefore urged his president to put his energies into passing the bill that could enable aid to South Asia via the 'Point IV' program. In fact, for all the insistence of the Indian government on non-alignment, Nehru and his officials had also gone out of their way to unofficially assure representatives from the United States that, should push actually come to shove, India would stand with the United States in the event of a world conflict.[24]

The most important method of securing South Asia's allegiance, therefore, had to rely on the promises of international aid, and food security. The Point IV program had been designed as an aid-giving project for infrastructural and developmental expenses for underdeveloped countries. The legislation was sponsored by Truman in 1948, and enabled the United States to offer economic and technical aid to India—a measure that received bipartisan support. In an address to Congress, Truman declared: 'The Point IV program was conceived as a world-wide continuing program of helping underdeveloped nations to help themselves through the sharing of technical information already tested and proved in the United States.'[25] The agreement had called for an 'interchange of technical knowledge and skills in related activities designed to contribute to the balanced and integrated development of the economic resources and productive capacities in India'.[26]

Pakistan was also a beneficiary of its terms: a paper concluded:

> We are prepared to offer Pakistan technical assistance under the Point IV program. We understand that such assistance is needed most in agriculture, geological surveys, transportation, light industries, etc.'[27] Liaquat was also warm in his praises for the benefits of Point IV: 'For we believe that this would be the most courageous, the wisest and the most far reaching method by which your country can assure the world of its goodwill and international outlook.[28]

George McGhee, the under-secretary for State for South Asian and Middle Eastern Affairs—an important point person in Truman's and Eisenhower's state department with regard to relations with South Asia, and an ardent champion of the strategic use of Pakistan against the Soviet Union—repeatedly encountered these arguments during a visit to Karachi in 1951. In preparation for the signing of the Middle Eastern Defence Treaty Organization, McGhee had visited Karachi on the back of a month-long tour of Saudi Arabia, Turkey, and Iraq. McGhee met with the editor of the Dawn newspaper, Altaf Hussain, who was markedly scornful of the US's efforts in the cultivation of its relations with Pakistan. Altaf Hussain—echoing, in some ways, CD Deshmukh's dark warnings to the White House about the dangers faced by India without the arrival of American aid—remarked at a dinner party that the onslaught of communism in South Asia was merely a matter of years, at the most, a decade. Certainly, he goaded, American attempts at combatting it were feeble, at best.[29] The telegram from the US embassy—which described and analysed this conversation in full—conceded that there seemed to be some truth to Hussain's hidden suggestion: 'The long delay in Congressional approval for Point IV; the small sums of money mentioned; and the continual emphasis on what the nations of Asia must do apparently dissipate what little hopes may be left'.[30]

Truman was warned however, that it would not be possible for the United States to meet all of India's demands for military aid.[31] 'We should, however, tell Nehru that we may not be able in the near future to make available to India any large quantity of military equipment... It results from our heavy commitments to other parts of the world.'[32] The memo argued that the American efforts in the region to provide military, technical, or infrastructural assistance ought to be strengthened. At the same time, it was also crucial to reassure the Indians that the US would always be available for additional help for India should the situations arise: 'Should extraneous developments place serious and unexpected strains on the Indian economy, this government would stand ready to consult with the government of India with respect to cooperative measures which might be taken to solve these extraordinary problems'.[33]

The propellants of India and Pakistan's foreign policy with regard to the United States were also perpetuated by patterns of thinking that had been well entrenched during the inter-war years, rather than only a new set of variables based on their antagonistic positioning after 1947. The antecedents and repercussions of Nehru's and Liaquat's visits to the United States in 1949 show a series of commonalties in the nature of transactions that both countries made during the Cold War. Furthermore the issues raised during these visits also serve to further highlight how the Cold War was a significant factor in the considerations about international positioning by India and Pakistan from the very earliest days of their existence: both leaders had been acutely aware of its potential over the decade that preceded the transfer of power, and, during their visit, determined to exploit their potential to the fullest. For all the claims made about India and Pakistan displaying different ideological trends in the conduct of their early foreign policy—of Pakistan displaying a marked turn towards a military alliance with the United States, while India remaining non-aligned and sympathetic to socialism—their actions are also indicative of two states that retained a deeply colonial apparatus for foreign policy, and whose reception on the world stage was primarily determined through this history, rather than their oppositional stances on Kashmir.

Indeed, the extent to which India's and Pakistan's international ambitions coincided in the 1950s is also striking. Arne Westad shows, for instance, how the early years of the Cold War also offered the opportunity for a new set of international configurations for recently decolonised countries: rather than this being a matter of allying with countries on the bases of ideological affinities towards communism or capitalism, many third world countries attempted to use the bipolar world order to their own advantage. [34] Certainly, neither India nor Pakistan saw the Cold War as being a demand for permanent alliances with either one super-power: they simply moved when they spotted incentive. Their appraisals of what constituted self-interest, moreover, as well as how to go about achieving it, were also characterised by a curious similarity.

Choreography at the United Nations

It was on the question of South Africa that the two delegations worked in particularly synchronised moves. The tactic of using the discriminatory practises of the government of South Africa to bolster their own anti-racist and independent credentials was in fact a familiar one to diplomats of the government of India in the years that followed the partition. The treatment of Indians in South Africa had rumbled on in the United nations and, before that, in the League of Nations since the 1920s. Given the policies of the South African government since the 1920s and, in 1946, the passing of the Asiatic Land Tenure Act (which, it was charged, essentially 'ghettoised' South Asian living in the country), the stage seemed set for a public confrontation between two members of the Commonwealth family in the United Nations. Obviously, M.A.H. Ispahani argued firmly, brushing aside the arguments of the South Africa delegation, 'the matter was a question of the fundamental human rights of South Asians in South Africa, and therefore well within the purview of the United Nations: The right to vote, to own property, to take part freely in commercial activities, to participate in public administration, were, without possible doubt, fundamental human rights.' Zafarullah Khan declared in November 1947 that 'The governments of India and Pakistan were in duty bound to take an interest in the fate of the Indians until they acquired full liberty.'

One correspondent of Jinnah's had even suggested that there was a reasonable case to be made for starting afresh with the South African government, asking for the extension of privileges to only Pakistani nationals, rather than to have to agitate on the behalf of all Indian origin migrants. After all, 'the Union of South Africa had extended the privileges of "whites" to Muslims of all countries, but that under the influence of Gandhi, but that the Muslims there would not accept the offer unless it were extended to the non- Muslim Indians in South Africa.'[35] Perhaps, the writer suggested, 'Such negotiations are, bound to succeed, and would bring in their wake such valuable commodities as coal and general mutual trade which we might then enter into with them'. An option, for embarking on a different strategy for negotiation was therefore available. Nonetheless, both India and Pakistan had moved in clear synchrony on the South Africa question. Indeed, a great deal of the substance of India's critique of South Africa's position in the United Nations, drew from arguments that Zafarullah Khan had made: South Africa's control over South West Africa, an arrangement made under the Mandatory system, was unlawful; that its annexation of this territory was against the spirit of the Mandatory system.

The United Nations then asked India and Pakistan to take part in the Round Table discussion on the issue with the government of South Africa. The matter came to very little, and within a few months, both governments resigned from the commission in protest of the continuing treatment of Indians and Pakistanis in South Africa. Nonetheless, a delegate from Pakistan declared: 'When the Union of South Africa recognised the Pakistanis and Indians in its territories as nationals in the full sense of that word, Pakistan and India would withdraw their complaint.'[36] When in February 1951, an international conference in Cape Town convened to examine the question of Indians in South Africa, the governments of India and Pakistan sent H.N. Kunzru and Dr Mahmoud Hussain as their representatives. The negotiations broke down, but the reason they did so are no less interesting: while India and Pakistan pressed for 'opportunities for the fullest development' of South African Indians, the government of South Africa pressed for the provision of repatriation. Both India and Pakistan protested vehemently against these proposals, and opted to leave the conference.[37]

The recently expanded number of nation states striving to enter the decision-making apparatus of the United Nations also provoked counter-veiling impulses: both the United States and the United Kingdom also strove to retain the balance of power in their favour while drafting the United Nations Charter.[38] As a consequences of the destruction and turmoil of the Second World War and Europe, and the beginnings of Cold War alignments in the continent—though not as a result of the 12 million who had been displaced by the partition—the question of the rights of stateless and displaced individuals acquired prominence and immediacy. In addition to thousands of Allied soldiers also looked to their governments for resources for resettlement and rehabilitation, Jews, ethnic Germans, Poles, Soviet prisoners, and Slovak and Czech populations, who either voluntarily or were forcefully relocated by 1946.[39]

In drawing up their plans of disentanglement and separation, the two governments were also following—or, at least attempting to—practises which had been well established in other parts of the world. And in the 1940s and 50s, many of the difficulties that India and Pakistan encountered when attempting to sort through the ramifications of the partition, was that this was in fact not a novel situation. A critical central question facing both governments in the 1950s: the movement of minorities, had also been thrashed out repeatedly, and in great detail, by governments all over the world, over the 1930s and '40s.[40]

During the war years, for instance, Mark Mazower estimates that the astounding figure of some 46 million people were uprooted, and 'displaced' in eastern and central Europe.[41]

During the United Nations deliberations on the Refugee Convention, India and Pakistan occupied a similar platform, due to their experiences with refugees at the time of partition. Both of them asked the UN to broaden its definition of the term refugee, and its provisions as to which sets of refugees would benefit from aid this body. At a meeting in 1950, Pakistan's representative during these deliberation went so far as to remark that '[t]he Governments of India and Pakistan had never thought it proper to link the question of settlement with any other issue outstanding between them',[42] and urged the committee in charge of drafting the criteria for the definition of refugees to extend it to those who could, in fact, claim a nationality, rather than, as would come to prevail, only to those deemed 'stateless' as a consequence of the aftermath of the Second World War in Europe.[43] Partly, their actions on the matter were under-girded by sheer necessity. Overwhelmed by the numbers of Europe's displaced persons or no, there was still no harm in petitioning the United Nations for additional assistance for India's and Pakistan's refugees on the basis of having become two separated nation states themselves, and therefore shaping their arguments around the need for the United Nations to offer protection to those who were not stateless, but nonetheless displaced. At the same time, it was also an assertion by both countries of their abilities to take part in international debates—and on terms that did not accentuate their differences with one another.

Both governments chose not to sign onto the United Nations Refugee Convention of 1951, owing to common concerns with regard to the rehabilitation of refugees. As Patricia Oberoi has pointed out, both India and Pakistan, no strangers to the question of mass migration and the problems posed by rehabilitation, had initially welcomed the activities of the United Nations in helping with the task of refugee rehabilitation in the subcontinent. They both urged the United Nations to accept a broader definition of the word refugee—which could be applied to communities which had become displaced because of the partition—and for a bigger jurisdiction of the United Nations High Commissioner for Refugees. When this ambition was foiled, neither signed on to the UN Refugee Convention of 1951.[44] The degree of difference in the position of the two countries was not determined on the basis of only their hostility to one another over the question of Kashmir, but on a more complicated praxis of self-interest. In carrying out these calculations moreover, they often occupied spaces characterised by a common set of objectives, and by being at the receiving end of a shared historical experience.

Furthermore, India and Pakistan's refugee regime in fact echoed the features of models of reconstruction after destruction and mass warfare which had been put in place in other parts of the world.[45] Indeed, an important principle that informed most of India's and Pakistan's exercises in refugee rehabilitation was about how it would give meaning and legitimacy to their claims to a viable statehood. But the shaping of the contours of the refugee debates at the United Nations—and India's and Pakistan's different opinions on this question—are significant: while the United States had argued that assistance ought to be provided for those who were 'stateless', India and Pakistan had argued that these protections ought to extend to those who could claim a nationality, but were still in need of rehabilitation and monetary assistance.

How to Live with a Partition

The prospect of the vote of Israel in the United Nations, some three months after their own creation as nation states, certainly tied both delegations into agonizing contortions about exactly how they should defend their decision to vote against the motion. Arguments for and against the principle of partition in the first place, or the compromise solutions within a confederative arrangement, could not have failed to remind India and Pakistan about the similarities with their own positions. Setting aside the rights and wrongs of the Palestinian question, my attempt here is to gauge the response of the Indian and Pakistani leadership to the issue in the 1950s, as a way of strengthening their own claims to nation-hood. This is important, since it reveals the belief of the leadership of both India and Pakistan on the merits on the principle of partition itself as a viable premise for the creation of a state, and therefore, also the basis of a viable coexistence.

The principle of partition itself was, unsurprisingly, very carefully handled by India and Pakistan in their dealings with the wider world. Yet, after their independence, their stances on the merits of partition were usually tinged with a measure of resignation: in the latter half of the twentieth century, after all, it was evident to all that partition was a phenomenon that was here to stay. In many ways, India's and Pakistan's positions on the various dilemmas thrown up by partition as a wider global phenomenon are comparable, and, in this section, I would like to highlight some of the commonalities that they had on these questions. The ways in which they moved on these issues were always designed to bolster their own claims to a separated statehood: in many ways, asserting this was as important to India as it was to Pakistan. While Nehru was frequently vocal in his condemnation of the evils of the two nation theory, despite his distaste, India's actions on the international stage also didn't shy away from recognising the force of arguments that arose in favour of it.

Interestingly enough, many of these questions were also embodied in the career of Henry Grady, the first American Ambassador to India. Before arriving in Delhi in 1947, Grady had also been a member of an Anglo American taskforce on the question of a Jewish state in Palestine. Grady's position on the principle of partition were mixed: while he disapproved of the notion of a unilaterally imposed Jewish state in Palestine, he was in favour of a settlement which gave the Arab and Jewish populations equal control over a federalised state. The best solution, he suggested, would be 'neither a Jewish state nor an Arab State'. On the whole, however, Grady felt that nationalist sentiments in favour of a separate state had to be recognized rather than suppressed by the United States. His taskforce came down strongly against any partition of Palestine, in part, due to the concerns of how majority communities would affect the rights of minorities. He argued that the solution lay in neither an Arab state nor an Israeli state, because both represented the form of 'extreme nationalism that the world should not condone'. Grady had pressed for a federal resolution to the Palestinian question: while he recognized that nationalist arguments needed to be factored into any situation involving the transfer of power, it was necessary to do this in ways that recognized all the claimants.

By 1947, however, Grady's views had been overruled by Truman, and the United States had decided that it would back the creation of an Israeli state sanctioned by a vote at the United Nations. While in India, Grady felt that the partition had had an enormous financial and military cost for India: had it not happened, he rued for instance, the prospects of the development of the jute mills of Calcutta would have been better.[46] Yet, he also argued that by and large, the British had done the only thing which could be done over the transfer of power to two states. The principle of partition itself was generally entertained with resignation—there was no denying that these forces were here to stay in the realm of international affairs, and the only question was how best they could be accommodated, while keeping in mind the requirements for regional and international stability.

In many ways, India's and Pakistan's treatment of the Palestine issue—disapproving, but also careful, and resigned to defeat—offers insights into the basis of the commonality of India's and Pakistan's positions on the international stage. Both India and Pakistan voted against the partition plan of Palestine, though their reasoning for doing this was carefully distinguished. On Palestine, both countries did argue to varying degrees that the way in which the decision was implemented was flawed and unfair. But the argument about the validity of partition as a reasonable premise to resolve the question was not questioned by either. The decisions on Palestine also show an adherence to a belief that partition could provide the basis for two separated and sovereign entities to have a stable coexistence—though in the Palestinian case, this had not been provided for adequately, and it was for this reason, rather than a fundamental disagreement about the idea of partition itself, that both India and Pakistan chose to vote against the motion.

During the 1930s, both the Congress and the Muslim League had made full-throated statements in favour of the Arab cause in Palestine. To Indira Gandhi, in 1938, for instance, Nehru outlined: 'We must remember that Palestine is essentially an Arab country, and must remain so, and the Arabs must not be crushed and supressed in their own homelands'. In the years that followed independence, however, while both countries voted against the creation of Israel in 1948, the reasoning behind their decisions became more complex, and rooted within a consideration of their own arguments about constituting a legitimate statehood.

The Pakistan delegation had consistently worked against the decision to partition at all, seeing this as a means of forcefully depriving the Muslim inhabitants of Palestine from their land. The delegation had also authored a minority report of the United Nations special commission on Palestine, which had argued that Palestine ought to remain a unitary country, with the transfer of power effective immediately. In 1948, however, Zafarullah Khan was put in the unenviable position of needing to defend this argument, when his own country had arrived onto the world stage via the same process. But Zafarullah Khan nonetheless reconciled the contradiction, arguing that his opposition was not based on the wrongs of partition itself as a principle, but rather the unfairness of the decisions in this particular case: unlike India and Pakistan, he argued, power had not been transferred to the majority community in Palestine. Indeed, when asked about the differences between the Indian partition and the Palestinian one, Zafarullah Khan argued that the former decision had been arrived at with the consent of all the parties involved: '[the Indian partition] had been based on the principle of ceding to the minority a number of areas in which they were in the majority. If that was what the Jews were asking for, Pakistan would be willing to grant their request'.[47]

Zafrullah's objections, therefore, were about providing frameworks that could be jointly accepted by both Jewish and Arab populations in Palestine, which could be equally acceptable to both groups. Moreover, his arguments did not discount the possibility about the potential for a formalised partition to provide a new framework in which these questions could also be dealt with more fairly. The provisions of the current solution, were not accepted by one group, and therefore, and would therefore not provide a viable model for partition: 'But how is the General Assembly going to set up the Arab State if the people say: no, we are not cooperating? Where are you going to get the services? Who is going in to keep order? These problems were put, but where have they been provided for?'.[48] But these words reflected concerns about the aftermath of the partition—whether its terms would be favorable to all the concerned parties—but not, in themselves, a repudiation of the principle of partition themselves.

The Indian delegation initially attempted to argue for what was known as the 'Nehru Plan': a scheme in favour of a confederation, with an autonomous area for Jews in the region, and a single economic union.[49] By 1948, Nehru had initially been in favour of abstention, and then, upon reflection and considering the solid Arab opposition to the prospect, instructed his delegation to vote against the partition. Yet, as P.R. Kumaraswamy shows, this decision was based on many contingencies, and Nehru had also closely considered the idea of recognizing Israel regardless of all the protests that had surrounded the vote. The fact of the matter was, Nehru admitted to H.V. Kamath, the state of Israel had come to stay, and had the full backing of the United States to boot. The writing about the creation of Israel was fairly clear on the wall when the United Nations met in Lake Success, where it was then head-quartered, in 1947. Sarwar Hassan, a diplomat from Pakistan involved in the United Nations, records how the vote on the Palestinian issue was rushed through, with the opinion of several dissenters on the question effectively marginalised. M.A.H. Ispahani, writing to Jinnah in 1948, gave a bleak appraisal about the chances of a unified Palestine: 'the more I see the U.N. at work, the more I arrive at the conclusion that reliance on this body to do justice is to expect the impossible. Every nation will have to rely on its own strength.'[50]

The difference between Nehru's and Liaquat Ali Khan's full-throated public vocalisation against the wrongs of partition, and their grudging concessions in private about how this could best be accommodated, is, in a sense, the subject of this book. The experiences of partition also enabled a set of choices that put India and Pakistan on the same side on a series of international questions, and it was the necessity of adhering to these standards, rather than a more narrow or knee-jerk opposition, that drove a great deal of the logic of their relationship. In 1940, Jinnah, commenting on the Irish situation, drew parallels between the distaste of the Unionists to be ruled by the Nationalists and the South Asian context, and argued that his reply to the Congress high command would be much the same as what the Irish Ulsterites had told the nationalists: 'I do not want to be ruled by you'.[51] And, in many ways, Jinnah's stances on this issue need not always be seen as diametrically opposed from those of Nehru's. In 1948, during a visit to India, Eamon de Valera, the Prime Minister of

Ireland, spoke against the ills of partition, portraying the attempts of the British to create a separate Northern Ireland as an illegal act. In this, he received Nehru's sympathy—the documentation of a warm personal relationship between Nehru and De Valera is also extensive, and Nehru himself spotted many parallels between the British course of actions in India and Ireland. [52] Yet in the end, De Valera's Indian campaign ended in failure. While Nehru's condemnation of the evils of British designs of 'divide and rule' were full-throated, distaste for the politics of partition had also not stopped him from examining how to go about consolidating, and benefitting from, its effects.

7

TRADE AND FINANCIAL RELATIONS BETWEEN INDIA AND PAKISTAN

In August 1953, M.H.A. Fazalbhoi, an influential solicitor, and from a powerful Bombay family himself, submitted a memorandum to the MEA on behalf of members of the trading community. He argued that Indian Muslim businessmen in particular were subject to suspicion and mistreatment by the Indian government:

> Evacuee property proceedings have been started on the flimsiest of grounds making them incur the cost of extensive legal proceedings and otherwise...It is therefore necessary that trade between the two countries should not only be made free... but a mandate should be given against undue suspicion on the part of government officials and the policy of black listing merchants having business dealings with Pakistan.[1]

Fazalbhai went on to number the ways in which conditions of trade could improve: establishment of branch offices in both countries to facilitate the exchange and movement of funds; facilities for prosecuting dishonesty in dealings between traders in both countries; and greater ease in travel, for, 'at present, if a person makes even a temporary visit to Pakistan, he has to face an enquiry from the evacuee officers'.[2]

Badruddin Tyabji, by then Commonwealth Secretary in the MEA, and who had signed off on files relating to different aspects in the relationship with Pakistan for some years now, headed a meeting to consider Fazalbhai's memorandum. There was no point, argued Tyabji, in implementing the evacuee property legislations to the extent that they were hurting India's commercial interests. Tyabji argued that Fazabhai's memorandum should be considered carefully: what it had asked for was not necessarily opposed to any hard and fast principle of the government of India. Yet his arguments did not convince for the time being. A representative from the Relief and Rehabilitation Ministry countered that 'while the evacuee property laws admittedly had abnormal features, they were inevitable in the context of current Indo-Pak relations.'[3] A letter from the Indian deputy high commissioner in Karachi on this matter was even blunter:

> It would be putting the cart before the horse because free trade between the two countries is quite obviously the result of good relations on the political sphere and it is meaningless to state that if there were free trade between India and Pakistan all the major problems that would have stood in the way of happy relations between the two countries would not have arisen.[4]

It was always clear that trade between India and Pakistan was going to be conducted as a product of a wider set of concerns. Trade did become a hostage to the other agendas that India and Pakistan were pursuing, both with one another, as well as with their arguments about demonstrating viability to the rest of the world. Ultimately, as the early policy makers on India–Pakistan trade rightly sensed, this was a situation which could only improve with political aspects of the relationship also improving. Bilateral trade could only really proceed with surety once the economic edifice of the states of India and Pakistan was sure of their own basis. Yet, in point of fact, bureaucrats in India actually found it quite difficult to go about separating their economic requirements from being dependent on supplies from Pakistan. Arguments about the necessity for cross-border trade rose at a variety of levels—at the regional level, along the eastern boundary line, by heavy industries that required jute, as well as at the international level by the requirement for maintaining the sterling balance.

In this chapter, I chart out how partition shifted the terms of trade between two points now divided by the boundary line. While, on the one hand, both governments made lofty declarations of carrying out trade with one another as independent nation states—taxable, and liable to regulations by both states—on the other, they were also forced to come to a series of arrangements to accommodate commercial transactions to continue in the way that they had always existed before the making of the boundary. In many instances, in fact, it was actually impossible to physically stop the process of commercial transactions between both sides of the border, and the boundary line. Therefore, the question this chapter is concerned with is the extent to which both governments' positions were amenable to the necessities of contingency, demand, and genuine emergency, in the face of a great deal of rhetoric about how the Indian and Pakistani economies had to be bolstered on their own merits.

In many ways the question of trade between India and Pakistan is also about the old conundrum of the extent to which free-flowing economic liberalism can trump the forces of nationalism. Both India and Pakistan more or less fastidiously adhered to the nationalist end of the spectrum of this debate, and consistently advocated policies which would strengthen the economic presence of the state as opposed to having a more lax set of arrangements that allowed for the free movement of trade and commodity exchange. The implications of this argument, moreover, made itself felt over the long term, and trade between the two countries dwindled in successive decades, to smaller and smaller levels.[5] Experts on trade and economic relations between India and Pakistan have also frequently argued that the path to a more prosperous subcontinent is in a better trading relationship. After all, implemented correctly, argues Ijaz Nabi, the prospect for bilateral trade can only bring about good and greater overall prosperity and growth in both countries. The case for a more integrated economic union between India and Pakistan is self-evident. The more practical, and cheaper path to greater economic growth on either side of the Punjab, it is argued, is via a network of trade that allows for the free flow of goods and commodities across the border. Indeed, the question that many analysts on India–Pakistan trade pose is: can the prospect of bilateral trade, bringing profitable returns, be a means of reducing the tensions between both states? I use this chapter to demonstrate that this was possible, but to some degree only.

During the 1950s, the necessity for bilateral trade was acknowledged, but only to the extent that the recognition of the requirements of two separated states was factored in. When, I argue, its presence was beneficial to either government, policies were usually put in place to make sure it took place. Its terms had to be conducted while recognizing the presence of both states, rather than by ignoring them. This chapter, therefore, is an evaluation of the capacity of the government to effect a better trading relationship, and an attempt to analyse how and why decisions were taken to enable this. The reasons for the resumption would also suggest that a straightforward linkage between greater amity on both sides, with more economic connectivity are misplaced. Throughout the period this book is concerned with, trade relations between India and Pakistan were structured in ways that prioritised the needs of two newly built economies, first and foremost. In the end, however, this was also a story about the state achieving a degree of compromise with rigid nationalist stances, when the situation did require it.

The Pursuit of Economic Self Sufficiency

The making of policy on bilateral trade in the 1950s is also an interesting example of the prevailing belief of that decade, in the capacity of the state. Both governments placed a high premium on strengthening their economic standing, as well as making them into self-sufficient entities. Such interventions were in keeping with the prevalent economic wisdom of the time. The foremost developmental economists of the fifties, such as Albert O Hirschman, were arguing that all international trade should be carried out according to the logic of states in the pursuit of their own strategic self-interest. Foreign trade could be a tool by which to consolidate military might, by importing the goods which were likely to strengthen the country.[6] Such trade would be more profitably carried out with countries that were in a weaker position, or with whom there already existed friendly ties. A second effect of foreign trade, argued Hirschman, was the influence effect, through which the foreign trade of a country might become a direct source of power. I will examine in the pages that follow the ways in which India and Pakistan went about pursuing these aims, what this meant for the prospect of bilateral trade, and the avenues these approaches also opened up for greater amounts of trade between India and Pakistan.

In India, the setting up of institutions such as the planning commission and the economic committee of the cabinet would provide the basis for the subsequent characterisation of the era as that of the heyday of state intervention in the management of the economy.[7] The economic committee of the cabinet included several familiar faces in leadership positions both within and outside the Congress. Key members of the committee included K.C. Neogy, Gopalaswami Ayyangar, and S.P. Mookherjee. Their stated priority was to build a strong Indian economy, and one in which the state held an important stake in heavy industries—steel, coal, cement, and civil engineering.[8]

Similarly, the government of Pakistan was also keen to be seen to be adopting a proactive role in the development of its economy from an early stage. Import substitution was a key concern in Pakistan: the Industrial Policy Document published in 1947 by the government of Pakistan, highlighted the need for industrialisation policy geared at reducing dependence on imports. By 1949, control of industrial development was made into a central subject.[9] A 'Council of Industries', consisting of representatives of strategic industries, trading interests, and members from state governments was formed to advise the government on its industrial policy, such as target setting for various industries, and regulations to be imposed by the centre. By 1950, the government of Pakistan had set up boards for the regulation of production and export of its key commodities, such as cotton, wool and jute.[10] Similarly, the Industries Development Corporation Act was passed in 1950, according to which a corporation would be set up for the promotion of those industries considered vital to the national interest. These industries included jute, paper, heavy engineering, heavy chemicals and fertilizers.[11] The provincial governments also directed their efforts at rehabilitating refugees by providing support for industrial and commercial ventures.[12]

The question of how the newly created states of India and Pakistan would regulate commercial flows across the boundary formed the subject of a fair amount of correspondence between both governments. In December 1947, the government of Pakistan sent a note arguing that in the case of excise duty on goods exported from India to Pakistan, the government of Pakistan was not currently entitled to collect her rightful share. Regarding the movement of raw jute from Pakistan to India, the government of Pakistan argued that it should be given a share in the revenue earned from the export duties in the port of Calcutta.[13] Under the present provisions, the note continued:

> no refund or rebate of excise duty is being granted on goods exported from India to Pakistan. On the other hand, cotton and other commodities produced in Pakistan are being exported to India without any payment of duty. The Pakistan government therefore consider that for the period of 7 ½ months ending on 31st March, 1948, Pakistan should be given a reasonable share of the total central excise revenue, on the basis of the quantity of excisable goods consumed in Pakistan territory.[14]

Similarly, S. Bhootalingam, a former student of economics at Cambridge, and the first finance secretary in India, submitted a note on the forecasted changes that the termination of the Standstill Agreement would bring: 'The effect of the termination of the present so-called standstill arrangement with Pakistan will be that Pakistan will become like any other foreign country for the purposes of our trade. Our exports to Pakistan will earn foreign currency, while our imports will be paid for in foreign currency.'[15] Payments for the supply of coal into Pakistan were made from the balances Pakistan continued to hold in the State Bank in India[16]. Bhootalingam however ended his note warning of the dangers of hasty changes being made with regard to trading conditions with Pakistan. For instance, he argued:

> We have to be extremely cautious before taking any steps to rashly to increase the production of raw jute in India which would merely have the result of a fall in all jute prices. In the long run both India and Pakistan gain by ensuring that their combined production of jute is not greater than the world demand.[17]

Unilaterally cutting off dependence on Pakistani jute by increasing production within India, Bhootalingam felt, would be to no one's gain. It was also evident to policy makers in India that in terms of economic relations, Pakistan possessed many advantages, and it would not be easy to cut off links entirely. A good deal of India's economy, in fact, was critically dependent on supplies from Pakistan. In terms of their commercial transactions, moreover, Pakistan had the upper hand, in terms of being able to dictate the terms according to which trade with India should be conducted.

In 1948, Pakistan had proposed that a currency exchange control be worked out between the two governments. Pakistan had argued that the trade with India be valued, and paid for, in terms of sterling; and the extent to which this could be agreed to by India was the subject of many of its discussions on the 'Payments Agreement' with Pakistan. Pakistan was, moreover, owed some £6 million sterling under the allocations of the sterling debt.[18] A note to the Cabinet Secretariat in India, however, warned against the costs of meeting these demands in full:

> It is not possible to consider the Commodities agreement in isolation, as our payments liabilities would be an important determining factor for our general as well as particular import and export control policies in regard to Indo–Pakistani trade. If our views on the payments question are not accepted by Pakistan, our objective should be to import from Pakistan only the minimum quantities of essential commodities and export to that country Indian goods as liberally as possible, in order to reduce our deficit in the balance of payments position.[19]

There was also consistently an emphasis placed on becoming 'self-sufficient' economically, so that dependence on Pakistan for vital goods could be reduced. This kind of rhetoric carried a great deal of weight in the early activities of both governments. Bilateral trade policies became part of a concerted effort to superimpose the interests of the state as a whole over differentiated patterns of cross-border trading. In India, for instance, a concerted effort was made to carry out all instances of cross border trading under a unified set of concerns, rather than to let them be carried forward in independent and discrete patterns.

This could be seen, for example, in a letter from Sardar Patel to Nehru, counselling him that 'discussions on trade, tariff policy, customs and economic control be carried out in a more "coordinated" manner, particularly when they concerned Pakistan.'[20] Patel argued that 'barter agreements' negotiated in isolation to one another would not serve India's economic position as a whole. For instance, he argued, isolated agreements that allowed for the exchange of cotton cloth for cotton, and wheat for rice—referring, in other words, to pre-partition patterns of trading—would, in the long run, endanger

India's positions of advantage with respect to Pakistan's. Agreements concluded in isolation of the complete picture, would, he argued present a 'substantial danger of our sacrificing the bargaining advantage which we undoubtedly hold in certain matters and of Pakistan securing advantage over us in certain others in which we are in a comparatively weak position.' Therefore, he suggested, a committee should be set up in cabinet 'to coordinate all our dealings with Pakistan on fiscal, financial, economic and other matters'. He also suggested that future negotiations with Pakistan be presided over by the Ministry of External Affairs. This committee would include secretaries of all ministries concerned in negotiations with Pakistan, such as Food, Relief and Rehabilitation, and Industry and Supply.

Patel also recommended that H.M. Patel, and H.V.R. Iengar—senior civil servants, who had had experience in dealing with matters arising out of partition—be placed on the committee. A committee was then created, headed by the prime minister, and composed of the ministers of finance, commerce, industry and supply, relief and rehabilitation, and food. Trade negotiations were structured according to the patterns of demand in each country: in India, the principle adopted was of a quid-pro-quo with regards to trading with Pakistan. For instance, the argument went, if Pakistan agreed to import on a larger scale Indian cotton textiles, then India would consider releasing a larger supply of coal, or cement. Yet, it was also not always possible to conduct the economic relationship between the two countries in such clear cut terms.

The Devaluation Crisis

It was the devaluation crisis that really made the government of India confront the viability of its own attempts at self-sufficiency. It was the devaluation crisis which hit prospects of bilateral trade with a thunderclap, but also forced the Indian government to take cognizance of the fact of its reliance on supplies from Pakistan. The value of Indian and Pakistani currency was pegged to the pound sterling at the end of the Second World War. In September 1949, Sir Stafford Cripps—a familiar figure to South Asian partition historians, and by now Chancellor of the Exchequer—announced that the pound sterling would be devalued by

30 per cent. One explanation offered for this was that sterling at its un-devalued rate would be unable to support the claims on it from the commonwealth area.[21] The issue of dollar-based imports acquired increasing significance in terms of trade in the sterling area. Thus the decision to devalue was made by a country hit by inflation and in an effort to catch up with the reduced value of its currency. Converting sterling balances into dollar purchases became an increasing worry to policy makers in Britain, as it increased the pressure on sterling to be able to maintain its standard. Maintaining an artificially high rate of the sterling was also, it was argued, impeding the development of Britain's post war economy. Devaluing the sterling exchange, therefore, was seen as a means of easing the flow of economic transactions between the UK and the rest of the world.

Nine other countries in the sterling area—Australia, New Zealand, India, South Africa, Ireland, Norway, Egypt and Israel—followed suit, and devalued their own currencies accordingly on the same day. B.N. Ganguli, faculty member at the Delhi School of Economics, and then a member of the Fiscal Commission in the government of India, for instance, argued that in view of the failure of the inflationary policies of the government with regard to currency exchange, there was 'no option' but to devalue along with sterling.[22] Similarly, C.D. Deshmukh wrote that 'Devaluation was forced on India by economic circumstances; its allegiance to and participation in the Sterling Area only influenced the timing of her decision.'[23] India was thus fairly willing to continue trading in the sterling area. In a speech on All India Radio following the devaluation of the rupee, Nehru argued 'The Sterling Area is important to us in our international economic relations. A great part of our international trade is with this area. Most of our export markets are also in this area, and it is important that we should not only maintain but improve our export position.'[24]

Pakistan announced its decision not to devalue its own currency. This announcement was met with consternation and anger in India, and led to apprehensions of lasting damage to the economies of both countries. It effectively became more expensive for India to trade with Pakistan. This decision found a great deal of support from business and trading lobbies, within Pakistan, who pointed out that the decision was based on sound reasoning. The *Economist* noted, for instance:

> First, Pakistan's balance of payments with the rest of the world, including the United States, is favourable. Secondly, Pakistan has embarked on a process of industrialisation and therefore needs to import capital goods as cheaply as possible. Thirdly, Pakistan government believes that its exports have inelastic demand. Finally, Pakistan wants to bring about a fall in domestic prices.[25]

The new rate of exchange would entitle Pakistan to a larger supply of coal, cotton textiles, vegetable oils, steel and tobacco from India, while being in an advantageous position in the balance of trade with India.[26] The devaluation crisis did have an acute impact on several sectors of the Indian economy. As a despatch from the British high commissioner in Delhi in February 1950 reported 'this has so far caused the complete closure of 15 mills, the partial closure of 20, and what a Press Note issued by the Bombay government describes as "widespread unemployment"'.[27] Another sector which suffered heavy losses in this period was the Bombay textile industry. Moreover, he said, steamer companies between East and West Bengal, were also at the receiving end of a sudden body blow to their income.

In India at the time it was nobody's case that all trade between the two countries ought to bought to a complete halt—indeed this was impossible. C.D. Deshmukh conceded, that trade in the commodities listed in the July 1949 agreement would have to carry on even without an agreement on an India–Pakistan exchange rate. This would have to be done, with 'one or more barter arrangements covering the commodities or groups of commodities to be supplied by each side.' Meetings of the economic committee of the cabinet began to consider options for damage control, if trade to Pakistan should suffer in the wake of the devaluation crisis. C.C. Desai was another erstwhile member of the ICS, secretary in the Ministry of Commerce in 1949, and who had also advocated greater de-regulation by the government of rationed commodities for the past year. Nonetheless, he pointed out, cutting off coal supplies to Pakistan, even after the devaluation, should only be carried out once the consequences of such an act had been apprehended as much as possible. 'It is not expected that in any such situation only Pakistan will be harmed. Naturally both countries may have to suffer hardships, but the final decision will depend on the relative degree of hardships and the comparative power of endurance.'[28] Moreover, a note from the Ministry of Commerce pointed out that the import of cotton seed from Pakistan would also have to continue, though if possible this should be secured at pre-devaluation prices.[29]

On the process of granting licenses for the import of cotton seed, for instance, the Ministry soon received a despatch from the High Commission in Karachi, jealously observing the high market prices of this commodity in Pakistan. The note attributed these prices to the demand for cotton seed in India, and recommended that the government of India not allow such advantages to go unnoticed:

> Several people are getting licenses from the government of India for importing cotton seed from Pakistan, and that they are, after profit making, selling them off to Muslims... [furthermore], if no import license was given, the price of cotton seed would fall further in Pakistan, and would further deteriorate the economic position in this country.[30]

In response, K.C. Neogy argued that 'I am anxious that this matter should not become a scandal of any kind', and so the economic committee of the cabinet should deliberate whether there was in fact, any pressing need for the licensing of imports of cotton seed.[31] Yet, regardless of how much Neogy wished to see India completely independent of supplies from Pakistan, the government of India was repeatedly forced to reckon with the grave dangers it faced should supplies of jute or cotton stop coming in from Pakistan altogether.

The report of the Indian government trade commissioner noted that '[a]ll elaborate plans for the expansion of the Indian textile industry will receive a serious setback if we were to lose a substantial portion of the cotton market in Pakistan.'[32] Similarly, he recommended to Delhi in May 1949 that the regulations for trading with Pakistan should be reduced. He argued that:

> It is true that the Pakistan government have used recently a portion of their foreign exchange for the importation of certain capital goods and a variety of consumer goods. The view usually put forth by the Pakistan government is that they have had to embark on substantial imports from other foreign countries because they could not get the required goods from India in time.[33]

In the annual report for inter-dominion trade in 1950, the Indian trade commissioner in Karachi admitted that 'Pakistan was in a happy position of having consumers at her door prepared to buy jute and cotton, practically at any price'.[34] International demand for jute and cotton sky-rocketed in the wake of the Korean War which created endless demand for raw materials for munitions. This situation could not be improved unless there was a reduction in the import and export duties for goods from Pakistan, accompanied by a simplification of import and export regulations.

By 1950, C.D. Deshmukh, the Indian Minister for Finance, approached the Pakistani high commissioner at the Commonwealth Conference in London to explore possible compromises.[35] In a conversation with the British high commissioner in India, Ambegaonkar the Indian finance secretary, stated that with regard to the International Monetary Fund's acceptance of Pakistan's exchange rate, '[a]lthough in fact India would have to accept whatever parity was approved by the IMF, (or cease to be a member of the fund), it was impossible on political grounds for her to give such assurances in advance.'[36]

This was also the predominant subject of discussion at the Commonwealth Conference for Finance Ministers, held in Columbo in January 1950. The question was discussed between Ghulam Muhammad, the Pakistani Finance Minister, Nehru and the British Secretary of State for Commonwealth Relations. The Secretary of State even pointed out that 'he had made considerable efforts to get rid of regulations for trade in Europe, and that considerable results had been achieved.'[37] He argued that 'continuation of conflict within the Commonwealth would be unfortunate from everybody's point of view'. But although both Nehru and Ghulam Muhammad politely agreed with this, there was no substantial change in the position of either with regards to the devaluation question. C.D. Deshmukh warned of the difficulties in arriving at such arrangements, sighing that he 'was not hopeful of a successful outcome of the proposed [Columbo] conference.'[38]

The problems relating to trading with Pakistan, and the latter's policies on devaluation, were loudly aired, both at forums of the Commonwealth, as well as the IMF. Bajpai met with Grafftey-Smith, the UK High Commissioner on 22 September 1949 to discuss the devaluation crisis. He sniped that while Pakistan had 'shown a most regrettable lack of commonwealth solidarity' in its decision not to devalue, and, finally, he concluded that India had 'in this, as in so many other matters, shown herself to be a reliable member of the Commonwealth, and a true friend of the United Kingdom'. Regardless of Pakistan's actions, Bajpai asserted, India would be able to procure the items hitherto received from Pakistan, such as jute and cotton, from other markets, such as Egypt, Uganda, and Australia.'[39]

Even in 1948 however, the impasse on arrangements for payments for trade between India and Pakistan were of concern to the United Kingdom, since, 'In these circumstances our only card of entry seemed to be to put the matter to the Indian delegation on the grounds that the dollars, involved in Pakistan's being compelled to buy coal from the USA, if her economy were not to come to a standstill, were an alarming and unnecessary drain on the control Reserves'.[40] This also offered an opportunity to define the role of the Commonwealth, as well as avenues for clearly positioning the economies of India and Pakistan within it.

One way of giving shape to the question of sterling balances owed to the colonies was to harness them for development plans in the commonwealth. In 1950, the Columbo Plan was finalised, according to which India, Pakistan and Ceylon would utilise a planned, annual drawings on the balances for the development expenditure in these countries. The Commonwealth Finance Ministers' Conference in London in November 1950 also floated the idea of the balances being used as a base for development of the Commonwealth area. Yet this was largely unsuccessful, since most countries opted to utilise the sterling balances for their own development, rather than as a collective resource.[41] It was also difficult to get agreement from all the members of the Commonwealth as how to how the balances could be used collectively. What was also increasingly discussed was how the claims on sterling could be settled with contributions from dollar based reserves.

Furthermore, difficult relations between the governments of India and Pakistan would also hamper the sterling balance negotiations, since the two countries would have to resort to importing essential items from other countries, and draw on their sterling reserves to do so. For instance, the sterling balances delegation was instructed to 'discuss with India and Pakistan the possibility of further dollar saving by the stepping up or the redirection of their own exports and the restriction of imports in certain cases'.[42] A meeting of the 'Overseas Negotiations Committee' in February 1948 noted that:

> It was difficult to judge the merits of any proposals for dealing with India without also considering the treatment of Pakistan. If we gave India less dollars than they had planned to spend, the Indian government might succeed in redressing their balance at the expense of Pakistan, in which case we should find it difficult to refuse additional assistance to Pakistan.[43]

Yet the importance of the Sterling Area as an economic unit steadily was being steadily chipped at over the 1940s and 50s, with a corresponding increase with their engagement with dollar based economies. The issue of dollar-based imports acquired increasing significance in terms of trade in the sterling area. Converting sterling balances into dollar purchases became an increasing worry to policy makers in Britain, as it was feared that, if uncontrolled, this would put pressure on the sterling to be able to maintain its standard. The team of British negotiators on the Sterling Balance question was headed by Jeremy Raisman, an erstwhile member of the Indian Civil Service, and who had held a variety of posts in his career in the government of India, including Finance Member of the Governor General's Council during the war.[44]

Much of the correspondence between the Treasury in London, and their representative in Delhi, Sir Raisman was on means by which to beat down the Indian and Pakistani claims on the sterling reserves. An anxious telegram was despatched to Sir Raisman as concerns about India's expenditure from the sterling reserves increased: 'The basic fact is that we are not in a position to afford the continuance of drawings by India upon reserves of Sterling Area in order to finance her dollar deficit, and we should find difficulty in accepting any agreement which does not start from this postulate.'[45] Yet, he also pointed out that 'there will be great difficulty in getting the Indian Ministers to agree to any proposals definitely limiting their dollar drawings on the sterling pool in the first half of 1948.'[46] The leader of the Indian Delegation told him privately that if this was forced upon them, the Indian government might have to dollar invoice the United Kingdom for essential goods such as jute.' Treasury officials, therefore, were concerned for their liabilities for payments against the dollar, for expenditure incurred by India in return for the Sterling Debt. The devaluation crisis exacerbated the concerns even further.

These issues also impacted on their patterns of trade with the rest of the world. The United Kingdom high commissioner, for example, noted in a telegram to the Commonwealth Relations Office:

> We are much exercised about the problem of Pakistan seeking from overseas supplies which she ought to get from India... The Pakistan delegation said that if their normal requirements of coal could be guaranteed them from India or elsewhere they would try to get out of the obligation to take the further 120,000 tons from the USA... We propose therefore, at this stage to try to maintain the attitude that we will not provide exchange for any purchases of coal and sugar by Pakistan from overseas beyond the 80,000 tons of coal and 20,000 tons of sugar already committed and that they would have to come to some sensible agreement with India on these and other similar matters in the forthcoming trade talks between them.[47]

The Indian government repeatedly complained of their supplies of jute, that had been paid for, being held up in East Bengal. A despatch from the U.K. High Commission in December 1949 noted that 'if India does not get satisfaction over the release of jute... she will suspend operation of inter-dominion commodities agreement, and cut off supplies of coal to Pakistan.'[48] The Commonwealth high commissioners as well as the Indian leadership thus kept a lookout for opportunities that could help them revive halted trade requirements.

In June 1949, India and Pakistan had ratified an agreement stating that both would grant rebates to excisable items that they exported to each other, provided that this was done on a mutual basis. In a telegram exchange between Ghulam Muhammad and K.C. Neogy, regarding the terms of tariff and rebates, Neogy argued that Pakistan's proposals that 'impairment should not result from any action taken by the Dominion granting the rebate only, and not the other Dominion' would surely 'detract from the scope of the agreement as a whole which is designed to increase Inter-dominion Trade. For example if Pakistan imposes an import duty on an excisable commodity at a level which would handicap our exports to Pakistan, the spirit in which the informal talks took place would be lost.'[49] Moreover, this agreement did not extend to jute or cotton—amongst the most important trading commodities for India and Pakistan—causing the Indian minister for industry and supply to complain that without these items within the purview of the agreement, it would be reduced to a 'façade of little value.'[50]

The deputy high commissioner in Dhaka urged that a better agreement for bilateral trade should be concluded soon, arguing, '[a] year ago, a suitable Trade Agreement could have been made for all goods without political considerations. Today, it is possible, but difficult. In another six months, to a year, Pakistan would attach political conditions to the resumption of trade. We have much to gain from a long-term arrangement'.[51] The secretary for food in the government of India also argued, in May 1950, that 'we shall need all we can get from Pakistan during the period the new agreement with Pakistan is likely to cover... to my mind, therefore import of grain from Pakistan is essential'.[52] By November 1950, almost a year into devaluation, the Economic Committee of the Cabinet in India held a meeting to ascertain just how much steel could be exported to Pakistan, and whether this quantity could be increased. The meeting was also attended by representatives from the Tata steel company. The meeting concluded by deciding that while it was not possible to meet the entirety of Pakistan's request for steel, for the time being, at least a partial supply from the steel industry could be sent across. [53]

The deadlock ensued in Indo–Pakistani trade for seventeen months, since it was feared that trading with Pakistan at the prevailing rate of exchange would disrupt India's economy. Eventually, however, in February 1951 a trade agreement was completed between India and Pakistan, according to which, exchange transaction would be permitted on the basis of the existing value of the Pakistani currency. The terms of the February 1951 trade agreement were, moreover, not to India's advantage in the post-devaluation financial context. India agreed to trade with Pakistan on the basis of the non-devalued Pakistani rupee; Rs. 100 Indian would be the equivalent of Rs. 69 Pakistani; such transactions could moreover be converted into sterling by the other country.[54] It was agreed that India would export coal, steel, pig iron, cement timber and textiles to Pakistan, and import from Pakistan jute, cotton, food grain, hides and skins.[55]

The trade agreement of February 1951was seen all over the world as a triumph of economic common sense over politics.[56] The agreement had been reached despite the differences in the value of currency after devaluation. Such an agreement was moreover also seen as a climb down on India's part since it had agreed to trade at the non-devalued rates. Many countries, including the Soviet Union, France, and Italy, sent in their congratulations to the Ministry of External Affairs for the conclusion of the treaty. But what many Indian files regarding trade talks acknowledged was that it was not possible at this stage to be intransigent over Pakistani demands for coal, cement, and steel; India's own jute and textile industries would suffer correspondingly. Furthermore, Pakistan's cooperation had to be secured if goods were to flow to Indian enclaves in East Pakistan, as well as to states such as Tripura, which could most easily be reached by crossing the border.

For the time being, however, India and Pakistan also entered into a series of rebate agreements with one another, allowing for the cross-border purchase of commodities at localised prices. The terms of these agreements were fractiously negotiated, but were, nonetheless, carried out. What they consistently upheld was the effort to make all bilateral trade an instrument to bolster the ability of both states to economically assert their rights as a whole.

Policies to wean off dependence on provisions from across the border were thus simultaneously adopted by both countries. While agreements on coal, jute iron and steel could not be avoided, both countries nonetheless also conducted in parallel the search for these supplies from other sources. For instance, after a bilateral trading agreement was signed in 1949, the economic committee of the cabinet issued a directive to the Ministry of Agriculture to 'devise plans for the expansion of production of cotton of the varieties imported from Pakistan, so as to make India independent of Pakistani cotton within a period of two years'.[57]

Both India and Pakistan were also now signatories of the General Agreement of Trade and Tariffs, and sent trade delegations at the second round of talks of the GATT in 1949. The object of these agreements was to reduce barriers for international trade, as a means of preventing further warfare between nations.[58] At these meetings, the Indian and Pakistani delegations raised the matter of the collection of excise duties. Pakistan argued that the terms of the MFN clause were being violated, because excise duty was still charged by India on the inflow of goods from Pakistan.[59] India's object of entering into a commodities agreement with Pakistan, as discussed at an inter-ministerial meeting, in May 1949, was to ask for an arrangement whereby the import and export controls for commodities flowing between India and Pakistan could be removed, given that both countries could specify the quantitative limits for allowing the flow of goods.[60] Yet, the fact that the contours of the discussion took the shape they did is significant for another reason: decisions on the controls over Indo–Pakistani trade, and whether certain rebates or tariffs need be abolished or not, were a way of ensuring that they were brought into the realm of international trade, and therefore regulated by the two governments.

Cross Border Trade

Bureaucrats of both states firmly went about insisting that all future economic exchanges between the two countries would have to take place along strictly formalised and legalised lines. In doing so, and in carrying out the process of negotiating on this issue, they were confronted with a curious problem: how to deal with a process in which cross-border activity and contact were going to carry on regardless. Bilateral negotiations on trade, therefore also had to accommodate pre-existing patterns of border trade into their agendas. But in defining the terms of this exercise, both states were also, in a sense, going about stamping their own existences onto a process that would have carried on regardless.

In many ways, the sets of policies made with regard to border trade were emblematic of the ways in which policies on bilateral trade were conducted: the fact of the trade, and all that it suggested was often politically inconvenient. It suggested that rather than relying on incomes that could be provided from within the nation state, people found it easier to rely on networks of trade that transcended the state in order to derive their livelihood. But the joint solutions that were fashioned out of these questions were also those that could favour the continuance of pre-partition patterns of economic exchange, rather than to attempt to remove them altogether, partly because it was not in either country's ability to be able to carry out successfully.

Bilateral trade treaties were usually divided into 'schedules' of goods, classified into goods that could be exported and imported within certain limits; goods that were exported and imported in any quantity, though taxes may be imposed on them on arrival; and a separate schedule of goods which were permitted under the heading of 'border trade'. Goods in the second schedule included fruit and vegetable, betel leaf, herbs, medicine, coir yarn, and mustard oil.[61] A large number of items in the second schedule were predominantly exchanged at the border—and the flows of these items indeed pre-dated the border. Items on the Open General License for import into India included 'fish—fresh and dried to be allowed into East Pakistan'. In return, the quota for trade of cattle into East Pakistan was to be fixed.[62]

The Indian Commerce Secretary H.V.R. Iyengar remarked to Pakistan's high commissioner on the 'serious difficulty in persuading the state governments that a trade agreement was of any value if it did not settle the problem of border trade.'[63] Border communities on both sides, particularly in the hill districts of Assam and Tripura, were dependent on supplies of fish, salt, kerosene, and a certain amount of food grains from the other side of the border.[64] In many ways, however, it was the government of Pakistan that had more to do with a completely open handed policy on border trade: valuable amounts of jute, a commodity whose prices were high and which would accrue valuable revenue to the coffers of its government, were liable to be smuggled through. Its stances on border trade, therefore, had to be drafted accordingly. Such uneasiness with the unavoidability yet undesirability of trade between India and Pakistan was manifested most clearly in the position of border trade: both governments acknowledged its necessity, and the fact that the partition and the boundary lines had disrupted a rich and self-contained ecosystem in Bengal, which had to be accommodated; yet, at the same time, conducting this trade had become a fractious, uneasy, and tense affair. Whatever the desires of either central government, it could not be stopped, so the question remained as to how to best regulate it.

For example, one issue was obtaining permission from Pakistan for the transportation of goods to other parts of India without circumnavigating the long border between India and East Pakistan. One bottleneck in the transport of goods into Tripura occurred in Akhaura—a railway station in East Pakistan, where goods headed for Tripura from the rest of India could most easily be off loaded—where they encountered East Pakistani customs barriers.[65] The Tripura Merchants Association made several representations to the government of India, as well as to the Ministry of External Affairs in particular to take this matter up at Indo–Pakistani forums. This was also mirrored by a similar set of policies along the eastern states in India: as J.N. Mandal had complained, India's policies with the 'economic strangulation' of East Bengal had cost the Hindu communities within that region heavily.

Both governments thus constructed an apparatus that could assert the existence of the state along the border: goods and services flowing between these areas had to reckon with the fact that two sovereign nations had come into being. At the same time however, cross-border trade was also accompanied consistently by what became the 'illegal' flow of goods across the border.[66] Trade along the border continued, whether sanctioned by the government or not, simply because it had done so for many years pre-dating partition. Indeed, between September 1948 and April 1950, when there was supposed to have been a complete deadlock in trade relations, it was reported that more than 300,000 bales of jute were smuggled into India from East Bengal.[67] A report from the Committee on Border Trade, compiled for the trade conference of 1953, concluded 'a certain amount of [illegal] trade continues to take place… By regularising it and properly defining its scope there was much less danger of smuggling and other evils than by driving it underground.'[68] Bilateral policy on economic relations could not merely be based on exercises of wishful thinking that simply and unilaterally declared an end to all pre-partition linkages of commerce and trade. They had to accommodate the necessity of a certain amount of co-dependency between the provinces on either side of the eastern boundary line. But they also placed a greater emphasis on the role of both states in regulating, controlling, or participating in the legal as well as illegal flows of commodities from across the border. The experience of partition encouraged both states therefore to conduct their trade relations in ways that recognized the imperatives of economic necessity, but made them part of a process that concerned the overall process of establishing the Indian and Pakistani state in relation to one another.

A later ambassador, Mohan Sinha Mehta, also found the question of border trade a difficult one, and blamed the break-down of trade talks in 1952 on petty interests and mutual suspicion. There was no reason, he pointed out, for the economies of India and Pakistan not to complement one another, particularly in border communities. Yet the Commerce Secretary, C.C. Desai, argued against this, claiming that 'he was at a loss to understand the approach of our High Commissioner'. Desai had argued that provisions for trade along the border were crucial to any success of a trade treaty between the two countries. This, he felt had to be incorporated into any treaty, although Mehta repeatedly found that this was difficult to push through. For Pakistan, the question of border trade was also vital due to the suspicion of illegal trading in jute, a commodity that fetched increasingly higher revenues from around the world. The trade treaties between India and Pakistan were revised annually, and when the two delegations met for discussion in February 1952, the talks broke down. The question of trade along the border provinces, however, proved to be the major stumbling block.[69]

The process of constructing the economic edifice of the states of India and Pakistan dealt a series of body blows to the patterns of pre-partition trade. It made sense for the two states arising out of a partition to declare that the economies that were crafted out of the process need not be dependent on each other, and that they were viable entities in their own right. A great deal of emphasis was placed on attempts to demonstrate that the Indian and Pakistani economies were not unduly reliant on commodities and labour flows from across the border. Yet, economic self-sufficiency, and independence from one another, while obviously a priority for both states, was palpably lacking, particularly in areas alongside the eastern boundary lines.

While governments of India and Pakistan certainly went about asserting the self-sufficiency of their economies, often, in the years that followed partition, the concrete policies they went about adopting contradicted such assertions. When necessity did demand it, various arrangements for commercial supplies could be negotiated by the bilateral machinery—which, in itself, was a significant achievement. But, as the official in Karachi had pointed out to Badrudin Tyabji, until the broader picture of India–Pakistan relations itself changed, placing any undue faith in the prospects of bilateral trade was also unwarranted. In the end, economics on its own could not solve the contradictions in the relationship—only political circumstances, borne out of two states that were fully confident in their self-sufficiency, could do that.

CONCLUSION

1950, then, was an interesting year: it had all the makings of the sets of causes that bring about both war and peace between India and Pakistan. Nehru and Liaquat Ali Khan had fulminated to their constituent assemblies over each other's duplicity over the refugee question; but they had also gone ahead with the shaping of a correspondence on the No War Pact. No 'permanent' solution—war, peace, or any of the intervening shades in between—was put into place, but a series of ad hoc, interim measures that could be countenanced by both states were devised in the meanwhile to patch things over. What was acknowledged on both sides was that the way to a lasting stability lay in finding answers that could lay the ghosts of partition to rest once and for all. And, to some extent at least, both governments made concerted efforts to bring this about.

At the time of writing, the state of India–Pakistan relations is bleak. Bilateral ties between India and Pakistan have been 'downgraded', owing to India's decision to revoke article 370 in Kashmir. How, then, are we to evaluate the contributions of the diplomatic infrastructure between India and Pakistan during the 1950s? In this book, as we saw, the bilateral machinery opened up interesting spaces for resolving problems in the aftermath of partition; as well as for enabling jointly sought after solutions to be implemented. At the very least, interactions between bureaucrats of India and Pakistan seemed to arrest the pace of the slide towards hostility; at their height—in exercises that are, perhaps of greater relevance today—they enabled a more proactive and integrated approach to seeking accommodative solutions to questions about a dense set of networks and loyalties that cut across the boundary line.

Indeed, the Bengal Pact would seem to offer several insights that are relevant today. At its heart, after all, the Nehru Liaquat agreement was a story of how bureaucrats from both states constructed a framework in which diverging and competing claims to multiple nationalities and allegiances that pre-dated the nation state could also be accommodated within a structure that both states put into place, as a means of further bolstering themselves in a jointly coordinated fashion. Obviously, there are many deeply structural differences between the positions of Bengal and that of Kashmir in the framework of the Indian and Pakistan union—which this present work does not claim to overlook. Yet the extent to which the comparison holds true is also the extent to which bilateral dialogue between India and Pakistan offers the potential for yielding dividends.

What also became clear is the deep seated necessity for the infrastructure of the relationship to stay in place at all: in many ways, the bilateral dialogue was the best instrument for defining the extent of the sovereignty and jurisdiction of both states. Such processes, moreover, tend to align with majoritarian leanings: the experiences of defining the basis of citizenship after partition, for instance, or navigating the maze of rules about evacuee property or even Tyabji's attempts to further the application of Fazalbhai for trade, also demonstrate the processes that the bilateral framework enabled did not necessarily favour the concerns of minority communities. But a bilateral dialogue, based on the agenda for finalising the partition—and therefore on the recognition of the basis of both states' existence—could also lead to outcomes that temper and accommodate these questions into a more fruitful result. A stronger diplomatic dialogue with Pakistan, moreover, also enabled the welfare of the minority populations of the subcontinent to become part of the government's agenda at a more structurally integrated level, than that of simply voicing optimistic intentions about the well-being of minorities.

Obviously, the story of India–Pakistan relations is also one of the process of state-finishing, and the consolidation of 'cartographically anxious' states.[1] Itty Abraham, for example demonstrates how India's emphasis on its territorial integrity also stems from an anxiety about the lack of any other unifying principle. In terms of language, or religion or ethnicity or even a fool-proof basis of claims to citizenship on the basis of being born on the same soil, the Indian union offers no unifying, cohesive principle for a diverse population. The anxiety about making the state territorially cohere, therefore, produces an unusual degree of emphasis on the integrity of its boundary lines—at the cost of its relations with its neighbours. South Asia is also witness to the development of states that are still chasing the nation. Of states, in other words, that are still varnishing the idea of the national community—who is to be in it, who is to be excluded, and which sets of people's historical imaginations are to be given the most salience to. Such questions continue to deeply affect how the terms of the bilateral relationship have been framed.

The gaps between reconciling these two ideals moreover—of shaping a 'strong state', territorially defined, and certain of the basis of the community it is in existence for, on the one hand, and the still incomplete process of determining who and what exactly is to be within these states on the other—is also in a sense responsible for the differences and inadequacies of the India–Pakistan relationship. Such debates were clearly in existence during the 1950s as well, and to a greater extent, and both states were able to address with a greater degree of circumspection and prudence. Yet, while it has also been argued that the decades prior to the 1965 war were easier on Indo–Pakistan relations, partly because of the continuance of cross border inter-personal contacts of an earlier generation, I would also argue that the differences between that decade and this also need to be viewed from the point of view of the declining power of the state as a whole: the 1950s in fact witnessed the height of the sense of possibility in the capacity of the state, and the capabilities, responsibilities, and accommodativeness of its institutions.

In a sense, however, the argument that the 1950s were a period of hectic cooperation and dialogue has a deeper significance: this generation, after all, had witnessed the very worst of the traumas that sub-continental politics could have thrown at them. The numbers of casualties arising out of the partition, and the ensuing ethnic genocide, quite easily dwarf the scale of violence seen in the more recent instances of violence between India and Pakistan. If, in these conditions, policy makers of India and Pakistan could conclude that the best remedy for the situation called for a series of detailed negotiations about how to put to rest the lingering questions arising out of the partition, because, in the long term, this would be in the interests of both states, then these arguments can also serve as a relevant guide to the maze of India–Pakistan relations today: their efforts were built on the principle of the acceptance of the irrevocability of partition, and the necessity of shaping two sovereign states in its wake.

APPENDIX I

Excerpted from A S Bhasin, (ed), India–Pakistan Relations, 1947–2007, A Documentary Study, Vol. IX, Sec XII, Public Diplomacy Division, Ministry of External Affairs, Geetika Publishers, New Delhi, 2012 'Agreement between Government of India and Government of Pakistan regarding treatment of Minorities', New Delhi, April 8 1950, p. 7310.

A. The Governments of India and Pakistan solemnly agree that each shall ensure, to the minorities throughout its territory, complete equality of citizenship, irrespective of religion, a full sense of security in respect of life, culture, property and personal honour, freedom of movement within each country and freedom of occupation, speech and worship, subject to law and morality. Members of the minorities shall have equal opportunity with members of the majority community to participate in the public life of their country, to hold political or other office, and to serve in their country's civil and armed forces. Both Governments declare these rights to be fundamental and undertake to enforce them effectively. The Prime Minister of India has drawn attention to the fact that these rights are guaranteed to all minorities in India by its Constitution. The Prime Minister of Pakistan has pointed out that similar provision exists in the Objectives Resolution adopted by the Constituent Assembly of Pakistan. It is the policy of both

Governments that the enjoyment of these democratic rights shall be assured to all their nationals without distinction.

Both Governments wish to emphasise that the allegiance and loyalty of the minorities is to the State of which they are citizens, and that it is to the Government of their own State that they should look for the redress of their grievances.

B. In respect of migrants from East Bengal, West Bengal, Assam and Tripura, where communal disturbances have recently occurred, it is agreed between the two Governments :

(i) That there shall be freedom of movement and protection in transit;

(ii) That there shall be freedom to remove as much of his moveable personal effects and household goods as migrant may wish to take with him. Moveable property shall include personal jewellery. The maximum cash allowed to each adult migrant will be Rs. 150 and to each migrant child Rs. 75;

(iii) That a migrant may deposit such of his personal jewellery or cash as he does not wish to take with him with a bank. A proper receipt shall be furnished to him by the bank for cash or jewellery thus deposited and facilities shall be provided, as and when required for their transfer to him, subject as regards cash to the exchange regulations of the Government concerned;

(iv) That there shall be no harassment by the Customs authorities. At each customs post agreed upon by the Governments concerned, liaison officers of the other Government shall be posted to ensure this in practice;

(v) Rights of ownership in or occupancy of the immoveable property of a migrant shall not be disturbed. If, during his absence, such property is occupied by another person, it shall be returned to him provided that he comes back by the 31st December, 1950. Where the migrant was a cultivating owner or tenant, the land shall be restored to him provided that he returns not later than the 31st December, 1950. In exceptional cases, if a Government considers that a migrant's immoveable property cannot be returned to him, the matter shall be referred to the appropriate Minority Commission for advice.

Where restoration of immoveable property to the migrant who returns within the specified period is found not possible, the Government concerned shall take steps to rehabilitate him.

(vi) That in the case of a migrant who decides not to return, ownership of all his immoveable property shall continue to vest in him and he shall have unrestricted right to dispose of it by sale, by exchange with an evacuee in the other country, or otherwise. A committee consisting of three representatives of minority and presided over by a representative of Government shall act as trustees of the owner. The Committee shall be empowered to recover rent for such immoveable property according to law.

The Governments of East Bengal, West Bengal, Assam and Tripura shall enact the necessary legislation to set up these Committees.

The Provincial or State Government, as the case may be, will instruct the District or other appropriate authority to give all possible assistance for the discharge of the Committee's functions.

The Provisions of this sub-paragraph shall also apply to migrants who may have left East Bengal for any part of India, or West Bengal, Assam or Tripura for any part of Pakistan, prior to the recent disturbances but after the 15th August, 1947. The arrangement in this sub-paragraph will apply also to migrants who have left Bihar for East Bengal owing to communal disturbances or fear thereof.

C. As regards the Province of East Bengal and each of the States of West Bengal, Assam and Tripura respectively the two Governments further agree that they shall :

(1) Continue their efforts to restore normal conditions and shall take suitable measures to prevent recurrence of disorder.

(2) Punish all those who are found guilty of offences against persons and property and of other criminal offences. In view of their deterrent effect, collective fines shall be imposed, where necessary. Special Courts will, where necessary, be appointed to ensure that wrong doers are promptly punished.

(3) Make every possible effort to recover looted property.

(4) Set up immediately an agency, with which representatives of the minority shall be associated, to assist in the recovery of abducted women.

(5) NOT recognise forced conversions. Any conversion effected during a period of communal disturbance shall be deemed to ***he*** forced conversion. Those found guilty of converting people forcibly shall be punished.

(6) Set up a Commission of Enquiry at once to enquire into and report on the causes and extent of the recent disturbances and to make recommendations with a view to preventing recrudescence of similar trouble in future. The personnel of the Commission, which shall be presided over by a Judge of the High Court, shall be such as to inspire confidence among the minority.

(7) Take prompt and effective steps to prevent the dissemination of news and mischievous opinion calculated to rouse communal passion by press or radio or by any individual or organisation. Those guilty of such activity shall be rigorously dealt with.

(8) Not permit propaganda in either country directed against the territorial integrity of the other or purporting to incite war between them and shall take prompt and effective action against any individual or organisation guilty of such propaganda.

D. Sub-paragraphs (1), (2), (3), (4), (5), (7) and (8) of C of the Agreement are of General scope and applicable according to exigency to any part of India or Pakistan.

E. In order to help restore confidence, so that refugees may return to their homes, the two Governments have decided

(i) to depute two Ministers, one from each Government, to remain in the affected areas for such period as may be necessary;

(ii) to include in the Cabinets of East Bengal, West Bengal and Assam a representative of the minority community. In Assam the minority community is already represented in the Cabinet. Appointments to the Cabinets of East Bengal and West Bengal shall be made immediately.

F. In order to assist in the implementation of this Agreement, the two Governments have decided, apart from the deputation of their

Ministers referred to in E, to set up Minority Commissions, one for East Bengal, one for West Bengal and one for Assam. These Commissions will be constituted and will have the functions described below:

(i) Each Commission will consist of one Minister of the Provincial or State Government concerned, who will be Chairman, and one representative each of the majority and minority communities from East Bengal, West Bengal and Assam, chosen by and from among their respective representatives in the Provincial or State Legislatures, as the case may be.

(ii) The two Ministers of the Governments of India and Pakistan may attend and participate in any meeting of any Commission. A Minority Commission or any two Minority Commissions jointly shall meet when so required by either Central Minister for the satisfactory implementation of this Agreement.

(iii) Each Commission shall appoint such staff as it deems necessary for the proper discharge of its functions and shall determine its own procedure.

(iv) Each Commission shall maintain contact with the minorities in Districts and small administrative headquarters through Minority Boards formed in accordance with the Inter-Dominion Agreement of December, 1948.

(v) The Minority Commissions in East Bengal and West Bengal shall replace the Provincial Minorities Boards set up under the Inter-Dominion Agreement of December, 1948.

(vi) The two Ministers of the Central Governments will from time to time consult such persons or organisations as they may consider necessary.

(vii) The functions of the Minority Commission shall be :

(a) to observe and to report on $he implementation of this Agreement and, for this purpose, to take cognizance of breaches or neglect;

(b) to advise an action to be taken on their reommendations.

(viii) Each Commission shall submit reports, as and when necessary, to the Provincial and State Governments concerned. Copies of such reports will be submitted simultaneously to the two Central Ministers during the period referred to in E.

(ix) The Governments of India and Pakistan and the State and Provincial Governments will normally give effect to recommendations that concern them when such recommendations are supported by both the Central Ministers. In the event of disagreement between the two Central Ministers, the matter shall be referred to the Prime Ministers of India and Pakistan who shall either resolve it themselves or determine the agency and procedure by which it will be resolved.

(x) In respect of Tripura, the two Central Ministers shall constitute a Commission and shall discharge the functions that are assigned under the Agreement to the Minority Commissions for East Bengal, West Bengal end Assam. Before the expiration of the period referred to in E, the two Central Ministers shall make recommendations for the establishment in Tripura of appropriate machinery to discharge the functions of the Minority Commissions envisaged in respect of East Bengal. West Bengal and Assam.

G. Except where modified by this Agreement, the Inter-Dominion Agreement of December, 1948 shall remain in force.

APPENDIX II

Republished in 'A S Bhasin, (ed), India–Pakistan Relations, 1947–2007, A Documentary Study, Public Diplomacy Division, Ministry of External Affairs, Geetika Publishers, New Delhi, 2012, Vol V, Sec II, 'Note by Prime Minister Jawaharlal Nehru to Secretary General of Ministry of External Affairs on the points raised by Pakistan in its Aide Memoire of 3rd January 1949, p. 4116.

The first thing is for both Governments to decide and declare that we rule out the resort to war in settling any differences, whatever they might be, and that we propose to settle them by peaceful methods. This statement is certainly rather vague. But in another sense it is definite enough and should go some way in reducing the tension, which unfortunately exists at present. In fact it will be easier to deal with the various problems when it is realized by all parties concerned that the only way of settlement is a peaceful one.

The Kashmir question,[1] as you have said, is in the hands of the United Nations and we can say nothing about it separately.

[1] The U.N.C.I.P., had on 28 August 1949, proposed that all points of difference between India and Pakistan with regard to the implementation of its Resolution should be submitted to arbitration. India rejected the proposal of arbitration because it amounted to placing the aggressor and the aggressed on an equal footing.

So far as we are concerned, there is no Junagadh case or any case in regard to other States. Not only can it not be reopened, but there is nothing to reopen.

As regards the dispute over canal waters[2] and evacuee property,[3] both of these should first be considered on the expert level by representatives of both parties. Where there is no agreement in the end, we are certainly prepared for a reference to a tribunal or to arbitration.

As regards the claim that Pakistan assets are being held back by India, so far as I know, there are many claims on our side that Pakistan is not paying what is our due. These matters should also be considered on the expert level first and then, if necessary, by reference to some impartial authority.

All these questions should not come in the way of the declaration. If the questions can be decided without the declaration, no need for the declaration arises. It is in order to ease the situation between the two countries and help in creating an atmosphere favourable to the settlement of disputes, that we have made our proposal. As soon as the declaration is made, we can discuss ways and means of settling outstanding disputes, as you have suggested.

---

[2] By the Inter-Dominion Agreement of 4 May 1948, India agreed to resume the supply of Indus waters to Pakistan and Pakistan agreed to develop in due course alternative resources for water supply.

[3] The Hindus and Sikhs who migrated from West Pakistan left behind 4,800,000 acres of agricultural land and housing property worth Rs. 5,000 crores. The Muslims who migrated from India left only 3,139,000 acres of land and houses worth Rs. 1000 crores. Negotiations with Pakistan on the repatriation of property and other assets left behind by refugees were deadlocked.

NOTES

INTRODUCTION

1. Fortnightly report from M.K. Kirpalani, Deputy High Commissioner for India in Lahore, 17 Sep. 1948, File No. 8-15/48-Pak I, NAI.
2. Akbar, M. J., *Blood Brothers:A Family Saga*, Roli Books, New Delhi, 2006.
3. Talbot, Ian (ed.), *The Deadly Embrace: Religion,Violence and Politics in India and Pakistan,* Oxford University Press, Karachi, 2007.
4. Talbot, Ian, *Pakistan: A Modern History*, St. Martin's Press, New York, 1998.
5. For a discussion of the chronology of India–Pakistan relations in this period, see, for example: Dasgupta, Jyoti Bhusan, *Indo-Pakistan Relations, 1947–1955,* Djambatan, 1960; Blinkenberg, Lars, *India–Pakistan: The History of Unsolved Conflicts,* Udenrigspolitisk Instituts,Odensk, 1999; Chaudhry, G. W., *Pakistan's Relations with India, 1947–1966*, Frederick A Praeger, New York, 1968.
6. Burke S. M. and Lawrence Ziring, *Pakistan's Foreign Policy: An Historical Analysis,* Oxford University Press, Karachi, 1990.
7. For some recent publications on this issue, see for instance, Christophe Jaffrelot, *The Pakistan Paradox, Instability and Resilience,* Oxford University Press, 2015; T.V. Paul, *The Warrior State, Pakistan in the Contemporary World*, OUP, New York 2014; Maya Tudor, *The Promise of Power: The Origins of Democracy in India and Autocracy in Pakistan,* Cambridge University Press, 2013.
8. 'Fortnightly political report of British High Commissioner in India, January 1950', File No. FO 371/84198, Public Records Office, London.

9. This is a growing field, aided by the recent opening of archives. Srinath Raghavan's *War and Peace in Modern India* provides the definitive account of the shaping of the strategic levers of war and peace by Nehru in the 1950s. See for instance, Bhagavan, M., *The Peace Makers: India and the Quest for One World*, Harper Collins, New Delhi 2012; Miller, Manjari C., *Wronged by Empire: Post Imperial Ideology and Foreign Policy in India and China,* Stanford University Press, 2013; Chaudhury, R., *Forged in* Crisis, Hurst & Co. London, 2013, and Andrew B. Kennedy, *The International Ambitions of Mao and Nehru: National Efficacy Beliefs and the Making of Foreign Policy*, CUP, Cambridge, 2012; Manu Bhagavan (ed.), *India and the Cold War*.
10. See also, for instance, on the tussle between Nehru and Patel on China: Dasgupta, C., 'Nehru, Patel and China', *Strategic Analysis,* Vol. 38, Issue 5, Sept. 2014.
11. Dubnov and Robson (eds), *Partitions, A Transnational History of Twentieth Century Territorial Separation,* Stanford University Press, 2019, p. 25.
12. Ganguly, S., *Deadly Impasse, Indo-Pakistani Relations at the Dawn of a New Century,* Cambridge University Press, 2016, p. 22.
13. Cohen, Stephen P., *The Idea of Pakistan*, Washington DC, 2004, p. 47.
14. Ibid, p. 46. See also for instance, Cohen, *Shooting for a Century: The India–Pakistan Conundrum,* Brookings Institution Press, Washington DC, 2013; Paul, T.V., *The Warrior State: Pakistan in the Contemporary World,* OUP, New York, 2014.
15. Thornton, Thomas Perry, 'Pakistan: Fifty Years of Insecurity', in Kux, D. et. al (eds), *India and Pakistan: The First Fifty Years,* Cambridge University Press, Cambridge, 1999.
16. See for example, Bose, S., 'To Partition or Not: A Comparative Perspective', *Ethnopolitics,* 10: 3–4, 2011; Downes, A., 'The Problem with Negotiated Settlements to Ethnic Civil Wars, *Security Studies,* Vol.. 13, Issue 4, 2004, Kaufman, CD, *When All Else Fails, Ethnic Population Transfers and Partitions in the Twentieth Century,* Quarterly Journal: International Security, vol. 23. no. 2. (Fall 1998): 120–56.
17. Frasier, T.G., 'Ireland and India', in Keith Jeffery (ed)., *An Irish Empire?: Aspects of Ireland and the British Empire*, Manchester University Press, Manchester, 1996, p. 92.
18. Khan, Y, *The Great Partition: The Making of India and Pakistan,* Yale University Press, New Haven, 2017, p. xxi.
19. Schaeffer, R., *Warpaths: The Politics of Partition*, Hill and Wang, New York, 1990, p. 5.
20. The Reminiscences of Sir Muhammad Zafrulla Khan, Interviews Conducted by Wayne Wilcox and Ainsley T Embree, Fazi-i-Umar

Press, Ohio, USA, p. 162 https://ia801300.us.archive.org/3/items/SirZafrullaKhanInterviews/Sir-Zafrulla-Khan-Interviews.pdf. Last accessed 21.09.2019.

21. See, for instance, Carole Fink, 'League of Nations and the Minorities Question', *World Affairs,* Vol. 157, No. 4, 1995.
22. Posen, B., 'The Security Dilemma and Ethnic Conflict', *Survival,* Vol. 35, No. 1, Spring 1993.
23. Blum, G., *Islands of Agreement: Managing Enduring Armed Rivalries,* Harvard University Press, Cambridge MA, 2007.

1. BILATERAL SOLUTIONS

1. Minutes of the First Meeting of Special Committee of the Cabinet held on 6 June 1947, *Partition Proceedings Vol IV,* pp. 5–13, Partition Secretariat, Govt. of India, National Archives of India, New Delhi (hereafter NAI).
2. Ibid.
3. Patel, H.M., *Rites of Passage: A Civil Servant Remembers*, Sucheta Mahajan (ed)., Rupa & Co., New Delhi, 2005, p. 185.
4. See also, for example, Ted Svensson, *Productions of Post-Colonial India and Pakistan: Meanings of Partition,* Routledge, Abingdon, 2013.
5. Gould, William, Taylor C. Sherman, and Sarah Ansari, 'The flux of the matter: loyalty, corruption and the everyday state in the post-partition government services of India and Pakistan', *Past and Present*, 219, 1 (2013): 237–79.
6. File No. 315 (1)-AD/ 47, EA& CR Dept., AD Branch, MEA Files, NAI.
7. Ibid.
8. Minutes of the 16th meeting of the Partition Council held on 6 August 1947; *Partition Proceedings,* Vol. IV, Partition Sect. Govt. of India, NAI, p. 425.
9. Document No. MB1/D14/12 Copy of a memorandum from the Partition Office, government of India, to members of the Partition Council, 12 August 1947, Mountbatten papers, University of Southampton.
10. Ibid.
11. Terms of Reference for Expert Committee No. 2, 'Assets and Liabilities', *Partition Proceedings, Vol. IV*, p. 30, Partition Secretariat, Govt. of India, NAI.
12. File No. 20 (18)-FSP/47, EA &CR Dept., FSP Branch, MEA File, NAI.
13. Document No. MB1/D11/1/2, Recommendations of the Steering Committee on an enclosed report by the External Affairs and Commonwealth Relations Department Sub-Committee, 5 July–27 July 1947, Mountbatten Papers, University of Southampton.

14. Dutt, Subimal, *With Nehru in the Foreign Office,* Calcutta, 1977.
15. See also Amit Das Gupta, *Serving India: A Political Biography of Subimal Dutt (1903–1992). India's Longest Serving Foreign Secretary.* New Delhi: Manohar Publishers & Distributors, 2017.
16. Document No. MB1/D5/5, Note about the setting up of the central Pakistan government in Karachi, 25 June 1947 by Liaquat Ali Khan to Partition Council, Mountbatten Papers, University of Southampton.
17. Ibid.
18. 'The Reminiscences of Sir Muhammad Zafarullah Khan', Interviews conducted by Professors Wayne Wilcox and Aislie T Embree for Columbia University, url: http://www.apnaorg.com/books/zafrullah-1/zafrullah.php?fldr=book, pp 168–73, last accessed 1 August 2012.
19. Ibid, p. 177.
20. See, for instance, Rakesh Ankit, *India in the Interregnum, Sept. 1946-Aug 1947*, OUP, 2018.
21. Reports from Chief of the General Staff of India to VCIGS, Jun–Jul 1947, File No. WO 216/669, Public Records Office, UK.
22. Ibid.
23. See also, for instance, Coombs, Catherine, Partition Narratives: Displaced Trauma and Culpability among British Civil Servants in 1940s Punjab, in Sherman, Taylor et al (eds), *From Subjects to Citizens: Society and the Everyday State in India and Pakistan, 1947–1970*, CUP, Delhi, 2014.
24. Marston. DM, The Indian Army, Partition, and the Punjab Boundary Force, 1945—1947, *War in History*, Volume 16 issue, Nov 2009.
25. J.S. Grewal, *Master Tara Singh in Indian History: Colonialism, Nationalism and the Politics of Sikh Identity*, OUP, New Delhi, 2017.
26. 'Minutes of the sixth meeting of the Joint Defence Council held at Government House, Lahore, 29 August 1947', Singh, Kirpal (ed.), *Selected Documents on Partition of Punjab-1947: India and Pakistan*, Delhi, 2006, p. 503.
27. 'Joint Statement of Pandit Jawaharlal Nehru and Liaquat Ali Khan', 4 Sep. 1947, in Singh, Kirpal (ed.), *Selected Documents on Partition of the Punjab,* p. 509.
28. Doc. No. MB1/D45/2, Agenda for a meeting of the Provisional Joint Defence Council from H.M. Patel, enclosing papers action to be taken in the event of disturbances in the boundary areas of the two dominions before and after partition, 28 Jul. 1947, Mountbatten Papers, University of Southampton.
29. See for instance, Marston, D., 'The Indian Army, Partition, and the Punjab Boundary Force, 1945–47', *War in History,* 16, 4 (November

2009); Jeffrey, Robin, 'The Punjab Boundary Force and the Problem of Order, August 1947', *Modern Asian Studies,* 8, 4 (1974).
30. Hamid, Shahid S., *Disastrous Twilight: A Personal Record of the Partition of India*, London, 1986.
31. Document No. MB1/D45/2, Agenda for a meeting of the Provisional Joint Defence Council from H.M. Patel, enclosing papers action to be taken in the event of disturbances in the boundary areas of the two dominions before and after partition, 28 Jul. 1947, Mountbatten Papers, University of Southampton.
32. Shahnawaz, J., *Father and Daughter: A Political Autobiography,* Ripon Press, Lahore, 1971, p. 231.
33. Dubnov, Arie M., and Laura Robson eds. *Partition: A Transnational History of Twentieth Century Territorialism,* Stanford University Press, 2019, Introduction.
34. See also, Kumar, R., The Troubled History of Partition, *Foreign Affairs,* January 1997.
35. Watenpaugh, K.D., 'The League of Nations' Rescue of Armenian Genocide Survivors and the Making of Modern Humanitarianism, 1920–1927', *American Historical Review* 115, 5 (2010): 1315–39.
36. Butalia, Urvashi, *The Other Side of Silence: Voices from the Partition of India*, London, 2000.
37. Virdee, P., 'Negotiating the Past: Journey through Muslim Women's Experience of Partition and Resettlement in Partition', *Cultural and Social History*, 6, 4 (2009): 467–84.
38. File No. 77-48/AP (Pak II), MEA File, NAI.
39. See also, Basu, A., *Mridula Sarabhai, Rebel with a Cause*, New Delhi, OUP, 1996.
40. See also Menon, Ritu, and K. Bhasin, *Borders and Boundaries: Women in India's Partition*, Rutgers University Press, New Jersey, 1998.
41. Gundevia, Y. D., *Outside the Archives,* Hyderabad, 1984, p. 38.
42. Ibid., Ch. 3.
43. File No. 77-48/AP (Pak II); AP Branch; MEA File, NAI.
44. File No. 77-48/AP (Pak II), MEA File, NAI.
45. Ibid.
46. Ibid.
47. Sri Prakasa, *Pakistan: Birth and Early Days,* Calcutta, 1965, p. 14.
48. 'Exodus of non-Muslims from East Bengal', File No. F.9-10/48- Pak I,MEA File, NAI.
49. Ibid.
50. Ibid.
51. Khaliquzzaman, C., *Pathway to Pakistan,* Lahore, 1961, p. 402.

52. Cited from Khaliquzzaman, C., *Pathway to Pakistan,* Lahore, 1961, p. 402.
53. Khaliquzzaman, C., *Pathway to Pakistan,* Lahore, 1961, p. 412.
54. Ibid, p. 410.
55. Kattan, V., 'Decolonizing the International Court of Justice: The Experiences of Judge Sir Muhammad Zafrulla Khan in the South West Africa Cases', *Asian Journal of International Law,* Sept. 2014, pp. 1-46.

2. THE NEHRU–LIAQUAT PACT

1. Ansari, S., *Life After partition: Migration, Community and Strife in Singh, 1947–1962,* OUP, 2005.
2. In Bengal, the politics of refugee rehabilitation had a long afterlife, manifested in various ways down to the present day. See for instance, Chatterji, J., *The Spoils of Partition: Bengal and India,* Cambridge University Press, 2007; Sen, Uditi, 'The Myths Refugees Live By: Memory and History in the Making of Bengali Refugee Identity', *Modern Asian Studies,* January 2014; Samaddar, Ranabir, *Refugees and the State: Practices of Asylum and Care in India*, New Delhi, 2003.
3. Zamindar, V., *The Long Partition and the Making of Modern South Asia: Refugees, Boundaries, Histories,* Columbia University Press, New York, 2007.
4. B.C. Roy to Nehru, 1 December 1949, in Das, Durga (ed.), *Sardar Patel's Correspondence, 1945–50,* Ahemdabad, 1974, Vol. IX, p. 37.
5. Minutes of Meeting on 22 October, 1948, 'Influx of Refugees from East Bengal', File No. F.9-10/48-Pak I, MEA, NAI.
6. Telegram, Gopalaswami Ayyangar to Nehru, 25 October 1948, File No. F.9-10/48-Pak I, MEA, NAI.
7. Ibid.
8. 'Proceedings of the inter-dominion Conference on 18th April 1948 at Writers Building, Calcutta'; File No. F. 8-15/48-Pak I; MEA, Pak I Branch; NAI.
9. Ibid.
10. Ibid.
11. Ibid.
12. Ibid.
13. 'Proceedings of the Inter-dominion Conference on 18th April 1948 at Writers Building, Calcutta'; File No. F. 8-15/48-Pak I; MEA, Pak I Branch; NAI.
14. Ibid.
15. 'Minutes of conference of representatives of two Dominions to be held on the 20 June 1948 regarding implantation of agreements at inter-dominion conference in April 1948', File No. F.8-2/48-Pak I, Min of EA, Pak I Branch, NAI.

16. 'Proceedings of the Inter-dominion conference on 18th April 1948 at Writers Building, Calcutta'; File No. F. 8-15/48-Pak I; MEA, Pak I Branch; NAI.
17. Telegram, 20 May 1950, File F. 23-4/50- Pak III, 'Protest from the Government of Pakistan against the enactment of the Immigrants (expulsion from Assam) Act, 1949; MEA Archives New Delhi.
18. 'Minutes of Meeting with Minister Without Portfolio, 18 July 1949', F.9-2/48-PakI (secret); Ministry of EA and CR wing, MEA File, NAI.
19. Ibid.
20. Ibid.
21. Ibid.
22. Press Note by Director of Publicity, Government of East Bengal, Dacca, 24 Dec. 1949; appendix to File F. 23-4/50- Pak III, 'Protest from the Government of Pakistan against the enactment of the Immigrants (expulsion from Assam) Act, 1949; MEA Archives New Delhi.
23. Ibid., p. 127.
24. Wright, T.P., 'Indian Muslim Refugees in the Politics of Punjab', *The Journal of Commonwealth and Comparative Politics*, XII, 2.
25. Joya Chatterji, *Spoils of Partition: Bengal and India, 1947–67*, Cambridge, 2007. See also Sen, U., *Citizen Refugee: Forging the Indian Nation after Partition*, CUP, 2018.
26. Raghavan, Srinath, *War and Peace in Modern India: A Strategic History of the Nehru Years*, Ranikhet, 2010.
27. Chatterji, J., *The Spoils of Partition*, Ch. 3.
28. P. Raghavan, 'Partition, An International History', *International History Review*, 2019.
29. Pederson, S., 'Back to the League of Nations', *The American Historical Review*, Vol. 112, No. 4, Oct. 2007.
30. Iqbal, 'Statement on the Report Recommending the Partition of Palestine, 27 July, 1937'; *Speeches and Statements of Iqbal*, Al Manar Academy Lahore, 1944, p. 295. See also Faisal Devji, *Muslim Zion, Pakistan as a Political Idea*, Cambridge, MA, 2013, Ch. 2.
31. Cited from D. N. Verma, *India and the League of Nations*, Bharti Bhavan Press, Patna, 1968.
32. Beni Prasad, *The Hindu Muslim Question*, Allahabad, 1940, p. 70, 'The Example of the Sudeten Germans'.
33. See, for instance, Fink, Carole, 'League of Nations and the Minorities Question', *World Affairs*, Vol. 157, No. 4, 1995; Pederson, S., 'Back to the League of Nations', *The American Historical Review*, Vol. 112, No. 4, Oct. 2007.

34. 'Text of Inter-dominion Agreement', File No. F.8-14/48-Pak I, Min of EA and CR, Pak I Branch, NAI.
35. Ibid.
36. Dutt, Subimal, *With Nehru in the Foreign Office,* Calcutta, 1977, p. 48.
37. 'Line of Approach for the Deputy High Commissioner at Dacca in dealing with the complaints from persons from minority community in East and West Bengal', File No. 23(44)-Pak III/50, MEA Archives.
38. Ibid.
39. Note by M. J. Desai, File No. PIII/53/66112/1-2, 'Indo-Pakistan Officials Conference at Calcutta regarding settlement of Eastern Zone Problems', MEA file, Pak III Branch, MEA Archives.
40. Copies of these complaints, and responses to them, are to be found in the Political Confidential Reports of the Home Department, National Archives Bhaban, Dhaka.
41. 'Exodus of non Muslims from East Bengal', File No. 9-10/48-Pak I, MEA, Pak I Branch, NAI.
42. 'Alleged communal incidents in Assam State', File No. L/52/6544/1, MEA, BL Branch, NAI.
43. Ibid.
44. Letter from High Commissioner of Pakistan to Ministry of External Affairs, 15 March 1950, File No. 12(21)-Pak III-50, Ministry of External Affairs, Pak III Branch, NAI.
45. Acharya to S. Dutt, 1 March, 1952, File No. L/52/6614/I, MEA, BL branch, NAI.
46. Ibid.
47. 'Fortnightly Reports from Deputy High Commissioner, Sept. 1948–January 1950', File No. 8-15/48-Pak I; MEA, Pak I Branch, NAI.
48. Minutes of conference of representatives of two Dominions to be held on the 20 June 1948 regarding implantation of agreements at inter-dominion conference in April 1948', File No. F.8-2/48-Pak I; MEA, Pak I Branch, NAI.
49. 'Non observance of the terms of the Calcutta Agreement by the Govt. of Pakistan', File No. 8/48-Pak I (Part II), MEA, Pak I Branch, NAI.
50. Ibid.
51. Letter from Pakistan High Commission to MEA New Delhi, 21 Feb. 1950; File No. 3(15)-BL/50, 'Communal Disturbances in Karimganj, Assam', MEA Archives, New Delhi.
52. Telegram from Liaquat Ali Khan to Nehru, 18 Feb. 1950, File No. 1-BL/50, 'Correspondence between the Prime Ministers of India and Pakistan', MEA Archives, New Delhi.
53. Ibid.

54. Text of Nehru Liaquat Agreement, 8 Apr. 1950, File No. 20(16)-R/C/50, Ministry of States, Rehabilitation Branch, NAI.
55. The full text of the Nehru–Liaquat Pact is available on the Government of India's MEA website: https://mea.gov.in/TreatyDetail.htm?1228, last accessed 9 May 2019.
56. Annexure to Nehru-Liaquat Pact, Press Note of Govt. of India, 16 Aug. 1950; File No. 20 (16)-R/C/50; Ministry of States, Rehabilitation Branch, NAI.
57. Address to the meeting of the Congress Working Committee, 11 November 1949,in Durga Das (ed.) *Sardar Patel Correspondence, 1945–1950*, Vol. 6.
58. 'Sardar Patel Appeals to the People of West Bengal to Give Indo-Pakistan Agreement a Fair Trial', in P.N. Chopra (ed.), *Collected Works of Sardar Vallabhai Patel*, Vol. 15, New Delhi, Konark Publishers Ltd. 1999.
59. Ibid.
60. 'Statement showing weekly arrival and departure of Hindus and Muslims from and to East Bengal and West Bengal from 13.2.1950', File No. 20 (16)-R/C/50; Ministry of States, Rehabilitation Branch, NAI.
61. 'A note on the implementation of the Indo Pakistan Agreement', File No. 20 (16)-R/C/50; Ministry of States, Rehabilitation Branch, NAI.
62. Ibid.
63. J.N. Mandal to Liaquat Ali Khan, 8 Oct. 1950, copy in Afzal, M. Rafique (ed.) *Speeches and Statements of Quaid-i-Millat Liaquat Ali Khan, 1941–1951*, Lahore, 1967.
64. Liaquat Ali Khan's statement in the Constituent Assembly of Pakistan, 14 Oct. 1950; in Afzal (ed.) *Speeches and Statements*.
65. Fortnightly Report of deputy high commissioner of India in Lahore, for 15–30 Apr. 1950, in File No. F10(11)Pak III/50, 'Implementation of Agreement on Evacuee Property' MEA Archives.
66. Note of S. Dutt on Meeting of the Information Consultative Committee in New Delhi on 6 May 1950, File No. 4(21) Pak/50 of 1950, MEA Archives.
67. Nehru's Note on Meeting with Editors, 7 May 1950, File No 4(21) Pak/50, MEA Archives.
68. *Dawn*, Editorial on 29 November 1950, Excerpted in File No. 23 (75)-Pak III/50, 'Joint Declaration by the governments of India and Pakistan', MEA Archives, New Delhi.

3. EVACUEE PROPERTY

1. Hosain, A., *Sunlight on a Broken Column,* Penguin Books, India, Gurgaon, 1988.

2. Zamindar, Vazira F. Y., *The Long Partition and the Making of Modern South Asia: Refugees, Boundaries, Histories,* New York, 2007.
3. Robinson, C. D., Too Much Nationality: Kashmiri Refugees, the South Asian Refugee Regime and a Refugee State, 1947–1974, *Journal of Refugee Studies,* Vol. 25, No. 3, August 2012.
4. Chatterji, J., 'From Subjecthood to Citizenship: Migrants and the Making of Nationality in South Asia, 1947–1955', *Historical Journal,* Vol. 55, No. 4 (Dec. 2012), pp. 1049–71.
5. Editorial, 12 May 1950, *Civil and Military Gazette,* in File No. F. 10 (55) Pak III/50; MEA Archives.
6. Kedar, Alexandre, 'Expanding Legal Geographies: A Call for a Critical Comparative Approach', in Kedar *et al* (eds), *The Expanding Spaces of Law: A Timely Legal Geography*, Columbia University Press, forthcoming.
7. Frank, M., 'Reconstructing the Nation State: Population Transfers in Central and Eastern Europe, 1944–1948', in Jessica Reisch and E. White (eds.), *The Disentanglement of Population: Migration, Expulsion and Displacement in Post-War Europe, 1944–49,* Palgrave Macmillan, Basingstoke, UK, 2011.
8. Schechtman, J. B., 'Evacuee Property in India and Pakistan', in Verinder Grover and R. Arora, *Fifty Years of India–Pakistan Relations: Partition of India, Vol. 1*, Deep Publications, New Delhi 1999.
9. Ibid, p. 32.
10. Ordinances promulgated by Governor General to Ensure Rehabilitation and Protection of Evacuee Property, Pakistan News, Issued from the Office of High Commissioner for Pakistan, London, File No. 12-20/49-Pak A, MEA File, NAI.
11. 'Press Note on Inter-dominion Conference on Urban Immovable Property, January 1949', File No. 11(4)- Pak III, NAI.
12. 'Minutes of the inter-dominion conference held in Lahore on 22nd July 1948', File No. F. 10 (55) Pak III/50; MEA Archives.
13. Agreed minutes, 'Secretariat Level meeting of Inter- Dominion Representatives', Dec.18-20 1947, Bhasin, A.S., (ed), *India–Pakistan Relations, 1947-2007, A Documentary Study,* Vol. IX, Geetika Publishers and Publicity Division, MEA.
14. Randhawa, M. S., *Out of the Ashes,* Patiala, 1978.
15. Ibid.
16. Fortnightly report of the High Commissioner for India in Pakistan for the period ending 30 June 1953, File No 45-R&I/53, Research and Information Branch, MEA File, NAI.
17. Ibid.
18. Schechtman, Joseph B., 'Evacuee Property in India and Pakistan', *Pacific Affairs,* Vol. 24, No. 4, December 1951.

19. Copy of telegram from Sardar Amir Azam to Mehr Chand Khanna, 9 March 1955, File No. PII/52/67237/201, MEA Archives.
20. Ibid.
21. I.H. Quereshi, Constituent Assembly of Pakistan debates, 6 April 1951.
22. 'Implementation of Karachi Agreement of January 1949', File No. 11(4)- Pak III, NAI.
23. I.H. Quereshi, Constituent Assembly of Pakistan debates, 6 April 1951; Constituent Assembly (Legislature) of Pakistan Debates, Official Report, Govt. of Pakistan Press, Karachi, p. 897.
24. Sucheta Kripalani to Constituent Assembly, 12 August 1949, *Constituent Assembly of India Debates (Proceedings), Vol. IX*.
25. 'Extract from note of Conversation between Prime Ministers of India and Pakistan, 26 and 27 April, 1950', File No. F. 10(55) Pak III/ 1950; MEA Archives.
26. Mehr Chand Khanna to Nehru, 12 January 1949, File No. 11(4)- Pak III, 'Implementation of Karachi Agreement of January 1949'; NAI.
27. Ilyas Chattha has shown, for example, how the government of West Punjab was ambivalent on its responsibility to rehabilitate refugees from 'non- agreed' areas, and had led to tensions with the Centre. The question led to the resignation of the Minister of Rehabilitation at the centre, Mian Iftikaruddin. See Chattha, Ilyas, *Partition and Locality: Violence, Migration and Development in Gujranwala and Sialkot, 1947–1961*, Karachi, 2011.
28. Telegram, 9 May 1950, G. Ayyangar to Khwaja Shahbuddin, File no. F. 10(55) Pak III/50; MEA Archives, New Delhi.
29. S. Dutt, File No. 10 (55) Pak III/50; MEA Archives.
30. Badruddin Tyabji on draft from Ministry of Relief and Rehabilitation, 7-2-1953; File No. PII/ 52/ 67820/201, Ministry of External Affairs Archives, New Delhi.
31. Ibid.
32. Editorial, 'Evacuee Property', *Economic and Political Weekly,* May 15 1954, Vol. VI, No. 20.
33. 'Implementation of Karachi Agreement of January 1949', File No. 11(4)- Pak III; NAI.
34. File No. 11(4)- Pak III, 'Implementation of Karachi Agreement of January 1949'; NAI.
35. Note from V. D. Dantyagi, Joint Secretary to GOI to Chief Secretaries of all Provinces, 3 November 1949, File No. D5111-R/49, Ministry of Relief and Rehabilitation File, NAI.
36. 'Inter-dominion Agreement on Evacuee Property: proposal to issue a Central Legislation covering all Agreed Areas', File No. 1(12)-G. (R),

Ministry of States, NAI; See also Jayal, Neerja Gopal, *Citizenship and its Discontents: An Indian History,* HUP, 2013; Introduction.

37. File No. 1(43)- H/49; Ministry of States, Hyderabad Branch, NAI.
38. N. C. Srivastava, Ministry of Rehabilitation to Y. K. Puri, Ministry of External Affairs; File No. PII/ 52/ 67820/201, Ministry of External Affairs Archives.
39. Letter to Y. L. Puri, Joint Secretary MEA from Ministry of Relief and Rehabilitation, 21 August, 1952, File No. PII/ 52/ 67820/201; MEA Archives.
40. Ibid.
41. Opening Address of Ajit Prasad Jain, Indian Minister for Rehabilitation, 17 Sep. 1952, File No. PII/ 52/ 67820/201; MEA Archives.
42. EBLA proceedings, 4th Session, 1949–1950; 30 November to 5 December, 1949; National Archives Bhabhan, Dhaka.
43. The East Bengal (Emergency) Requisition of Property Bill, 1948, East Bengal Legislative Assembly Proceedings, Official Report, Second Session, Vol. II, 7–15 June 1948, Proceedings on 9 June 1948, National Archives Bhabhan, Dhaka, p. 73.
44. Ibid, p. 74.
45. Gundevia, Y. D., *Outside the Archives,* Hyderabad, 1984.
46. 'Some Feelings about the Evacuee Problem', note by M. Sarabhai, File No. F. 10 (11) Pak III/50; Ministry of External Affairs, Pak III Branch, 1950, 'Evacuee Property-Agreement on Movable Evacuee Property-Implementation of'; MEA Archives, New Delhi.
47. Ibid.
48. Ibid.
49. V. D. Dantyagi, July 1949, File No. 10 (27)- Pak III/ 50; Ministry of External Affairs Archives, New Delhi.
50. Nehru's letter to chief ministers, 1 December 1949, *Selected Works of Jawaharlal Nehru*, Second Series, Vol. 14, Part 1, p. 369.
51. 'Administration of the Evacuee property Ordinance of East Punjab, Delhi etc'; File No. 1(7)-R, Ministry of Relief and Rehabilitation, 1949; NAI.
52. Fortnightly report of the Deputy High Commissioner for India in Dhaka, for the fortnight ending 15 August 1949, File No. D2576- Pak A/49, MEA File, NAI.
53. File No. D 798- G (R) 49; Ministry of Relief and Rehabilitation, 1949, NAI.
54. Note to State Governments, 14 January 1950, File No. 7-R(Sec), Min. of States File, NAI.
55. Note by Rehabilitation Ministry, 16 June 1949, File No. PII/52/67829/ 201 (Vol.1), MEA File, Pak II Section, MEAA.

56. Note by Min. of Rehabilitation, 10 April 1956, in ibid.
57. S. K. Bannerji to Chief Secretary, Govt. of Punjab (Pakistan), 'Properties Belonging to the Chamba and Tehri Garwal States in Lahore', 14 Jan. 1953, Ibid.
58. Note by N.C Ray, Maw Ministry, 4 Nov. 1949, Ibid.
59. Note by Y. K. Puri, 23 Aug. 1952, Ibid.
60. De, Rohit, 'Taming of the Custodian: Evacuee Property Law and Economic Life in the Indian Republic', in Gyan Prakash, Nikhil Menon, and Michael Laffan (eds), *The Postcolonial Moment in South and Southeast Asia*, London, Bloomsbury Academic, 2018.

4. NO WAR PACT: 'ALL MEN OF GOOD WILL'?

1. *Times of India,* Editorial on 30 November 1950, Excerpted in File No. 23 (75)- Pak III/ 50, 'Joint Declaration by the governments of India and Pakistan', MEA Archives, New Delhi.
2. *Correspondence which has taken place between the Prime Ministers of India and Pakistan on the subject of No War Declaration,* New Delhi, Ministry of External Affairs, 1950.
3. Ibid.
4. For a detailed account of these developments, see also: Raghavan, Srinath, *War and Peace in Modern India: A Strategic History of the Nehru Years,* Ranikhet, 2010.
5. Nehru to C Rajagopalachari, 19 March 1950, *Selected Works of Jawaharlal Nehru, Second Series*, 14, pt I: p. 126.
6. Speech to Constituent Assembly, February 1950; *Selected Works of Jawaharlal Nehru, Second Series*, Vol. 14, part 1, p. 35.
7. Telegram from UK High Commissioner in India to Commonwealth Relations Office, 28 March 1950, File No. FO 371/84253, 'India–Pakistan Relations', PRO.
8. Telegram from Liaquat Ali Khan to Attlee, March 10, File No. FO 371/84253, 'India–Pakistan Relations', PRO.
9. 'Proposed Joint Declaration by Governments of India and Pakistan re: Method of Settlement of all Matters in Depute between the two Countries', File No. 31/54/NGO, MEA Archives, New Delhi.
10. Ibid.
11. File No. 23 (75)- Pak III/ 50, 'Joint Declaration by the governments of India and Pakistan', MEA File, MEA archives.
12. For perspectives from the government of Pakistan relating to the No War Pact, I have worked mainly from sections of their correspondence enclosed within the files of the MEA, kept both in the National Archives of India, as well as in the MEA Archives. I have also consulted 'White

Paper' publications of the government of Pakistan during this decade, published memoirs of officials serving in Pakistan's Foreign Ministry during this time, as well as files containing their letters and telegrams in the Public Record Office in London.

13. SWJN, SS, Vol 14, Part 1, p.1.
14. File No. 23 (75)- Pak III/ 50, 'Joint Declaration by the governments of India and Pakistan', MEA File, MEA archives.
15. Ibid.
16. Ibid.
17. Note by S. Dutt, 12 Dec.49, 'Proposed Joint Declaration by Government of India to Pakistan re: methods of settlement of all matters in dispute between the two countries', F.23 (3) Pak III/50; 31/54/NGO, MEA file.
18. Ibid.
19. Text of Briand Kellogg Pact, https://avalon.law.yale.edu/20th_century/kbpact.asp.
20. Note by G. S. Bajpai, dated 18 Feb. 1950, File No. 31/54/NGO, 'Proposed Joint Declaration by Governments of India and Pakistan re: Method of Settlement of all Matters in Depute between the two Countries', MEA Archives, New Delhi.
21. Letter from Patel to Nehru, 25 Feb. 1950, Ibid.
22. Sardar Patel to Nehru, 25 February 1950, File No. 31/54/NGO, 'Proposed Joint Declaration by Governments of India and Pakistan re: Method of Settlement of all Matters in Depute between the two Countries', MEA Archives, New Delhi.
23. Ibid.
24. To S. Gopal, for instance, 'Nehru's sustained endeavour in the face of discouragement to control the development of nuclear weapons, his courageous and outspoken resistance to United States policy and his achievement in holding together the South Asian governments on Indo- China ensured for him a commanding stature in world politics.' Gopal, S., *Jawaharlal Nehru: A Biography*, Vol. II, 1947–1956, OUP, New Delhi, 1979, p. 192. See also, for instance, McGarr, Paul M., 'India's Rasputin?: V. K. Krishna Menon and Anglo American Misperceptions of Indian Foreign Policymaking, 1947–1964', *Diplomacy and Statecraft*, 22:2, 2011, pp. 239–60. McGarr usefully illustrates how, regardless of Krishna Menon's many, and widely known, failings, he was consistently promoted by Nehru, in part, due to his search for allies within the cabinet. See also Brown, J.M., *Nehru: A Political Life*, Yale University Press, 2003.
25. *Selected Works of Jawaharlal Nehru, Second Series*, Part II, Vol 14, p. 48.

26. Telegram from U. K. High Commissioner in India to Commonwealth Relations Office, 28 March 1950, File No. FO 371/84253, 'India–Pakistan Relations', PRO.
27. Ibid.
28. Ibid.
29. Memorandum by Gordon Walker, May, 1950, 'Note of Meeting with Pakistan Prime Minister', File Number FO 371/84198, PRO.
30. For a copy of the Government of Pakistans's position on the No War Pact, see, A S Bhasin, *India–Pakistan Relations, A Documentary Study: 1947–2009*, Aide Memoire of the Government of Pakistan reacting to the proposal for a No War Declaration, Karachi, December 1949, p. 4114.
31. *Times of India,* 30 November 1950.
32. *White Paper on No War Correspondence*, Ministry of External Affairs, New Delhi, 1950
33. Speech in Parliament, 28 Nov. 1950; *Jawaharlal Nehru's Speeches*, Vol. 2; Publications Division, GOI.
34. File No. 31/54/NGO, 'Proposed Joint Declaration by Governments of India and Pakistan re: Method of Settlement of all Matters in Depute between the two Countries', Ministry of External Affairs Archives, New Delhi.
35. *White Paper on No War Correspondence*, Ministry of External Affairs, New Delhi, 1950; *No War Declaration and Canal Water Dispute: Correspondence between the Prime Ministers of India and Pakistan, 18 January–24 November,* Karachi, Govt. of Pakistan, 1950.
36. Ibid.
37. Letter from Nehru to Liaquat Ali Khan, File No. 31/54/NGO, 'Proposed Joint Declaration by Governments of India and Pakistan re: Method of Settlement of all Matters in Depute between the two Countries', MEA Archives, New Delhi.
38. Telegram dated 21st November, 1950, Ibid.
39. Makieg, Douglas C, 'War, No War, and the India–Pakistan Negotiating Process', *Pacific Affairs,* Vol. 60, No. 2, pp. 271–94.
40. *Dawn*, Editorial, September 1950, Excerpted in File No. 23 (75)- Pak III/ 50, 'Joint Declaration by the governments of India and Pakistan', MEA File, MEA archives.
41. Amin, S. M, *Pakistan's Foreign Policy: A Reappraisal*, OUP, Karachi, 2000, p. 119.
42. Ibid.
43. J. Nehru Speech in Parliament on 7 December 1949 on the role of Realism and Idealism in Foreign Policy; cited from Appadorai, A. (ed.), *Documents on India's Foreign Policy. 1947–1972,* New Delhi, 1982.

5. INDUS WATERS

1. See also Daniel Haines, *Rivers Divided, Indus Basin Waters in the Making of India and Pakistan,* London & New York, 2017.
2. ND Gulhati to SK Banerji, 13 Feb.51, 6(1)-Pak III/51, Pak III Branch, Ministry of External Affairs, MEA Archives.
3. 'The Reminiscences of Sir Muhammad Zafrullah Khan', Interviews conducted by Professors Wayne Wilcox and Aislie T Embree for Columbia University, url: http://www.apnaorg.com/books/zafrullah-1/zafrullah.php?fldr=book, last seen 31 August 2012.
4. *Emergence of Pakistan*, p. 321.
5. Nehru to Gopichand Bhargava, 28 April 1948, *Selected Works of Jawaharlal Nehru, Second Series,* Vol. 6, p. 61.
6. Ibid.
7. N.D. Gulhati, *Indus Waters Treaty, An exercise in International Mediation*, Bombay, 1973.
8. J. Nehru, 'Temples of the New Age', speech at Bhakra dam site, 8 July, 1954, Cited in Michel, A. A. *The Indus Rivers: a Study of the Effects of Partition,* Yale University Press, New Haven and London, 1967.
9. Ibid, p. 151.
10. Note from Min. of Natural Resources and Scientific Research, File No. 6(1)—Pak III/51, 'Canal Waters Dispute', p. 50.
11. Excerpted in File PIII/54/2821/2-Vol. V—"Canal Waters—Anti India propaganda in Pakistan and abroad and counter measures adopted by India', p. 20.
12. Ibid.
13. C.M. Trivedi to Nehru, 2 September 1950, *Sardar Patel's Correspondence, 1945–1950*, Vol 10, Ch. 15, p. 427.
14. Ibid.
15. Nehru's Record of an Interview with Ghulam Muhammad, 3 May 1948, *Selected Works of Jawaharlal Nehru, Second Series*, Vol. 6, p. 61.
16. Ibid.
17. File No. 6- Pak III/51, 'Canal Water Charges, Payment by Pakistan to India', MEA Archives, New Delhi.
18. Ibid.
19. Ibid.
20. Ibid.
21. Canal Waters Charges, Payment by Pakistan to India, File 6—Pak III/51, 22 June 1951, Letter from Pakistan High Commissioner.
22. File No. 23(106) Pak III/50, 'Inter-dominion Agreement on the Canal Waters Dispute between East and West Punjab', MEA Archives, New Delhi.

23. Ibid.
24. File No. 23 (106) Pak III/50 (Secret), 'Inter- Dominion Agreement on the Canal Waters Dispute—Question whether the Agreement should be registered with the UNO Secretariat', MEA, Pak III Branch, p. 15.
25. Ibid.
26. File No. 23 (106) Pak III/50 (Secret), 'Inter-Dominion Agreement on the Canal Waters Dispute—Question whether the Agreement should be registered with the UNO Secretariat', Min of EA, Pak III Branch, p. 15.
27. File No. 23 (106) Pak III/50 (Secret), 'Inter- Dominion Agreement on the Canal Waters Dispute—Question whether the Agreement should be registered with the UNO Secretariat', Min of EA, Pak III Branch, p.6, Note by Gopalaswami Ayyangar.
28. Statement of R. S. Chattrari, Representative to the United Nations, Government of Pakistan, 10 May 1950, File No. 23 (106) Pak III/50 (Secret), 'Inter-Dominion Agreement on the Canal Waters Dispute, p. 154.
29. Rietzler, Katharina, 'Counter-Imperial Orientalism: Friedrich Berber and the politics of international law in Germany and India, 1920s–1960s', *Journal of Global History*, 11, 1 (2016). pp. 113–34.
30. Reply to Dr. Berber's Query from the partition Secretariat, Note by BS Bhatnagar, 18 Sep. 1951, File 6/1—Pak III/51, Canal Waters Dispute, India–Pakistan, MEA Archives.
31. Note by Subimal Dutt on Berber's Query, File 6/1—Pak III/51, Canal Waters Dispute, India–Pakistan, MEA Archives.
32. Note from Pakistan Ministry of Foreign Affairs to High Commissioner for India in Pakistan. Karachi, November 23, 1949; Bhasin, Vol. VII, p. 5650.
33. Note by Prime Minister J. Nehru on the Canal Water dispute with Pakistan, 28 Sep. 1949, A.S. Bhasin (ed.), *India–Pakistan Relations, A Documentary Study,* Public Diplomacy Division, Ministry of External Affairs, Geetika Publishers, New Delhi, Vol VII, p. 5643.
34. Statement on River Waters handed over to India by Pakistan, 21 July, 1948, A.S. Bhasin (ed.), *India–Pakistan Relations, A Documentary Study,* Public Diplomacy Division, Ministry of External Affairs, Geetika Publishers, New Delhi, Vol VII, p. 5615.
35. Ali, Chaudhry Muhammad, *Emergence of Pakistan*, p. 324. The Thal project was also commenced, which also provided employment and opportunities for settlement for refugees in West Punjab.
36. Nehru to Liaquat Ali Khan, 18 May 1948, *Selected Works of Jawaharlal Nehru, Second Series*, Vol. 6, p. 66.

37. Letter from Prime Minister Jawaharlal Nehru to Minister of Irrigation and Power Gulzarilal Nanda, New Delhi, 23 March 1953, *India–Pakistan Relations, A Documentary Study,* Public Diplomacy Division, Ministry of External Affairs, Geetika Publishers, New Delhi, Vol VII, p. 5743.
38. Ibid.
39. Ibid., p. 5744.
40. Haines, D., *Rivers Divided, Indus Basin Waters and the Making of India and Pakistan,* New York, Oxford University Press, 2017.
41. Khan, Muhammad Ayub, *Friends, Not Masters: A Political Autobiography*, London 1967.
42. Mehta, J., 'The Indus Water Treaty: A Case Study in the Resolution of an International River Basin Conflict', *Natural Resources Forum*, Vol. 12, No 1, Feb. 1988.
43. Ibid.
44. Undala Z. Alam, Water Rationality: Mediating the Indus Waters Treaty, unpublished PhD Dissertation, University of Durham, 1998.

6. SHAPING INTERNATIONAL PERSONALITIES

1. Halberstam, D., *The Fifties*, Villard Books, Random House, 1993, p. xi.
2. Mansergh, N., *Survey of British Commonwealth Affairs: Problems of Wartime Cooperation and Post War Change, 1939–1952*, Oxford University Press, Oxford, 1958.
3. See, for instance, Louis, Wm. Roger, *The British Empire and the Middle East, 1945–1951: Arab Nationalism, the United States and Post War Imperialism*, OUP, Oxford and New York 1984.
4. Note on India's position on Commonwealth membership, from J. Nehru to Krishna Menon, 2 Dec. 1948, N. G. Gopalaswami Ayyangar papers, Sub. File No. 24, Teen Murti Archives.
5. McGarr, P., *The Cold War in South Asia, Britain. The United States and the Indian Subcontinent*, CUP, 2013; Anita Inder Singh, *The Limits of British Influence, South Asia and the Angle American Relationship, 1947–56*, Bloomsbury, London, 1990.
6. Speech at the East and West Association, New York, October 1949.
7. Ibid.
8. Dean Acheson to Truman, Nov. 1949, Papers of H.S. Truman, Official File, OF-48-H, Box 298.
9. Haqqani, H., *Magnificent Delusions: Pakistan, the United States and an Epic History of Misunderstanding,* HUP, 2014, p. 49.
10. Ibid, p. 50.
11. Ibid.

12. See for instance, Brobst, P.J., *The Future of the Great Game: Sir Olaf Caroe, India's Independence, and the Defence of Asia*, University of Akron Press, 2005.
13. Cited in Brobst, P.J., *The Future of the Great Game*.
14. See also Rudolph, Lloyd I., and Susanne Rudolph, 'The Making of US Foreign Policy for South Asia: Offshore Balancing in Historical Perspective', *Economic and Political Weekly*, 25 Feb. 2006.

    For more recent discussions about the making of the US relationships with India and Pakistan, see, for instance Chaudhuri, R., *Forged in Crisis: India and the United States since 1947*, London, 2013; Haqqani, H., *Magnificent Delusions: Pakistan, The United States and an Epic History of Misunderstanding*, New York, 2013; McMahon, R. J., *The Cold War and the Periphery: The United States, India, and Pakistan,* New York, 1996; Kux, Dennis, *Disenchanted Allies: Pakistan and the United States*, 2001.
15. Bowles to Allen, July 15, 1952, Chester Bowles' Correspondence, Psychological Strategy Board Files, 1951–1953, Truman Archives.
16. Bowles to Averill Harriman, Sept. 1952, Box 1426, OF 426, Official File, Papers of H.S. Truman, Truman Archives.
17. Report for the National Security Council: 'Trade between Pakistan and the Soviet Bloc, September 1951', National Security Council Files, Box 6., Truman Archives, Missouri, USA.
18. Ibid.
19. Ibid.
20. Ibid.
21. Bowles to Avril Harriman, Sept. 1952, File No. OF 426, Box. 1426, Truman Archives.
22. Truman, Address to US Congress, Feb. 1952.
23. Chester Bowles to Truman, September 20, 1952, Official File No. 426, 'Aid to India', Truman Archives.
24. See also, for instance, Paul McGarr, *The Cold War in South Asia, Britain. The United States and the Indian Subcontinent*, CUP, 2013, Ch. 1.
25. Geselbracht, Raymond H., (ed), *Foreign Aid and the Legacy of Harry S Truman,* p. 206.
26. Point IV General Agreement for the Technical Cooperation between India and the Unites States of America, signed December 1950, Appadorai A., *Select Document on India's Foreign Policy and Relations,* Vol. 2, OUP, New Delhi, 1985.
27. Background memoranda of Visit to the United States of Liaquat Ali Khan, May 1950, Pt. VII, 'United States-Pakistan Relations', Presidents Secretary Files, Truman Archives, Box. 141.
28. Town Hall Speech, Liaquat Ali Khan, 8 May, 1950, Pakistan: Heart of Asia.

29. South Asia Regional Conference of United States Diplomatic and Consular Officers, Ceylon, March 1951, George McGhee Papers, Box 2, Truman Library and Archives.
30. Ibid.
31. Ibid.
32. Background Memoranda on Visit to the United States of Jawaharlal Nehru, October 1949, President's Secretary Files, Foreign Affairs No. 158, Truman Archives.
33. Ibid.
34. Westad, O.A., 'Rethinking Revolutions: The Cold War in the Third World', *Journal of Peace Research,* Vol. 29, No., 4, (Nov. 1992); See also Westad, O.A., *The Global Cold War: Third World Interventions and the Making of Our Times,* Cambridge University Press, Cambridge, 2007.
35. Zaidi, ZH. (eds). *Jinnah Papers*, First Series, Vol. VII, Quaid-i-Azam papers Project, Islamabad, 2002; Ali Muhammad Khan to Jinnah, 16 Jan. 1948. p. 41.
36. Hasan, K Sarwar, *Pakistan and the United Nations*, p. 217.
37. Tinker, H., *The Banyan Tree: Overseas Emigrants from India, Pakistan and Bangladesh*, OUP, 1977, p. 29.
38. Mazower, M., *Dark Continent: Europe's Twentieth Century,* London 1998.
39. See, for instance Jessica Reinisch and E. White (eds), *The Disentanglements of Populations: Migration, Expulsion and Displacement in Post War Europe, 1944–1949*, Palgrave Macmillan, Basingstoke, 2011.
40. See also, for instance Frank, M., 'Reconstructing the Nation State: Population Transfers in Central and Eastern Europe, 1944–1948', in Jessica Reisch and E. White (eds), *The Disentanglement of Population: Migration, Expulsion and Displacement in Post-War Europe, 1944–49,* Palgrave Macmillan, Basingstoke, UK, 2011.
41. Mazower, M., *Dark Continent: Europe's Twentieth Century*, Knopf, New York, 1998, p. 214.
42. Cited from Oberoi, P., *Exile and Belonging: Refugees and State Policy in South Asia*, OUP, New Delhi, 2006; Minutes of UN, Fifth Session, Ad Hoc Political Committee, 4 December 1950, para 26, UN Archives.
43. Oberoi, P., South Asia and the Creation of the International Refugee Regime', *Refuge*, Vol. 19, No. 5 (2001).
44. Ibid.
45. Mazower, M., *Dark Continent: Europe's Twentieth Century*, Knopf, New York, 1998, p. 214.
46. McNay, John T. (ed.), *The Memoirs of Ambassador Henry F Grady, From the Great War to the Cold War*, University of Missourie Press, 2009.

47. Cited from Hasan, K., Sarwar, *Pakistan and the United Nations* Prepared for the Pakistan Institute of International Affairs and Carnegie Endowment; Manhattan Publishing Company, New York, 1960. p. 170 (Zafrullah Khan to UN Ad Hoc Committee on the Palestinian Question, 13 Oct. 1947).
48. Speech by Zafarullah Khan, On the UN vote for Palestine; cited in Hasan, K., Sarwar, *Pakistan and the United Nations*, Prepared for the Pakistan Institute of International Affairs and Carnegie Endowment; Manhattan Publishing Company, New York, 1960.
49. Kumaraswamy, P. R., *India's Israel Policy*, Columbia University Press, New York, 2010.
50. Ispahani to Jinnah, May 19, 1948, Z. H. Zaidi (ed.), *MA Jinnah–Ispanahi Correspondence, 1936–1948,* Forward Publications Trust, Karachi, p. 596.
51. Cited from T.G. Fraser, 'Ireland and India', Keith Jeffrey (ed.), *An Irish Empire?: Aspects of Ireland and the British Empire*.
52. See, for instance, Kelly, Stephen. (2011). 'A Policy of Futility: Eamon de Valera's Anti-Partition Campaign, 1948–1951', *Études irlandaises*, doi:10.4000/etudesirlandaises.2348.

7. TRADE AND FINANCIAL RELATIONS BETWEEN INDIA AND PAKISTAN

1. Memorandum from Mr. MAH Fazalbhai, Indo Pakistan Relations–Commercial and Finance, File. No. PII/53/67819/1-2; MEA Archives.
2. Ibid.
3. Ibid.
4. Ibid.
5. See, for instance, Nisha Taneja and Sanjib Pohit (ed), *India Pakistan Trade, Strengthening Economic Relations,* Springer India, 2015.
6. Hirschman, Albert O., *National Power and the Structure of Foreign Trade*, University of California Press, 1945.
7. See, for instance, Kudaisya, M. 'A Mighty Adventure: Institutionalising the Idea of Planning in Post Colonial India, 1947–60'. *Modern Asian Studies* (2009).
8. Frankel, Francine R, *India's Political Economy, 1947–1977; The Gradual Revolution*, Princeton University Press, 1978.
9. Industrial Development was a provincial subject under the Government of India Act 1935.
10. Annual Economic Report for the year 1950- 51from the India Government Trade Commissioner in Karachi, Pakistan, File No. 2-30/51- Pak- I; MEA File; MEA Archives, New Delhi.

11. Annual Economic Report for the year 1950–51 from the India Government Trade Commissioner in Karachi, Pakistan; File No. 2-30/51- Pak- I; MEA File, MEA Archives, New Delhi.
12. Talbot, Ian, 'A Tale of two Cities: The Aftermath of Partition for Lahore and Amritsar, 1947–1957', *Modern Asian Studies,* 41, 1 (2007).
13. Ibid.
14. Extracts from Pakistan's Aide Memoire, dated 13 December, 1947, Annexure to White Paper on Indo–Pakistani Trade Relations, in *Indo Pak Relations: A Documentary Study*.
15. Mr Bhootalingam's note, dated February 1948. File No. 15(27) ECC/49; Economic Committee of the Cabinet, Cabinet Secretariat Files, National Archives of India.
16. White Paper on Indo- Pakistan Trade Relations (15August 1947–31 December 1949); Government of India; in Sreedhar and Kaniyalil, J (ed.) *Indo-Pak Relations: A Documentary Study*; New Delhi 1993.
17. Mr Bhootalingam's note, dated February 1948. File No. 15(27) ECC/49;Economic Committee of the Cabinet, Cabinet Secretariat Files, National Archives of India.
18. Note of conversation between Secretary of State for Commonwealth Relations, Nehru and Ghulam Muhammad at Columbo Conference, File No. 142/ 201, 'Pakistan Decision not to Devalue Rupee'; PRO.
19. 'Summary for the Economic Committee of the Cabinet', September 1949, File No. 15(27) ECC/49; Cabinet Secretariat File, NAI.
20. Note by Sardar Patel, 3 February 1948; File No 94/CF/47, Part II; Cabinet Secretariat File, NAI.
21. Schenk, Catherine R., *Britain and the Sterling Area: From Devaluation to convertibility in the 1950s,* London, Routledge, 1994.
22. Ganguli, B.N., 'Devaluation of the Rupee: What it means to India'; *Occasional Papers of the Delhi School of Economics.*
23. Deshmukh, C. D., *Economic Developments in India: 1947–1956: A Personal Retrospect*, Bombay, 1957.
24. Nehru's broadcast to the nation, All India Radio, 20 September 1949, SWJN, SS, Vol. 13, p. 41.
25. 'Pakistan at Par', in *The Economist*, 15 November 1949, excerpted in File no. 142/183, 'Repercussions of Pakistan's decision not to Devalue Rupee', PRO.
26. Jalal, Ayesha, *The State of Martial Rule: The Origins of Pakistan's Political Economy of Defence,* Cambridge University Press, 1990.
27. UK high commissioner to Commonwealth Relations Office, Report from 19 January to 2 February 1950; File No. DO 142/183, 'Repercussions of Pakistan's decision not to Devalue Rupee', PRO.

28. Note by C.C. Desai, November 1949, File No. 15 (116)- P/49; Economic Committee of the Cabinet, Cabinet Secretariat File, NAI.
29. 'Indo Pakistan trade', File No. 3(IV)- ECC/50; Economic Committee of the Cabinet, Cabinet Secretariat File, NAI.
30. 'India–Pakistan Trade', Economic Committee of the Cabinet, File No. 3(IV) – ECC / 50; Cabinet Secretariat File, NAI.
31. Ibid.
32. Letter from Indian government trade commissioner, Karachi, May 1949 to C.C. Desai, Commerce Secretary; File number File No. 15(27) ECC/49; Cabinet Secretariat File, NAI.
33. File No. 15(27) ECC/49; Cabinet Secretariat File, 1949, National Archives of India.
34. Annual Economic Report for the year 1950–1951, from the India government trade commissioner in Pakistan, Karachi; File No. 2-30/51-Pak-I, MEA File, MEA Archives, New Delhi.
35. 'Indo-Pakistan Trade Talks and Agreement', File No. PII/52/2316/2; MEA File, MEA Archives.
36. Telegram from UK high commissioner to Commonwealth Relations Office, 7 February 1950, File No. DO 142/183, 'Repercussions of Pakistan's decision not to Devalue Rupee', PRO.
37. Telegram from UK delegation at Columbo, of meeting between Gordon Walker, Ghulam Muhammad and Nehru; 12 January 1950; File No. DO 142/ 201, 'Decision not to Devalue Pakistani Rupee', PRO.
38. Ibid.
39. Telegram from Grafftey-Smith to Commonwealth Relations Office, 22 Sep. 1949, File No. DO 142/183, 'Repercussions of Pakistan's decision not to Devalue Rupee', PRO.
40. Telegram from UK High Commissioner in India to Commonwealth Office, 11 Feb. 1948, File no. IOR: L/E/9/303,' Sterling Balance negotiations 1948', Economic and Overseas Department Collections, India Office Records, British Library.
41. Catherine R. Schenk, *Britain and the Sterling Area: From Devaluation to convertibility in the 1950s,* London, 1994.
42. 'India and Pakistan: Note by the Treasury', March 1948, File no. IOR: L/E/9/303,' Sterling Balance negotiations 1948', Economic and Overseas Department Collections, India Office Records, British Library.
43. Extract from Draft Minutes of a Meeting of the Overseas Negotiation Committee held on 2 Feb, 1948, File no. IOR: L/E/9/303,' Sterling Balance negotiations 1948', Economic and Overseas Department Collections, India Office Records, British Library

44. See, Chadavarkar, Anand, 'Sir (Abraham) Jeremy Raisman, Finance Minister, Government of India (1939–1945): Portrait of an unsung Hero Extraordinaire', *Economic and PoliticalWeekly,* Vol. 36, No. 28, (14–20 July 2001).
45. Telegram from Raisman to Commonwealth Relations Office, 21 January 1948, File no. L/E/9/303, Sterling Balance negotiations 1948, Economic and Overseas Department Collections, India Office Records, British Library.
46. Ibid.
47. Telegram from U.K. high commissioner in India, 11 Feb. 1948, File No. E(B) Coll. 50/4, 'Sterling Balance Negotiations: Question of Sterling/ Dollar Sources of Raw Material', IOR, BL.
48. Telegram from U. K. high commissioner in Pakistan, 20 December 1949, File No. DO 142/ 201, 'Decision of Pakistan not to Devalue Rupee', PRO.
49. Neogy to Ghulam Muhammad, File No. F 20 (8)-Jute 14/51, Ministry of Commerce and Industry, Jute (Pakistan) Section, NAI.
50. Ibid.
51. Trade Report from deputy high commissioner, Dhaka, January 1950, File No. F 20 (8) -Jute 14/51.
52. File No. 15(27)/ECC-49; NAI.
53. File No. 15(27) ECC/49; Cabinet Secretariat File, 1949, National Archives of India.
54. Pillai to Ikramullah, File No. F 20 (8) -Jute 14/51, Ministry of Commerce and Industry, Jute (Pakistan) Section, NAI.
55. Ibid.
56. A copy of this agreement is also available on the MEA website: https:// mea.gov.in/bilateral-documents.htm?dtl/6737/Trade+Agreement.
57. Record of Meeting of Economic Committee of the Cabinet, on 28 June, 1949, File No. 15 (27)ECC/ 49; Cabinet Secretariat File; National Archives of India.
58. Yoffie, David, *Power and Protectionism: Strategies of the Newly Industrialising Countries*, Columbia University Press.
59. File No. 15 (27)ECC/ 49; Cabinet Secretariat File; NAI.
60. Ibid.
61. Summary of Trade Agreement, Note for Economic Committee for Cabinet, File No. 28- Pak (15)/52; 'India Pakistan Trade Agreement, 1952', MEA File, MEA Archives.
62. Letter from N. Ikramullah to B Pillai, 25 February 1951, File No. F 20(8) -Jute 14/51, Ministry of Commerce and Industry, Jute (Pakistan) Section, NAI.

63. 'Indo–Pakistan Trade Talks, March 1953'; File No. PII/ 53/ 2341/1-2; Ministry of External Affairs Archives.
64. 'Indo–Pakistan Trade Talks and Agreement, July 1952'; File no. PII/52/2316/2; MEA File, Pakistan II Section, MEA Archives.
65. 'Difficulties of Agartala Merchants in connection with the in-transit goods through Pakistan via Akhuara'; File No. PII/ 54/2341/202; Ministry of External Affairs Archives.
66. Van Schendel, W. *The Bengal Borderland: Beyond State and Nation in South Asia*, Anthem Press, London 2005.
67. Vakil, C. N. *Economic Consequences of Divided India*, New Delhi, 1950.
68. 'Indo- Pakistan Trade Talks, March 1953'; File No. PII/ 53/ 2341/1-2; Ministry of External Affairs Archives.
69. Indo–Pakistan Trade Talks and Agreement, July 1952; File no. PII/52/2316/2; MEA File, Pakistan II Section, MEA Archives.

CONCLUSION

1. Itty Abraham, *How India Became Territorial, Foreign Policy, Diaspora, Geopolitics,* Stanford University Press, 2014.

BIBLIOGRAPHY

Primary Sources

Archives and Records Management, Ministry of External Affairs, New Delhi
Ministry of External Affairs Files from Archive and Record Management Section:
– Pakistan Branch
– Bengal Branch

National Archives of India, New Delhi
Files from Ministry of External Affairs:
– Pakistan Branch
– Bengal Branch
Ministry of States Files, Hyderabad Branch
Ministry of Home Affairs Files
Ministry of Relief and Rehabilitation Files
Ministry of Commerce and Industry Files, Jute Branch
Files of Economic Committee of the Cabinet, Cabinet Secretariat Papers

Bangladesh National Archives, Dhaka
Political and Confidential Files
East Bengal Legislative Assembly Proceedings
Home Department Files, Political Branch

Public Records Office, Kew, London
Dominion Office Files (DO 142 Series)

Foreign and Commonwealth Office Files (FO 371 Series)
Cabinet Office Papers

Nehru Memorial Museum and Library, New Delhi
Gopalaswami Ayyangar Papers
Sri Prakasa Papers
B. N. Rau Papers
Subimal Dutt Papers
Gopinath Bardoloi Papers
C. D. Deshmukh Papers
Mohan Sinha Mehta Papers
Vijayalakshmi Pandit Papers

India Office Records, British Library, London
Economic Department Records, (L/E Series)
India Office: Accountant General's Records, (L/AG Series)

Truman Presidential Library and Archives
Chester Bowles Papers
Henry Grady Papers
National Security Council Files
Papers of HS Truman, Official File

Official and Semi-Official Publications and Compilations

Gopal, S. (ed.), *Selected Works of Jawaharlal Nehru*, New Delhi, 1972.

Zaidi, Z. H. (ed.), *Quaid-i-Azam Muhammad Ali Jinnah Papers*, Islamabad, 1993.

Durga Das (ed.), *Sardar Patel's Correspondence, 1945- 1950*, Ahemdabad 1974.

Constituent Assembly of India Debates (Proceedings), Lok Sabha Secretariat, Govt. of India.

Constituent Assembly of Pakistan Debates, National Assembly of Pakistan, Manager of Publications, Govt. of Pakistan, 1950.

Partition Proceedings, (6 Vols.), Partition Council, Partition Sectt., Govt. of India 1948.

Mansergh, N. and E. W. R. Lumby (ed.), *Transfer of Power 1942–7*, London, 1970–1983.

Ahmad, R. (ed.) *The Works of Quaid-i-Azam Mohammad Ali Jinnah*, Islamabad, 1993–2002.

Phillips, C. H. and M. D. Wainwright (ed.), *The Partition of India: Policies and Perspectives 1935–47,* London, 1970.

Muhammad Ali Jinnah, Speeches as Governor General, 1947- 48, Karachi, Ministry of Information and Broadcasting, 1950.

Afzal, M. Rafique (ed.) *Speeches and Statements of Quiad-i-Millat Liaquat Ali Khan, 1941-1951*, Lahore, 1967.

Garewal, Sher Muhammad, *Jinnah- Mountbatten Correspondence, 22 March- 9 August 1947*, Lahore 1998.

Papers Relating to the Foreign Relations of the United States, Washington, U. S. Govt. Printing Office, 1943.

Sreedhar and Kaniyalil, J (ed.) *Indo- Pak Relations: A Documentary Study*; New Delhi 1993.

A S Bhasin, *India–Pakistan Relations, A Documentary Study,* Public Diplomacy Division, Ministry of External Affairs, Geetika Publishers, New Delhi, 2012.

Sadullah, M. M. (eds), *The Partition of the Punjab 1947: A Compilation of Official Documents*, Lahore 1983.

Singh, Kirpal, (ed.), *Select Documents on Partition of Punjab- 1947, India and Pakistan,* Delhi, 1991.

Aziz, K. K. (ed.), *Prelude to Pakistan, 1930- 1940: Documents and Readings Illustrating the Growth of the Idea of Pakistan*, Lahore, 1992.

Khan, L. A., *Pakistan: The Heart of Asia, Speeches in the United States and Canada, May and June 1950, by the Prime Minister of Pakistan*, London, 1950.

'Boundary Dispute between India and Pakistan relating to the Interpretation of the Reward of the Bengal Boundary Commission', *Reports of the International Arbitral Tribunal*, Vol. XXI, United Nations Secretariat.

Memoirs and First Person Accounts

Ali, C.M., *The Emergence of Pakistan*, New York, 1967.

Akhund, I., *Memoirs of a bystander: A Life in Diplomacy*, Karachi 1997.

Ambedkar, B.R., *Pakistan or the Partition of India*, Bombay, 1946.

Ansari, S., *Pakistan: The Problem of India,* Lahore, 1944.

Azad, A., *India Wins Freedom: An Autobiographical Narrative*, Bombay, 1959.

Bannerji, S.K., *From Dependence to Non Alignment: Experiences of an Indian Administrator and Diplomat,* New Delhi, 1987.

Bowles, C., *Ambassador's Report,* London, 1954.

Chakrabarty, S., *My Years with BC Roy: A Record upt o 1962, a Documentary in depth study of the Post Independence Period*, Calcutta, 1958.

Darling, M., *At Freedom's Door,* London, 1949.

Dayal, R., *A Life in Our Times*, New Delhi 1998.

Dutt, Subimal, *With Nehru in the Foreign Office,* Calcutta, 1977.

Gulhati, N.D., *Indus Waters Treaty: An Exercise in International Mediation*, Bombay, 1973.

Gundevia, Y.D., *Outside the Archives*, Hyderabad, 1984.
Hamid, S., *Disastrous Twilight: A Personal Record of the Partition of India*, London, 1993.
Chagla, M.C. *Roses in December*, New Delhi, 1974.
Noon, Feroz Khan, *From Memory,* Karachi, 1966.
Ismael, Mirza, *My Public Life*, London 1954.
Johnson, A.C., *Mission With Mountbatten*, New York, 1953.
Johnson, Alan C., *Mountbatten in Retrospect*, London, 1997.
Khaliquzzaman, C., *Pathway to Pakistan*, Lahore, 1961.
Khan, A.W., *India wins Freedom: The Other Side*, Karachi, 1961.
Khan, Sir Zafrullah, *Pakistan's Foreign Relations*, Karachi 1950.
Khosla, G.D., *Stern Reckoning: A Study of the Events Leading up to and following the Partition*, New Delhi 1989.
Menon, V.P., *Transfer of Power in India*, Princeton, 1957.
Menon, V.P., *The Story of the Integration of Indian States*, Bombay, 1961.
Moon, P., *Divide and Quit*, New Delhi, 1998.
Moon, P. (ed.), *Wavell: The Viceroy's Journal,* Karachi, 1973.
Panikkar, K.M., *Asia and Western Dominance,* London 1953.
Patel, H.M., *Rites of Passage: A Civil Servant Remembers,* New Delhi, 2005.
Patel, H.M., *The First Flush of Freedom: Reflections and Recollections,* New Delhi, 2005.
Prasad, R., *India Divided,* Bombay, 1947.
Shahnawas, J., *Father and Daughter: A Political Autobiography,* Lahore, 1973.
Sri Prakasa, *Pakistan: Birth and Early Days,* Calcutta, 1965.
Nehru, B.K., *Nice Guys Finish Last*, New Delhi, 1997.
Randhawa, M.S., *Out of the Ashes,* Patiala, 1978.
Tuker, F., *While Memory Serves: The Last Two Years of British Rule in India*, London, 1950.
Tyabji, Badr-ud-din, *Memoirs of an Egoist,* (2 vols.), New Delhi, 1988.
Rai, S.M., *Partition of the Punjab: A Study of its Effects on the Politics and Administration of the Punjab (I), 1947–1956*, New Delhi, 1965.
Randhawa, M.S, *Out of the Ashes: The Story of Rehabilitation in the Punjab*.

Secondary Literature

Abraham, I., *How India Became Territorial, Foreign Policy, Diaspora, Geopolitics,* Stanford University Press, 2014.
Ahmed, Akbar S., *Jinnah, Pakistan and Islamic Identity: The Search for Saladin,* London 1997.
Akbar, M.J., *Blood Brothers: A Family Saga*, New Delhi, 2006.

Alam, Undala Z., Water Rationality: Mediating the Indus Waters Treaty, Unpublished PhD Dissertation, University of Durham, 1998.

Alavi H. and Harris S. (ed), *The Sociology of Developing Societies*, Basingstoke, 1989.

Amin, Shahid M., *Pakistan's Foreign Policy: A Reappraisal*, Oxford, 2000.

Andrew B. Kennedy, *The International Ambitions of Mao and Nehru: National Efficacy Beliefs and the Making of Foreign Policy*, CUP, Cambridge, 2012.

Andrus, J.R. and Muhammad, A. F., *The Economy of Pakistan,* London, 1958.

Anita Inder Singh, *The Limits of British Influence, South Asia and the Angle American Relationship, 1947–56*, Bloomsbury, London, 1990.

Anita Inder Singh: *The Limits of British Influence: South Asia and the Anglo American Relationship, 1947–56*; London, 1993.

Ansari, S., *Life After Partition: Community, Migration and Strife in Sindh, 1947–1962*, Oxford University Press, 2005.

Ayub Khan, Muhammad, Friends, Not Masters: A Political Autobiography, London, 1967.

Aziz, K.K., *The Making of Pakistan: A Study in Nationalism*, Lahore, 1967.

B.N. Ganguli, 'Devaluation of the Rupee: What it means to India'; *Occasional Papers of the Delhi School of Economics.*

Bajpai, K. and S. Mallavarapu (ed.), *International Relations in India: Bringing Theory Back Home,* Hyderabad, 2005.

Bajpai, K., 'To War or Not to War: The India–Pakistan Crisis of 2001–2', in Sumit Ganguly and S. Paul Kapur, ed., *Nuclear Proliferation in South Asia: Crisis Behaviour and the Bomb*, Oxford, 2008.

Bajpai, K., (ed.), *Brasstacks and Beyond: Perception and Management of Crisis in South Asia*, New Delhi, 1995.

Bandopadhyay, J., *The Making of India's Foreign Policy: Determinants, Institutions, Process and Personalities*, Bombay, 1970.

Bandyopadhyay S., Caste, Protest and Identity in Colonial India: The Namasudras of Bengal, 1872–1947, Surrey, 1997.

Bandyopadhyay S., Transfer of Power and the Crisis of Dalit Politics in India', *Modern Asian Studies,* Vol. 34(4), 2000.

Bandyopadhyay, S., 'From Alienation to Integration: Changes in the Politics of Caste in Bengal, 1937–47', *The Indian Economic and Social History Review,* Vol. 31(3), 1994.

Barnds, William J., *India, Pakistan and the Great Powers*, London 1972.

Basu, A., *Mridula Sarabhai, Rebel with a Cause*, New Delhi, OUP, 1996.

Beard, C., *The Idea of National Interest: An Analytical Study in American Foreign Policy*, New York, 1934.

Beate, J., (ed.), *Classical Theory in International Relations*, Cambridge 2006.

Benjamin Zachariah, *Nehru*, London, 2002.

Bhagavan, M., 'A New Hope: India, the United Nations and the Making of the Universal Declarations of Human Rights', *Modern Asian Studies,* Vol. 44, No. 2, March 2010.

Bhagavan, M., *The Peace Makers: India and the Quest for One World*, Harper Collins, New Delhi, 2012.

Bin Sayeed, K., *Pakistan, The Formative Phase, 1857–1948,* Karachi, 1968.

Blinkenberg, Lars, *India–Pakistan: The History of Unsolved Conflicts,* Odensk, 1999.

Blum, G., *Islands of Agreement: Managing Enduring Armed Rivalries,* Harvard University Press, Cambridge MA, 2007.

Bose, S., 'To Partition or Not: A Comparative Perspective', *Ethnopolitics,* 10:3-4, 2011.

Bose, Sumantra, 'Kashmir: Sourced of Conflict, Dimensions of Peace', *Economic and Political Weekly,* Vol. 34, No. 13 (March 27- April 2, 1999).

Bose, Sumantra, *Contested Lands: Israel-Palestine, Kashmir, Bosnia, Cyprus and Sri Lanka*, Cambridge MA, 2007.

Braibanti, R., 'Public Bureaucracy and Judiciary in Pakistan' in LaPalombara (ed.), *Bureaucracy and Political Development*, Princeton, 1963.

Brecher, M., *India and World Politics: Krishna Menon's View of the World*, London 1968.

Brobst, P.J., *The Future of the Great Game: Sir Olaf Caroe, India's Independence, and the Defence of Asia*, University of Akron Press, 2005.

Brodkin, E.I., 'United States Aid to India and Pakistan: The Attitude of the Fifties', *International Affairs*, Vol. 43, (Oct. 1967).

Brown, Judith, *Nehru: A Political Life*, New Haven, 2002.

Brown, W.N., *The US, India and Pakistan,* Harvard University Press, 1953.

Burke S.M. and Lawrence Ziring, *Pakistan's Foreign Policy: An Historical Analysis,* Oxford, 1990.

Burke, S.M., *Mainsprings of Indian and Pakistani Foreign Policies*, Minneapolis, 1974.

Butalia, Urvashi, *The Other Side of Silence: Voices from the Partition of India*, London, 2000.

Chatterji, J., 'From Subjecthood to Citizenship: Migrants and the Making of Nationality in South Asia, 1947–1955', *Historical Journal,* forthcoming.

Chatterji, J., *Bengal Divided, Hindu Communalism and Partition, 1932–1947*, Cambridge 1994.

Chatterji, J., The Fashioning of a Frontier: The Radcliffe line and Bengal's Border Landscape, 1947–1952', Modern Asian Studies, Vol. 33, No. 1, February 1999.

Chatterji, J., *The Spoils of Partition: Bengal and India, 1947–1967*, Cambridge 2007.

Chattha, I., *Partition and Locality: Violence, Migration and Development in Gujranwala and Sialkot, 1947–1961*, Karachi, 2011.

Chaudhry, G.W., *Pakistan's Relations with India, 1947–1966*, London, 1968.

Chaudhury, R., *Forged in* Crisis, Hurst & Co. London, 2013.

Chester, Lucy P., *Borders and Conflict in South Asia: The Radcliffe Boundary Commission and the Partition of Punjab*, Manchester, 2009.

Cloughley, B., *A History of the Pakistani Army: Wars and Insurrections*, Karachi, OUP 1999.

Cohen, S. and R.L. Park, *India: Emergent Power?* New York, 1978.

Cohen, S., *The Pakistan Army*, University of California, 1984.

Cohen, *Shooting for a Century: The India–Pakistan Conundrum,* Brookings Institution Press, Washington DC, 2013.

Cohen, Stephen P., *The Idea of Pakistan,* Washington DC, 2004.

Coombs, Catherine, 'Partition Narratives: Displaced Trauma and Culpability among British Civil Servants in 1940s Punjab', in Sherman, Taylor et al (ed.), *From Subjects to Citizens: Society and the Everyday State in India and Pakistan, 1947–1970*, CUP, Delhi, 2014.

Copland, Ian, 'The Master and the Maharajas: the Sikh Princes and the East Punjab Massacres of 1947', *Modern Asian Studies,* Vol. 36, July 2002.

Darwin, J., *Britain and Decolonisation: The Retreat from Empire in the Post War World*, Basingstoke, 1998.

Das Gupta, Amit, *Serving India: A Political Biography of Subimal Dutt (1903–1992). India's Longest Serving Foreign Secretary*, New Delhi: Manohar Publishers & Distributors, 2017.

Dasgupta, C., 'Nehru, Patel and China', *Strategic Analysis,* Vol. 38, Issue 5, Sept. 2014.

Dasgupta, C., *War and Diplomacy in Kashmir, 1947–1948*, New Delhi 2002

Dasgupta, Jyoti Bhusan, *Indo-Pakistan Relations, 1947–1955,* Djambatan, 1960.

Davis, K., 'India and Pakistan: The Demography of Partition, *Pacific Affairs,* Vol. 22, (Sep. 1949).

De, Rohit, 'Taming of the Custodian: Evacuee Property Law and Economic Life in the Indian Republic', in Gyan Prakash, Nikhil Menon, and Michael Laffan (eds), *The Postcolonial Moment in South and Southeast Asia*, London, Bloomsbury Academic, 2018.

Deshmukh, C.D., *Economic Developments in India: 1947–1956: A Personal Retrospect*, Bombay, 1957.

Devji, F., *Muslim Zion: Pakistan as a Political Idea*, Cambridge, MA, 2013.

Dhulipala, V., *Creating a New Medina, State Power, Islam, and the Quest for Pakistan in Late Colonial North India,* CUP, New Delhi, 2016.

Dixit, J.N., *India and Regional Developments: Through the Prism of Indo-Pakistan Relations*, New Delhi, 2004.

Donnan, H., and Wilson, T., *Borders: Frontiers of Identity, Nation and State*, Oxford, 1999.

Downes, A., 'The Problem with Negotiated Settlements to Ethnic Civil Wars, *Security Studies,* Vol. 13, Issue 4, 2004.

Dubnov and Robson (eds), *Partitions, A Transnational History of Twentieth Century Territorial Separation,* Stanford University Press, 2019.

Dutt, Subimal, *With Nehru in the Foreign Office,* Calcutta, 1977.

Fink, Carole, League of Nations and the Minorities Question, *World Affairs,* Vol. 157, No. 4, 1995.

Frankel, Francine R, *India's Political Economy, 1947–1977; The Gradual Revolution*, Princeton University Press, 1978.

Fraser, T.G., 'Ireland and India', in Keith Jeffrey (ed.), *An Irish Empire?: Aspects of Ireland and the British Empire*, Manchester, 1996.

Ganguly, S., *The Origins of War in South Asia,* New Delhi, 1999.

Ganguly, Sumit, *Conflict Unending: India–Pakistan Tensions since 1947*, New York, 2002.

Gilpin, A.C. *India's Sterling Balances: A Report prepared for the Indian Affairs Group of the Fabian Society*, April, 1946.

Goodnow, H.F., *The Civil Service of Pakistan: Bureaucracy in a New Nation,* Yale University Press, 1964.

Gopal, S., *Jawaharlal Nehru: A Biography* (3 vols.), Cambridge (Mass.), 1976.

Gould, H.A., *The South Asia Story: The First Sixty Years of U. S. Relations with India and Pakistan,* London, 2010.

Gould, William, Taylor C. Sherman, and Sarah Ansari, 'The flux of the matter: loyalty, corruption and the everyday state in the post-partition government services of India and Pakistan', *Past and Present*, 219, 1 (2013): 237–79.

Gulhati, N.D., *Indus Waters Treaty, An exercise in International Mediation*, Bombay, 1973.

Gundevia, Y.D., *Outside the Archives,* Hyderabad, 1984.

Gupta, S., *Kashmir: A Study in India–Pakistan Relations*, Bombay, 1967.

Haqqani, H., *Magnificent Delusions: Pakistan, the United States and an Epic History of Misunderstanding,* HUP, 2014.

Hasan, K. Sarwar, *Pakistan and the United Nations*, New York, 1960.

Hasan, M. (ed.), *India's Partition: Process, Strategy and Mobilisation*, Delhi, 1994.

Hasan, M., *Legacy of a Divided Nation: India's Muslims since Independence*, London, 1997.

Hasan, S.M., *Muhammad Ali Jinnah: A Political Study,* Lahore, 1953.

Hashmi, B. 'The Beginnings of the US Pakistan Alliance' *Pakistan Forum*, Vol. 3 (March–April 1973).

Hirschman, Albert O., *National Power and the Structure of Foreign Trade*, University of California Press, 1945.

Hosain, A., *Sunlight on a Broken Column,* Penguin Books, India, Gurgaon, 1988.

J.S. Grewal, *Master Tara Singh in Indian History: Colonialism, Nationalism and the Politics of Sikh Identity*, OUP, New Delhi, 2017.

Jaffrelot, Christophe, *The Pakistan Paradox, Instability and Resilience,* Oxford University Press, 2015.

Jalal, A., 'Inheriting the Raj: Jinnah and the Governor-Generalship Issue', *Modern Asian Studies,* Vol. 19 (1985).

Jalal, A., *Democracy and Authoritarianism in South Asia: A Comparative and Historical Perspective*, Cambridge, 1995.

Jalal, A., *The Sole Spokesman: Jinnah, the Muslim League and the Demand for Pakistan*, Cambridge, 1985.

Jalal, A., *The State of Martial Rule: The Origins of Pakistan's Political Economy of Defence*, Cambridge, 1990.

Jeffrey, Robin, 'The Punjab Boundary Force and the Problem of Order, August 1947', *Modern Asian Studies,* Vol. 8, No. 4 (1974).

John T. McNay (ed.), *The Memoirs of Ambassador Henry F Grady, From the Great War to the Cold War*, University of Missourie Press, 2009.

Kamran, T., *The Unfolding Crisis in Punjab, March- August 1947: Key Turning Points and British Responses*, Journal of Punjab Studies, Vol. 14, No. 2, (Fall 2007).

Kamtekar, Indivar, 'A Different War Dance: State and Class in India, 1939–1945', *Past and Present*, No. 176, (August 2002).

Kaufman, C.D., *When All Else Fails, Ethnic Population Transfers and Partitions in the Twentieth Century, Quarterly Journal: International Security*, vol. 23. no. 2. (Fall 1998): 120–56.

Kazimi, Muhammad Reza, *Liaquat Ali Khan: His Life and Work*, Karachi 2004.

Kedar, Alexandre, 'Expanding Legal Geographies: A Call for a Critical Comparative Approach', in Kedar *et al* (eds), *The Expanding Spaces of Law: A Timely Legal Geography*, Columbia University Press, forthcoming.

Kelly, Stephen, A Policy of Futility: Eamon de Valera's Anti-Partition Campaign, 1948–1951. *Études irlandaises*, 2011, doi: 10.4000/ etudesirlandaises. 2348.

Kennedy, Paul M., *Realities behind Diplomacy: Background Influence on British External Policies, 1865–1980*, London, 1985.

Khalid bin Sayeed, *The Central Government of Pakistan, 1947–1951* (Department of Economics and Politics, McGill University).

Khan, Humayun and G. Parthasarathy, *Diplomatic Divide: Cross Border Talks,* Delhi, 2004.

Khan, Y., *The Great Partition: The Making of India and Pakistan*, Yale University Press, 2007.

Kudaisya, G., *Region, Nation, "Heartland": Uttar Pradesh in India's Body Politic*, New Delhi, 2006.

Kudaisya, M., 'A Mighty Adventure: Institutionalising the Idea of Planning in Post Colonial India, 1947– 60'. *Modern Asian Studies* (2009).

Kumar, R., The Troubled History of Partition, *Foreign Affairs,* January 1997.

Kumaraswamy, P.R., *India's Israel Policy*, Columbia University Press, New York, 2010.

Kux, D. (et al.) *India and Pakistan: The First Fifty Years*, Cambridge, 1999.

Kux, D., *India–Pakistan Relations: Is Past still Prologue?* Washington, 2006.

Kux, Dennis, *Disenchanted Allies: Pakistan and the United States*, 2001.

Kux, Dennis, *Estranged Democracies: India and the United States, 1941–1991,* New Delhi 1994.

Lamb, A., *Incomplete Partition: The Genesis of the Kashmir Dispute, 1947–1948,* Karachi, 2002.

Louis, W.M., *The British Empire and the Middle East, 1945–1951: Arab Nationalism, the United States and Post War Imperialism*, OUP, Oxford and New York, 1984.

Low, D.A. (ed.), *The Political Inheritors of Pakistan*, Cambridge, 1991.

Makieg, D., 'War, No War, and the India Pakistan Negotiating Process, *Pacific Affairs,* Vol. 60, (Summer, 1987).

Malik, I.H., *State and Civil Society in Pakistan*, New York, 1997.

Manela, Erez, *The Wilsonian Moment: Self Determination and the Ideological Origins of Anti Colonial Nationalism*, New York, 2006.

Mansergh, D. (ed.), *Independence Years: The Selected Indian and Commonwealth papers of N. Mansergh,* New Delhi, 1999.

Mansergh, N., *Documents and Speeches on Britain's Commonwealth Affairs,* London, 1953–1963.

Mansergh, N., *Survey of British Commonwealth Affairs: Problems of Wartime Cooperation and Post War Change, 1939–1952*, Oxford University Press, Oxford, 1958.

Mansergh, N., *The Commonwealth and the Nation: Study in British Commonwealth Relations*, London, 1948.

Mansingh, S., and Charles H. Heimsath, *A Diplomatic History of Modern India,* Bombay, 1971.

Marston, D., 'The Indian Army, Partition, and the Punjab Boundary Force, 1945–47', *War in History,* Vol. 16, No. 4, November 2009.

Mazower, M., *Dark Continent: Europe's Twentieth Century*, Knopf, New York, 1998.

Mazower, Mark, *No Enchanted Palace: The End of Empire and the Ideological Origins of the United Nations*, Princeton, 2009.

McGarr, P., *The Cold War in South Asia, Britain. The United States and the Indian Subcontinent*, CUP, 2013.

McLeod, Duncan, *India and Pakistan: Friends, Rivals or Enemies?,* Hampshire, 2008.

McMahon, R.J., *The Cold War on the Periphery: The United States, India and Pakistan,* New York, 1994.

Mehta, J., 'The Indus Water Treaty: A Case Study in the Resolution of an International River Basin Conflict', Natural Resources Forum, Vol. 12, No. 1, Feb. 1988.

Menon, R., and K. Bhasin, *Borders and Boundaries: Women in India's Partition*, New Delhi, 1998.

Michel, A.A., *The Indus River: A Study of the Effects of Partition*, New Haven, 1967.

Miller, Manjari C., *Wronged by Empire: Post Imperial Ideology and Foreign Policy in India and China,* Stanford University Press, 2013.

Morgenthau, Hans, *Politics Amongst Nations*, New York, 1948.

Oberoi, P., '*Exile and Belonging: Refugees and State Policy in South Asia*', OUP, New Delhi, 2006.

Oberoi, P., South Asia and the Creation of the International Refugee Regime', *Refuge*, Vol. 19, No. 5 (2001).

OLeary, B., Debating Partition, Justifications and Critiques, Working Paper 28, Mapping Frontiers, Plotting Pathways, https://www.qub.ac.uk/research-centres/CentreforInternationalBordersResearch/Publications/WorkingPapers/MappingFrontiersworkingpapers/Filetoupload,175429,en.pdf.

Pandey, G., *Remembering Partition: Violence, Nationalism and History in India,* Cambridge, 2001.

Pandey, G., *Routine Violence: Nations, Fragments, Histories*, Stanford, 2006.

Patel, H.M., *The First Flush of Freedom: Recollection and Reflection*, A. Abraham (ed.), Rupa & Co., New Delhi, 2005.

Paul, TV, *The Warrior State: Pakistan in the Contemporary World,* OUP, New York, 2014.

Posen, B., The Security Dilemma and Ethnic Conflict, *Survival,* Vol. 35, No. 1, Spring 1993.

Raghavan, S., *War and Peace in Modern India: A Strategic History of the Nehru Years,* Ranikhet, 2010.

Ranadive, B.T., *The Sterling Balances Betrayal*, Bombay, 1948.

Rao, Uma Bhaskar, *The Story of Rehabilitation,* Govt. of India Publications Division, Delhi, 1967.

Reisch, Jessica and E. White (eds), *The Disentanglement of Population: Migration, Expulsion and Displacement in Post-War Europe, 1944–49,* Palgrave Macmillan, Basingstoke, UK, 2011.

Rietzler, Katharina (2016), *Counter-Imperial Orientalism: Friedrich Berber and the politics of international law in Germany and India, 1920s–1960s.* Journal of Global History, 11 (1). pp. 113–134.

Rizvi, Hasan A., *Pakistan and the Geo-Strategic Environment: A Study in Foreign Policy*, New York, 1993.

Robert Jervis, 'Cooperation Under the Security Dilemma', *World Politics,* Vol. 30, No. 2, Jan 1978.

Robinson, C.D., 'Too Much Nationality: Kashmiri Refugees, the South Asian Refugee Regime and a Refugee State, 1947–1974', *Journal of Refugee Studies,* Vol. 25, No. 3, August 2012.

Rotter, Andrew Jon, *Comrades at Odds: The United States and India, 1947–1964*, Ithaca, 2000.

Rudolph, Lloyd I., and Susanne Rudolph, 'The Making of US Foreign Policy for South Asia: Offshore Balancing in Historical Perspective', *Economic and Political Weekly,* 25 Feb. 2006.

Samaddar, R. (ed.), *Reflections on Partition in the East,* Calcutta, 1997.

Samaddar, R. (ed.), *Refugees and the State: Practises of Asylum and Care in India, 1947–2000*, London, 2003.

Samaddar, R., *The Marginal Nation: Transborder Migration from Bangladesh into West Bengal,* London, 1998.

Sankaran, Krishna, 'Cartographic Anxiety: Mapping the Body Politic in India', Alternatives: Global, Local, Political, Vol. 19, No. 4, Fall 1994.

Sattar, Abdul, *Pakistan's Foreign Policy, 1947–2005: A Concise History*, Oxford, 2002.

Schaeffer, R., *Warpaths: The Politics of Partition*, Hill and Wang, New York, 1990.

Schechtman, J.B., Evacuee Property in India and Pakistan, in Verinder Grover and Arora R., '*Fifty Years of India–Pakistan Relations: Partition of India, Vol. 1*, Deep Publications, New Delhi, 1999.

Schenk, Catherine R., *Britain and the Sterling Area: From Devaluation to convertibility in the 1950's,* London, 1994.

Sen, Dwaipan, '"No Matter How, Jogendranath had to be Defeated": The Scheduled Castes Federation, and the Making of Partition in Bengal, 1945–1947', *Indian Economic and Social History Review*, Vol. 49, No. 3, (July- September 2012).

Sharma, Jayeeta, *Empire's Garden: Assam and the Making of India*, Durham, 2011.

Singh, Anita Inder, *The Limits of British Influence: South Asia and the Anglo American Relationship, 1947–1956*, London, 1993.

Spake, O.H.K., 'The Partition of India and the Prospects for Pakistan', *Geographical Review,* Vol. 38, (Jan., 1948).

Svensson, Ted, *Productions of Post-Colonial India and Pakistan: Meanings of Partition,* Routledge, UK, 2013.

Symonds, R., *The Making of Pakistan*, London, 1950.

Talbot, I., *Pakistan: A Modern History*, London, 1998.

Talbot, Ian, 'A Tale of two Cities: The Aftermath of Partition for Lahore and Amritsar, 1947–1957', *Modern Asian Studies,* 41, 1 (2007).

Talbot, Ian, and G. Singh (ed.) *Region and Partition: Bengal, Punjab and the Partition of the Subcontinent*, Karachi, 2000.

Talbot, Ian, *Freedom's Cry: The Popular Dimensions in the Pakistan Movement and Partition Experience in North West India,* Karachi, 1996.

Talbot, Ian, *India and Pakistan: Inventing the Nation*, New York, 2000.

Talbot, Ian (ed.), *The Deadly Embrace: Religion, Violence and Politics in India and Pakistan,* Oxford University Press, Karachi, 2007.

Tan, Tai Yong and Gyanesh Kudaisya (eds), *The Aftermath of Partition in South Asia*, New York, 2000.

Tan, Tai Yong, *The Garrison State: The Military, Government and Society in Colonial Punjab, 1849*–1947, New Delhi, 2005.

Thornton, Thomas Perry, 'Pakistan: Fifty Years of Insecurity', in Kux, D. et. al (eds), *India and Pakistan: The First Fifty Years,* Cambridge University Press, Cambridge, 1999.

Tinker, H., 'Pressure, Persuasion, Decision: Factors in the Partition of the Punjab, August 1947', *The Journal of Asian Studies*, Vol. 36, No. 4, Aug 1977.

Tinker, H., *The Banyan Tree: Overseas Emigrants from India, Pakistan and Bangladesh*, OUP, 1977.

Tomlinson, B.R., 'Indo British Relations in the Post Colonial Era: The Sterling Balances Negotiations, 1947–1949', *Journal of Imperial and Commonwealth History,* vol. 13, no. 3, May 1985.

Vakil, C.N. and G. Raghava Rao, *Economic Relations between India and Pakistan: Need for International Cooperation*, Bombay, 1950.

Van Schendel, Willem, *Chittaging Hill Tracts: Living in a Borderland,* Dhaka, 2001.

Van Schendel, Willem, 'I am Not a Refugee: Rethinking Partition Migration', *Modern Asian Studies,* Vol. 37, No. 3, pp. 551–584.

Van Schendel, Willem, *Reviving a Rural Industry: Silk Producers and Officials in India and Bangladesh, 1880s to 1980s*, Dhaka, 1995.

Van Schendel, Willem, *The Bengal Borderland: Beyond State and Nation in South Asia,* London, 2007.

Varshney, A., 'India, Pakistan and Kashmir: Antimonies of Nationalism', *Asian Survey,* Vol. 31, (Nov. 1991).

Verma, D.N. *India and the League of Nations*, Bharti Bhavan Press, Patna, 1968.

Virdee, P., 'Negotiating the Past: Journey through Muslim Women's Experience of Partition and Resettlement in Partition', *Cultural and Social History*, 6, 4 (2009): 467–84.

Visaria, P., 'Migration between India and Pakistan, 1951–1961', *Demography,* Vol. 6 (Aug. 1969).

Waltz, K., *Man, the State and War: A theoretical Analysis*, New York, 2001.

Watenpaugh, K.D., 'The League of Nations' Rescue of Armenian Genocide Survivors and the Making of Modern Humanitarianism, 1920–1927', *American Historical Review* 115, 5 (2010): 1315–39.

Westad, O.A., Rethinking Revolutions: The Cold War in the Third World, *Journal of Peace Research,* Vol. 29, No., 4, (Nov. 1992).

Westad, O.A., *The Global Cold War: Third World Interventions and the Making of Our Times,* Cambridge University Press, Cambridge, 2007.

Wright, T.P., 'Indian Muslim Refugees in the Politics of Punjab', *The Journal of Commonwealth and Comparative Politics*, Vol. XII, No. 2.

Zachariah, B., *Nehru,* London, 2002.

Zaheer, Hasan, *The Times and Trial of the Rawalpindi Conspiracy Case 1951: The First Coup Attempt in Pakistan,* Karachi, 1998.

Zaidi, ZH. (eds), *Jinnah Papers*, First Series, Vol. VII, Quaid-i- Azam papers Project, Islamabad, 2002; Ali Muhammad Khan to Jinnah, 16 January 1948.

Zamindar, V.F.Y., *The Long Partition and the Making of Modern South Asia: Refugees, Boundaries, Histories,* Columbia University Press, 2007.

Ziring, L., *Pakistan in the Twentieth Century: A Political History,* OUP, 1997.

INDEX

Abducted Persons Act (1949), 37
abducted women, 3, 20, 23, 32, 34–9, 62
Abraham, Itty, 185
Acharya, B.K., 63
Acheson, Dean, 144, 148
Afghanistan, 144
Ahmed, Azizuddin, 63
Ajmer Merwara, 84
Akal Sena, 32
Akhaura, 180
Ali, Chaudhury Muhammad, 24–5, 122
Ali, Tafazzal, 91
Ali, Wajed, 54
Allen, Raymond, 146
Alwar State, 31
Ambegaokar, K. G., 172
Amin, Nurul, 90
Amin, Shahid M., 115
Anand Bazaar Patrika, 69
Arbitral Tribunal, 121, 122, 124, 125, 128
Armenian genocide (1914–23), 35
Asiatic Land Tenure Act (1946), 152
Assam
  border trade, 179
  evacuee property in, 89
  Maintenance of Public Order Act (1947), 55
  migrants and refugees, 52, 53–5, 62–3, 64
Atlantic Charter (1941), 30
Attlee, Clement, 103, 110
Auchinleck, Claude, 33
Australia, 29, 106, 110, 169, 173
Awadh, 42, 73
Ayyangar, Gopalaswami
  and Assam migration policy, 54
  and abducted women, 37
  and economic policy, 165
  and evacuee property, 75, 85, 87, 90, 91
  and Indus rivers, 119–20, 128, 133, 134
  and No War Pact, 106
  and refugee crisis, 49, 50, 54
Azam, Amir, 83

Badaber, 144
Baghdad Pact, 145
Bahawalpur, 96, 124
Bahawalpur House, Delhi, 96, 97
Bajpai, Girija Shankar, 30, 102–3, 107, 112–13, 143, 148, 172–3
Baluchistan, 84

Banerji, S. K., 94, 96
Bangladesh Liberation War (1971), 7
Banpur, 66
Barcelona Convention (1920), 130
Bardoloi, Gopinath, 53, 54–5
Bari Doab Canals, 121, 122, 132
barter agreements, 167
Benapole, 66
Bengal
  border trade, 179
  communal violence in, 109
  evacuee property in, 89, 90, 93–4
  minority rights in, 16, 41–2, 44–5, 56–7, 60–71
  refugee crisis, 41–2, 44–5, 48, 49–57, 102, 103, 111
  steamer companies, 170
Bengal Pact (1950), 16, 47, 57, 60, 65–71, 85, 102, 110–11, 184
Berber, Frederich, 128–30
betel leaf, 179
Bevin, Ernest, 142
Bhakra Nangal Dam, 120, 123–5
Bharatiya Janata Party, 24
Bhargava, Gopichand, 122
Bhatinda, 31
Bhoothalingam, Subrahmanya, 166
Bihar, 55, 56, 89
bilateral trade, 161–82
Biswas, Charu Chandra, 66
Black, Eugene, 131, 135–6
Blum, Gabriella, 18
Bombay, 30, 56, 85, 91, 161, 170
Bongaon, 66
border trade, 178–81
Bose, Surjit, 61, 62
Bowles, Chester, 146, 148, 149
Branch Secretariat, 61
Brexit, 14
British Broadcasting Corporation (BBC), 73
British India (1858–1947)
  Civil Service, 28, 30, 50, 170, 174
  Commerce Department, 28
  External Affairs and Commonwealth Relations Department, 25, 26, 29
  Foreigners Act (1946), 55
  Joint Defence Council, 32–3, 80
Bulgarians, 78
Burke, Samuel Martin, 5
Burma, 29, 144

Cabinet Mission Plan, 15
Calcutta
  Branch Secretariat in, 61
  Inter-Dominion Conference on Minorities (1948), 50–53, 60, 64, 66, 93–4
  jute mills, 157
  Pakistani High Commission in, 62–3
Campbellpore, 37
Canada, 106, 110
canal waters, 101, 103, 104, 105, 107, 108–9, 117–36
Caroe, Olaf, 145–6, 147
cattle, 179
cement, 168, 177
Central Treaty Organisation (CENTO), 145
Ceylon, 29, 172–3
Chamba estate, Lahore, 95–8
Chandra, C.N., 93
Chatham House, 78
Chatta, Ilyas, 85
Chatterji, Joya, 57, 76
China, 9, 10, 28, 146, 147
Chowdhry, Abdul Hamid, 63
citizenship, 3, 65, 66, 77, 79
  evacuee property and, 75, 77, 79, 98

Civil and Military Gazette, 76, 124
civil society, 36
coal, 64, 152, 165, 166, 168, 170, 175, 176
Coeh, T. B., 87
coir yarn, 179
Cold War, 101, 142, 143, 150–51, 153
Columbo Plan, 172–3
Commerce Department, 28
Commonwealth, 28, 103, 139, 141, 142–3
  and devaluation crisis, 172–3
  and Indo–Pakistani war, prospect of, 109, 110–11
communism, 10, 144, 146–7, 148, 150, 151
Constituent Assembly, Pakistan, 20, 84, 113, 183
continualist foreign relations, 142
cotton, 165, 166, 167, 168, 170, 171–2, 173, 176, 177
Council for the Protection of Rights of Minorities, 64
Council of Industries, Pakistan, 165
Coyajee, Jehangir Cooverji, 59
Cripps, Stafford, 168
Custodians of Evacuee Property, 74, 79, 80–88, 92–3, 94
Cyprus, 35
Czechoslovakia, 15, 59, 106, 153

Dandakaranya, 57
Dantyagi, V.D., 92
Darsana, 66
Daultana, Mumtaz, 121
Dawn, 69, 70, 114, 150
De Valera, Eamon, 159–60
De, Rohit, 98
Delhi, 52, 96, 110
Delhi Pact (1950), 16, 47, 57, 60, 65–71, 85, 102, 110–11, 184
Delhi School of Economics, 169
Department of External Affairs and Commonwealth Relations, 25, 26, 29
Desai, C.C., 170, 181
Deshmukh, Chintaman Dwarakanath, 143, 148, 150, 169, 170, 172
devaluation crisis, 168–78
Dhaka, 61, 62, 94, 176
Dipalpur, 122, 132
displaced persons, 74, 153–4
Dubnov, Arie, 11, 34
Dutt, Subimal, 30, 60–61, 64, 85–6, 105, 127, 130

East Bengal/Pakistan, 20, 42, 49, 50, 52–6, 63
  Assam, relations with, 53–4
  Bangladesh Liberation War (1971), 7
  border trade, 179–80
  evacuee property in, 89, 90, 93–4
  jute, 175, 180
  minority rights in, 16, 41–2, 44–5, 56–7, 60–71
  refugee crisis, 41–2, 44–5, 48, 49–57, 102, 103, 111
  State Acquisition and Tenancy Act (1950), 90
  steamer companies, 170
  West Bengal, relations with, 55
East Punjab, 32
  abducted women in, 39
  Bhakra Nangal Dam, 120, 123–5
  evacuee property in, 76, 80–83
  Indus waters, 118, 120–38
Eastern League of Nations, 58–9
Economic and Political Weekly, 87

economic liberalism, 163
economic self-sufficiency, 164–8
Economist, 169
Egypt, 28, 169, 173
Eisenhower, Dwight David, 148
Embree, Ainsley, 15
Enemy Property Acts, 77
ethnic cleansing, 17, 32
evacuee property, 3, 8, 20, 73–98
 agreed areas, 81, 83, 84–7, 94
 Custodians of Evacuee Property, 74, 79, 80–88, 92–3, 98
 individual exchange, 81
 Inter-Dominion conferences on, 74, 75, 79–83, 87
 intending evacuees, 87–95
 No War Pact correspondence and, 101, 103, 104, 108, 112
Evacuee Property Law
 India, 89
 Pakistan, 96, 97
Expert Committees, 25–6, 28
External Affairs and Commonwealth Relations Department, 25, 26, 29

family feud metaphors, 5
Fazalbhai, M.H.A., 161–2, 184
feminism, 35
Ferozepur, 102
fertilizers, 165
first generation of partition, 15
First Information Reports (FIRs), 54
Fiscal Commission, India, 169
fish, 179
Foreigners Act (1946), 55
France, 106
Franks, Matthew, 79
Frasier, T.G., 14
'Frontier of Public Opinion', 100, 111–16
fruit, 179

Gandhi, Indira, 7, 143, 157
Gandhi, Mohandas Karamchand, 152
Ganguli, B.N., 169
Ganguly, Sumit, 12
General Agreement of Trade and Tariffs (GATT), 177–8
Germany, Germans, 15, 59, 106, 129, 153
Goalpara, Assam, 54
Grady, Henry, 156–7
Grafftey-Smith, Lawrence, 111, 172
grain, 176
Great Game, 146
Greece, 18, 78
Guarantee System, 59
Gujarat, 37
Gulhati, Niranjan Das, 119–21, 123, 124, 126, 129, 134–5
Gundevia, Yezdezard Dinshaw, 38–9
Gupta, D.M., 63
Gurdaspur, 37
Gurmani, Mushtaq Ahmed, 39

Haines, Dan, 137
Hajj, 28
Halberstam, David, 139
Haldar, Surendranath, 62
Hamid, Shahid, 33
Haqqani, Hussain, 144
Hassan, Sarwar, 159
heavy engineering, 165
Henderson, Loy, 110
herbs, 179
High Commission for India, 1, 23, 26, 40–42, 51
 and abducted women, 38–9
 and economic policy, 171, 176
 and evacuee property, 94
 and minorities, 41–2, 51, 63, 64, 70

High Commission for Pakistan, 23, 26
    and minorities, 62–3
Hilaly, Aga, 28–9
Himachal Pradesh, 95, 96
Hinduism, 4, 6, 15, 17
Hindustan Times, 143
Hirschman, Albert Otto, 164
Hope Simpson, John, 78, 83
Hossain, Attia, 73
Hungary, 15, 147
Hussain, Altaf, 150
Hussain, Mahmoud, 153
Hussain, Zahid, 103
Hyderabad, 8, 9, 89

Iengar, Haravu Venkatanarasimha Varadaraja, 168, 179
Iftikaruddin, Mian, 75, 85, 144
Immigrants (Expulsion from Assam) Act (1949), 55
India
    Abducted Persons Act (1949), 37
    Article 370 revocation (2019), 183
    bilateral trade with Pakistan, 161–81
    Cabinet Economic Committee, 165
    currency exchange, 166–7
    Custodian of Evacuee Property, 74, 80–88, 92–3, 94, 98
    devaluation crisis, 168–78
    Evacuee Property Law (1950), 89
    Fiscal Commission, 169
    High Commission in Pakistan, *see* High Commission for India
    Immigrants (Expulsion from Assam) Act (1949), 55
    Influx from Pakistan (Control) Act (1949), 55
    Israel, creation of (1947–8), 155–9
    Ministry of Agriculture, 177
    Ministry of Commerce, 170–71
    Ministry of External Affairs, *see* Ministry of External Affairs
    Ministry of Law and Justice, 95–6, 97, 127
    Ministry of Relief and Rehabilitation, 35, 36, 38, 82, 89–90, 92, 94–5, 97, 162
    Ministry of Science and Power, 119
    Payments Agreement with Pakistan, 167
    Passport Act (1967), 55
    State Bank, 166
    Trade Agreement with Pakistan (1951), 177
    United States, relations with, 101, 142, 143–4, 147–9, 150
    Zamidari Abolition Act (1950), 90
Indian National Congress, 5, 13, 17, 40, 157
Indian Passport Act (1967), 55
Indo-Pakistani War
    1947: 8, 37, 140–41
    1965: 185
Indus Basin Development Fund, 137
Indus rivers, 4, 8, 117–38
    Arbitral Tribunal, 121, 122, 124, 125, 128
    Bari Doab Canals, 121, 122, 132
    Bhakra Nangal Dam, 120, 123–5
    4 May Agreement, 125–8
    Indus Waters Treaty (1960), 7, 117–21, 136–7
    Mangla Dam, 133
Indus Waters Treaty (1960), 7, 117–21, 136–7

Industrial Policy Document (1947), 165
Industries Development Corporation Act (1950), 165
Influx from Pakistan (Control) Act (1949), 55
intending evacuees, 87–95
Inter-Dominion conferences, 7
 on aftermath of partition, 37
 on evacuee property, 74, 75, 79–83, 87, 93–4
 on minorities, 49, 50–53, 56, 60, 64, 66, 93–4
International Bank, 147
International Court of Arbitration, 130
International Court of Justice (ICJ), 44
 and evacuee property, 86–7
 and Indus waters, 107, 119, 124, 126–7, 129, 131, 133, 134
International Monetary Fund, 172
Iqbal, Muhammad, 58–9
Iran, 144, 145
Iraq, 145
Ireland, 15, 35, 106, 159–60, 169
irrigation canals, 27
Islam, 4, 15, 17
 Hajj, 28
Islands of Agreement, 18
Ismael, Mirza, 26
Ispahani, Mirza Abul Hassan, 144, 152, 159
Israel, 18, 77, 78, 155–9, 169

Jain, Ajit Prasad, 86, 90
Jaintia Hills, Assam, 54
Jaipur, 84
Jammu, 115
Jan Sangh, 50
Jenkins, Ivan, 32, 34
Jessore, 62, 68
Jews, 153
Jhelum, 37
Jhelum river, 133
Jinnah, Fatima, 35
Jinnah, Muhammad Ali, 30, 34, 40, 42, 43, 152, 159
Jodhpur, 84
Joint Defence Council, 32–3, 80
Joint Technical Mission, 117, 133–4
Joint Valuation Board, 81
Jullundar, 82, 97, 102
Junagadh, 9, 103, 104, 108
jute, 157, 162, 165, 166
 border trade, 179, 180, 181
 devaluation crisis and, 171, 172, 173, 175, 177
 smuggling of, 180, 181

Kamath, Madhav Vittal, 159
Kangra, 37
Karachi
 census (1951), 56
 Indian High Commission in, 1, 8, 40–42, 51, 64, 171
 McGhee's visit (1951), 149–50
 migration to, 30, 56
 Ministry of Foreign Affairs in, 28, 30, 87
Karimganj, Assam, 65
Kashmir, 2, 4, 5, 8, 9, 12, 20, 115, 140–41, 155
 Article 370 revocation (2019), 183
 Indo-Pakistani War (1947), 8, 37, 140–41
 Indo-Pakistani War (1965), 185
 line of control, 30
 No War Pact correspondence and, 103, 104, 108, 112, 183
Kasur, 124

Kattan, Victor, 43
Kedar, Alexandre, 77
Kellogg–Briand Pact (1928), 105–6
kerosene, 179
Khaliquzzaman, Chaudhry, 40, 42–4
Khan, Ikramullah, 28
Khan, Liaquat Ali, 140, 141, 183
  evacuee property, policies on, 80
  Indus waters dispute, 131, 133
  Israel, creation of, 159
  on Karachi, overcrowding in, 30
  minorities, policies on, 32, 64
  Nehru–Liaquat Pact (1950), 16, 47, 50, 65, 69, 102
  No War Pact correspondence, 8, 99–116
  United States, relations with, 142, 144, 150
Khan, Muhammad Ayub, 7, 33–4, 136
Khan, Muhammad Zafarullah, 15, 30–31
  and Indus waters, 122, 131, 133
  and Israel, 158
  and Kashmir, 30–31
  and minority rights, 15, 42–5, 103
  and South Africa, 152
  and war preparations (1949), 110
Khan, Rana Liaquat Ali, 144
Khan, Shaukat Hayat, 121
Khan, Yasmin, 15
Khanna, Mehr Chand, 75, 85
Khasi, Assam, 54
Khosla, G.D., 131
Khuhro, Muhammad Ayub, 48
Khulna, 68
King George's Avenue, Delhi, 110
Kirpalani, M.K., 64
Korean War (1950–53), 172
Kripalani, Jivatram Bhagwandas, 1
Kripalani, Sucheta, 84
Kumar, Radha, 35
Kumaraswamy, P.R., 159
Kunzru, Hridya Nath, 153

Lake Success, New York, 159
Lahore
  abducted women in, 37, 38–9
  Chamba estate, 95–8
  Indian High Commission in, 1, 38–9, 70
League of Nations, 16, 36, 57, 58–60, 62, 130, 151
Lebanon, 18
Liaquat–Nehru Pact (1950), 16, 47, 57, 60, 65–71, 85, 102, 110–11, 184
Liberal Party (UK), 78
Lilienthal, David, 135
Line System, 55
Locke, John, 86
'Long Partition, The' (Zamindar), 75–6
Louise, Roger, 142
Lucknow, 73
Ludhiana, 102
Lutyens, Edwin Landseer, 110

majoritarianism, 15, 16, 44, 184
Malaya, 29
Malerkotla State, 84
Malik, Abdul Motaleb, 66
Mandal, Jogendra Nath, 64, 69, 180
Manela, Erez, 140
Mangla Dam, 133
Mankekar, D.R., 143
Mansergh, Nicholas, 141
Marshall Plan, 148
Mathai, M.O., 143
Matsya Union, 84
Mazower, Mark, 154

McGhee, George, 149–50
medicine, 179
Mehta, Jagat, 137
Mehta, Mohan Sinha, 181
Menon, Krishna, 109, 113
Menon, P. Achuta, 26
Middle Eastern Defence Treaty Organization, 145, 149
migrants, 6, 8, 30, 34, 41–5, 47–71, 74, 153
  Liaquat–Nehru Pact (1950), 16, 47, 57, 60, 65–71
  Calcutta conference (1948), 50–53, 60
  definition of, 52
  No War Pact correspondence and, 99–100, 102
  over-crowding and, 78
  property rights, 3, 8, 20, 73–98, 101
  rights, defining of, 56–65
Military Evacuation Organisation, 36
Ministry of Agriculture, India, 177
Ministry of Commerce, India, 170–71
Ministry of External Affairs, India, 20, 30, 60
  and economic policy, 161, 168, 180
  and evacuee property, 74, 79, 87, 94, 95, 97
  and Indus waters, 123, 126, 130
  and No War Pact, 105, 112
  and refugee crisis, 65
Ministry of Foreign Affairs, Pakistan, 28–9, 30, 104
Ministry of Law and Justice, India, 95–6, 97, 127
Ministry of Relief and Rehabilitation, India, 35, 36, 38, 82, 89–90, 92, 94–5, 97, 162
Ministry of Science and Power, India, 119
minorities, 2, 3, 8, 14, 15, 41–5, 47–71, 153
  Calcutta conference (1948), 50–53, 60
  Liaquat–Nehru Pact (1950), 16, 47, 57, 60, 65–71
  majoritarianism and, 15, 44
  rights, defining of, 56–65, 153
Mirza, Iskander, 26
MLAs (Members of the Legislative Assembly), 90–91
Montgomery district, 124
Mookerjee, Syama Prasad, 49, 50, 68, 165
Mountbatten, Louis, 1st Earl Mountbatten of Burma, 24, 80
Mridula Sarabhai, 38
muhajir, 76
Muhammad, Ghulam, 50, 51, 52–3, 66, 121, 122, 125, 172, 175
Multan district, 124
Musharraf, Parvez, 6
Muslim League, 5, 13, 17, 40, 42, 124
  abducted women, recovery of, 39
  Assam agreement (1945), 53
  Israel, creation of, 157
  National Guard, 32
mustard oil, 179
Mysore, 28

Nabi, Ijaz, 163
Naidu, Sarojini, 38
Nanda, Gulzarilal, 134–5
National Security Council, US, 146
nationalism, 163, 164
Nazi Germany (1933–45), 129
Nazimuddin, Khwaja, 60

Nehru, Jawaharlal, 8, 9–11, 32, 40, 140, 141, 183
  Bardoloi, confrontations with, 54
  Commonwealth, views on, 142–3
  Commonwealth Conference for Finance Ministers (1950), 172
  evacuee property, policies on, 80, 83, 85, 93, 101
  foreign policy, 20, 109, 116
  Indus waters dispute, 120, 122, 123, 125, 127, 129–35
  Ireland, relations with, 160
  Israel, creation of, 157, 159
  Kellogg–Briand Pact, influence of, 105–6
  Liaquat–Nehru Pact (1950), 16, 47, 57, 65, 68, 70, 102
  minorities, policy on, 32, 42, 47, 49, 50
  No War Pact correspondence, 8, 99–116, 183
  two nation theory, views on, 156
  United States, relations with, 101, 142, 143–4, 147–9, 150
Nehru, Rameshwari, 38
Nehru–Liaquat Pact (1950), 16, 47, 57, 60, 65–71, 85, 102, 110–11, 184
Neogy, Kshitish Chandra, 49, 50, 54, 68, 165, 171, 175
New Zealand, 106, 169
No War Pact, 6, 8, 99–116, 183
Non Military Pre-Emptive Action, 18
North Atlantic Treaty Organization, 145
North West Frontier, 84, 145, 147
Northern Ireland, 160
Norway, 169
Nye, Archibald, 102, 110

Oberoi, Patricia, 154
oil, 145
Open General License, 179
Orissa, 55
Overseas Negotiations Committee, 174

Pai, A. V., 26
Pakistan
  bilateral trade with India, 161–81
  Constituent Assembly, 20, 84, 113, 183
  Council of Industries, 165
  currency exchange, 166–7
  Custodian of Evacuee Property, 74, 80–88, 98
  devaluation crisis, 168–78
  East Bengal State Acquisition and Tenancy Act (1950), 90
  Industrial Policy Document (1947), 165
  Industries Development Corporation Act (1950), 165
  Israel, creation of (1947–8), 155–9
  Ministry of Foreign Affairs, 28–9, 30, 87, 104
  High Commission in India, 23, 26
  military, preponderance of, 6
  Payments Agreement with India, 167
  Protection of Evacuee Property Ordinance (1948), 80, 93–4
  Trade Agreement with India (1951), 177
  United States, relations with, 142, 144–7, 149–51
Pakistan Newspapers Editors Conference, 70
Palestine, 15, 44, 59, 77, 78, 83, 155–9
Pandit, Vijaya Lakshmi, 113

paper, 165
Partition (1947)
 abduction of women, 3, 20, 23, 32, 34–9
 assets, division of, 27
 ethnic cleansing, 32
 High Commissions, establishment of, 23, 26
 Indus rivers and, 4, 8, 117–38
 migrants and refugees, *see under* migrants; minorities; refugees
 property and, *see under* evacuee property
 Radcliffe Boundary Commission, 44
 riots, 24, 25, 26, 32, 35
Partition Council, 23–8
 abducted women, ruling on, 38
 Expert Committees, 25–6, 28
 High Commissions, establishment of, 23, 26
 Standstill Agreement, 121, 166
 Steering Committee, 24, 27, 50
Patel, Hirubhai Mulljibhai, 24–5, 27, 41, 50–51, 168
Patel, Vallabhbhai Jhaverbhai 'Sardar', 50, 68–9, 107–8, 167
Patiala, 118, 123
Patiala and East Punjab States Union (PEPSU), 82, 123
pig iron, 176
Point IV program, 149, 150
Poland, Poles, 15, 58, 106, 147, 153
Posen, Barry, 16–17
pound sterling, 162, 167, 168–78
Prakasa, Sri, 40–42, 44, 45
Prasad, Beni, 59
Princely States, 8, 12, 20, 28, 31–2
Protection of Evacuee Property Ordinance (1948), 80, 93–4
public opinion, 100, 111–16
Punjab
 abducted women in, 36–9
 Boundary Force, 20, 23, 31–4, 35, 137
 ethnic cleansing in, 32
 evacuee property in, 76, 80–83, 84, 94, 95–8
 Indus waters, 118, 120–38
 migrants and refugees, 52
 partition riots (1947), 24, 26, 32, 81
Punjab Boundary Force, 20, 23, 31–4, 35, 137
Puri, Yogendra Krishna, 39, 97, 126

Qureshi, Ishtiaq Hussain, 84

Radcliffe Boundary Commission (1947), 44
Raghavan, Srinath, 9, 57
Rai, Lala Lajpat, 41
railways, 27
Raisman, Jeremy, 174
Rajagopalachari, Chakravarti, 102, 142
Rajaji Marg, Delhi, 110
Rajasthan Union, 84
Rashtriya Swayamsevak Sangh (RSS), 32, 92
Rau, Benegal Narsing, 87
Rau, K. Rama, 143
Rawalpindi, 37
refugees, 6, 14, 15, 32, 41–5, 47–71, 73, 74, 153
 Liaquat–Nehru Pact (1950), 16, 47, 57, 60, 65–71
 Calcutta conference (1948), 50–53, 60
 definition of, 52
 land exchanges for, 41

  No War Pact correspondence and, 99–100, 102
  over-crowding and, 78
  property rights, 3, 8, 20, 73–98, 101
  rights, defining of, 56–65
  UN Refugee Convention (1951), 141, 154–5
Reizler, Katherina, 129
rice, 167
riots, 24, 25, 26, 32
  abduction of women, 35
  Assam (1950), 54
  partition (1947), 24, 25, 26, 32, 35, 81
Robson, Laura, 11, 34
Roy, Bidhan Chandra, 41, 49, 50, 54, 60, 62
Russian Empire (1721–1917), 146
Russian Federation, 17

Sachdev, Mulk Raj, 39, 126, 131
salt, 179
San Francisco, California, 101
Sarabhai, Mridula, 38, 92
Saurashtra, 84
Saxena, Mohanlal, 49
Schaeffer, Robert, 15
schedules of goods, 179
Second World War (1939–45), 15, 30, 77, 145, 153–4
security dilemma, 16–19
self-sufficiency, 164–8
Semiruddin Munshi, 54
Sen, S., 61
Shahbuddin, Khwaja, 39, 51, 53, 75, 85
Shahnawaz, Jahanara, 33
Shimla, 95
Sialkot, 37
Sikander Road, Delhi, 96
Sikhism, 37
Silchar, Assam, 62–3
Sindh, 30
  Bhakra Nangal Dam, opposition to, 124
  Indus waters dispute, 118, 124
  migrants and refugees, 41, 48, 52, 56
  evacuee property, 75, 84
Singh, Lakshman, 97
Slovaks, 153
Smith, Arthur, 31
South Africa, 28, 29, 44, 141, 151–3, 169
South West Africa (1915–1990), 44, 152
Southeast Asia Treaty Organisation (SEATO), 145
Soviet Union (1922–91), 17, 28, 144, 146–7, 149, 153
Standstill Agreement, 121, 166
state completion, 19
State Department, US, 146, 147, 148
steamer companies, 170
steel, 64, 165, 170, 176, 177
Steering Committee (Partition Council), 24, 27, 50
sterling, 162, 167, 168–78
Stern Reckoning (Khosla), 131
Sudeten Germans, 59
Suez crisis (1956), 143
sugar, 175
Sunlight on a Broken Column (Hossain), 73
Sutlej river, 123, 124, 134

Taluqdar, 73
telegraph lines, 27
Tennessee Valley Authority, 135
textiles, 168, 170, 171, 177

Thapar, Premvati, 37
Third Force, 143
timber, 177
Times of India, 101, 112, 143
tobacco, 170
Trade Agreement (1951), 177
Tripura, 52, 89, 177, 179–80
Trivedi, Chandulal Madhavlal, 125
Truman, Harry S., 142, 144, 148, 149
Turkey, 18, 78
two nation theory, 41, 45, 156
Tyabji, Badruddin, 86, 161–2, 182, 184

Uganda, 173
Ukraine, 17
unemployment, 170
United Kingdom, 140, 141–3
  Foreign Office, 139
  Great Game, 146
  and Indo–Pakistani war, prospect of, 110, 111
  Kellogg–Briand Pact (1928), 106
  Northern Ireland, 160
  and refugee crisis, 103
  sterling, 162, 167, 168–78
  and United Nations, 153
  Wilsonian Moment, 140
United Nations, 4, 14, 28, 104, 110, 113
  Charter, 127, 153
  and Kashmir, 30, 108, 115, 141
  and Indus rivers, 117, 126–8
  and Israel, 78, 155–9
  Refugee Convention (1951), 141, 154–5
  and refugee crisis, 42, 45, 103
  and South Africa, 151–3
United Provinces, 40, 84, 88
United States, 20, 141–51
  Bhakra Nangal Dam, lack of aid for, 120
  Cold War, 144, 146–51
  India, relations with, 101, 110, 120, 142, 143–4, 147–9, 150
  and Indo–Pakistani war, prospect of, 110
  and Israel, creation of, 156–7, 159
  Kellogg–Briand Pact (1928), 106
  Liaquat's visit (1949), 142, 144, 150
  Nehru's visit (1949), 101, 142, 143–4, 147–8, 150
  oil, search for, 145
  Pakistan, relations with, 28, 29, 110, 142, 144–7, 149–51
  Point IV program, 149, 150
  United Nations, founding of, 153
Upper Bari Doab Canals (UBDC), 121, 122, 132
Uttar Pradesh, 52, 56, 89

Vajpayee, Atal Bihari, 6, 7
vegetable oils, 170
vegetables, 179
Virdee, Pippa, 36

Wagah, 125
Walker, Gordon, 111
Watenpaugh, Keith, 35
Wells of Power, The (Caroe), 145
West Bengal, 41, 48, 49, 50, 52, 53, 54
  East Bengal, relations with, 55
  evacuee property in, 88, 89, 93–4
  minority rights in, 16, 41–2, 44–5, 56–7, 60–71
  refugee crisis, 41–2, 44–5, 48, 49–57, 102, 103
  steamer companies, 170